Also by JEAN-PIERRE AUMONT

Plays:
L'Empereur de Chine (My Name is Aquilon)
L'Ile Heureuse
Un Beau Dimanche
Farfada
Lucy Crown (from the novel by Irwin Shaw)
Ange
Madame Mousse
Objection, votre Honneur

Books:
Souvenirs Provisoires
La Pomme de son Oeil
Le Soleil et les Ombres
Prix des Critiques
and *Prix de l'Académie Française*

SUN AND SHADOW

Translated from the French by Bruce Benderson

Sun and Shadow

Jean-Pierre Aumont

With a Foreword by François Truffaut

W · W · Norton & Company · Inc · New York

Translation copyright © 1977 by W. W. Norton & Company, Inc.
Published simultaneously in Canada by George J. McLeod Limited,
Toronto. Printed in the United States of America.
All Rights Reserved

Originally published under the title *Le Soleil et les Ombres*
© Opera Mundi 1976
Library of Congress Cataloging in Publication Data

Aumont, Jean-Pierre.
Sun and shadow.
Translation of Le soleil et les ombres.
1. Aumont, Jean-Pierre.   2. Actors—France—Biography
I. Title.
PN2638.A88A2913 1977   791'.092'4 [B] 76–58878

ISBN 0 393 07511 7
2 3 4 5 6 7 8 9 0

This book was designed by Antonina Krass
Typefaces used are Janson and Bauer Text Initials
Manufacturing was done by Vail-Ballou Press

Photograph from the MGM release 'THE CROSS OF LOR-
RAINE' © 1943 Loew's Inc. Copyright renewed 1970 by
Metro-Goldwyn-Mayer, Inc., courtesy of MGM.

Photograph from the MGM release 'Lili' © 1953 Loew's Incorpo-
rated, courtesy of MGM.

To my two sons:

My Jean-Claude, my Patrick, because I know you pretty well, I'm sure you will glance through this book looking only for the paragraphs where you happen to be mentioned. But if, by chance, you open it to this page, you will see that it is dedicated to you.

With love.

"Pleasure is not to be found in specific things, but in the way we apprehend them all."

—Jean Cocteau

CONTENTS

FOREWORD BY
FRANÇOIS TRUFFAUT

Written in the first person and with disarming candor by Jean-Pierre Aumont, *Sun and Shadow* is a fascinating and witty account of his life, his work as an actor, his travels, and his loves. One of the most refreshing aspects of the book is that there is not the slightest attempt on the part of the author to glorify his public image.

With *The Emperor of China*, the best of his plays, as well as through a collection of short stories titled *The Apple of His Eye*, Aumont had already demonstrated that he is a born writer. In contrast to many limelight personalities, he has no need for an "as told to" collaborator. Aumont is the sole author of this book, and every page reflects his literary gifts, as well as his enjoyment in writing it.

That enjoyment is infectious: Without ever resorting to the familiar Gallic epigrams, or to the raconteur's laborious build-up toward a colorful punchline, Aumont's memoirs generate laughter through a spontaneous, true-to-life brand of humor. The poetic milkman of Marcel Carne's *Drôle de Drame*, the seductive magician of *Lili*, the continental lover of *Day for Night* is obviously incapable of taking himself seriously, for he is constantly aware of the little absurdities of man.

I have enormous admiration for such anti-solemn artists as Sacha Guitry, Claude Dauphin, Ernst Lubitsch, Jean Renoir, and David Niven. Through his wit, which is essentially mischievous but never malicious, Jean-Pierre Aumont is related to that family of entertainers. He is essentially a *blagueur*, a term the French use to define the irreverent, good-natured laughter of an adolescent upon discovering that the adult world is made up of puppets who dangle around with an air of self-importance while someone else pulls the strings.

Because of his relaxed style and manner, Jean-Pierre Aumont is ranked as a light comedy actor, a genre which is not as easy as it seems. The reason I prefer "light" actors to their more serious counterparts is that they can, when necessary, perform with gravity, whereas most so-called serious actors are incapable of injecting a light touch into their performance.

Most of the actors I know experience periods of appalling anxiety between the final day of shooting of one picture and the starting day of the following one, but Jean-Pierre Aumont is the exception to the rule, for he always has a literary project in the works. How fortunate it is for an actor to be a writer! Instead of sitting tensely, waiting for the phone to ring, Aumont simply grabs a fistful of blank pages and immerses himself in his writing.

Since the congenial shooting of *Day for Night*, we have gone our separate ways, and in his book Aumont wonders whether I feel as warmly toward him as he does toward me. I welcome this chance to reply to that question with an emphatic yes!

Readers who are already attached to the public figure are bound to enjoy their discovery of his cheerful, glowing off-screen personality. I have no doubt that after reading *Sun and Shadow*, many of them will feel that if they had the chance to spend their next vacation in the company of an actor, it would be a fabulous bit of good luck if that actor should happen to be Jean-Pierre Aumont.

François Truffaut

ACKNOWLEDGMENT

My deepest appreciation to Bruce Benderson and to my editor, Starling Lawrence, for having patiently helped to translate my book into English. Or, at least, what they assured me was English.

PART ONE

I

Born at Sixteen

I was born at the age of sixteen.

Is there any other birth for an actor than the first day he finds himself standing in the wings of a theater?

Of my childhood, I remember almost nothing. Nothing except the taste of revolt and a pressing need for freedom. I've been told that I was an impossible child. I doubt it. I've been told that at the age of seven I was excited by a nearby fire and, out of envy, tried to burn down our apartment so that the firemen would come to our house, too. I've been told that I tried to blind my grandmother by using her eyes as targets for my darts . . . Where is the child who hasn't indulged in similar pranks?

When I was nine my parents decided to put me in boarding school. They dragged me to one of those oppressive cobblestone villas in the suburbs of Paris which some people have the audacity to call "quaint." Here lurked a one-armed professor whose system of education was a series of daily lashes with a whip. He had so much power over us that not one of us dared complain to our parents about the tortures we were enduring.

Every morning he whipped us with might and main under the pretext that he knew we'd been up all night engaging in certain "forbidden practices." What these practices could be, we had not the slightest idea. But since we were being beaten for them anyway, we decided to look into the subject more carefully . . .

Whoever goes in search of pleasure, "those pleasures which are thoughtlessly called physical,"* finds it. From then on we knew why we were being beaten. And as for the professor, well . . . I suspect he had secretly discovered in himself a certain propensity for children and whips . . . Such vices are committed in thy name, O Virtue!

Was it out of viciousness that he made me cut off the golden curls which had been the pride and joy of my mother? When I climbed out of the barber's chair I was as bald as an egg.

A few days later I went to the Gare de Lyon to see my parents off on a vacation. I got there just as their train was pulling out. I caught a glimpse of my parents at the door of the Pullman. I removed my hat and waved it excitedly. Suddenly, a shriek reverberated across the platform and the train screeched to a halt. My mother had pulled the emergency brake. In vain my father tried to calm her, but her screams sent the whole station into a panic. And when the train got underway again, my mother, in the voice of Sarah Bernhardt, could be heard wailing: "A wig! Somebody, buy him a wig!"

I was ten years old when my grandmother took me to the Comédie Française. I had never before set foot in a theater. In that hushed red auditorium, brilliant with lights, I felt as if I were at the center of a volcano. It was a performance of *Andromaque*. I didn't understand a word, but a strange warmth spread through my chest.

Returning to my schoolmaster at Ville-d'Avray, I told him of my intention to become an actor. If I had murdered my brother, it would have been considered a less serious crime. "An actor! . . . an actor! . . . do you understand the enormity of what you are saying? Maybe a good whipping after dinner will help you put your ideas in order!"

* Colette

From that day on, life was hell. I couldn't say a word without somebody answering, "Come on now, you're not on the stage, you know!" That didn't matter to me. In the deepest part of my soul I knew my destiny was to be an actor.

My parents never really opposed my passion for the the-ater. As a matter of fact, I think that they secretly approved of it. My mother had an innate gift for poetic exaggeration. She distorted and dramatized everything. Was it André Gide who wrote: "It takes exaggeration to bring out the truth in a story. Otherwise, the incident loses the colors of reality"? My mother subscribed to this theory by exaggerating, transforming, and embellishing everything . . . At the beginning of the war she'd been warned against excitement or strong emotion by the doc-tor, because of a severe heart ailment. Though she remained calm and indifferent to the air raid sirens and the bombs crash-ing down around us, a small spoon dropped accidentally would send her rushing out of her room to revile the culprit. When we laughed at her, she defended herself with perfect logic: "We can't do anything about the bombs, but when it comes to little spoons . . ."

She always treated me more like a lover than a son. But she regained her maternal impatiences as soon as she worried about my health or my career: "My poor darling, what *have* you been doing to yourself? I think your friends want to see you dead. Otherwise they wouldn't try to drink you under the table at Maxim's every night! If you continue at this rate, we'll be shop-ping for your coffin in a week or two . . . To say nothing of your career. I know you think I'm an idiot when it comes to that, and maybe you're right, but I do have a little common sense. How long has it been since you've had a film offer? Three days? Of course, you know I'd rather see you on the stage—but if it's films you want . . ."

Every Christmas she forced me to offer my blessings and gifts to the servants. As a child, I hated the uncomfortable mo-ment when I was supposed to slide some bills into their palms and stammer: "Here, buy yourself something."

"What did the m-a-i-d say?" worried my mother. When she

was talking about the servants, even when they weren't in the house, she spelled out the key words.

"The m-a-i-d asked me for a r-a-i-s-e again."

"Well, she can go straight to h-e-l-l."

My younger brother, François, who was nicknamed "Poum," was a red-haired butterball. When he was five or six, I would make him help me practice my lines in tragedies by Racine. I would rig him out in an old curtain as Andromaque, and ask him: "And what wilt thou do?"

Under the threat of a slap he was forced to answer: "Go we to hith tomb. I shall there conthult my huthband."

In spite of such provocations, we are still the best of friends today.

My father was just as good-natured. Right up until his death at eighty-three he tried to understand the problems of others and excuse their faults. He loved humanity. His acute critical sense, rather than rendering him uncompromising, helped him to discover the best in everyone.

Can my passion for the theater be traced to an ancestor? My great-uncle, Georges Berr, had been a famous actor, but he had become disgusted with the intrigues of the Comédie Française and had resigned from it by the time I became interested in acting. He did everything in his power to deter me from the theater.

His own career had been a happy and paradoxical one. Small, myopic, and awkward-looking, he seemed more like an asthmatic notary from the provinces than a stage celebrity. The fact that he had built his reputation on parts which called for fire and swaggering was all the more surprising: Figaro, Scapin, Cyrano—these were heroic roles. In the last years of his career he had become almost blind. Off stage he got around gropingly. But on stage he jumped over benches in *Fourberies de Scapin*, tumbled down chimneys in *Ruy Blas*, and leaped across hedges in *The Marriage of Figaro*. As soon as the curtain rose, he found his youth again, his agility and his sight: it's the miracle of the theater.

His sister, my grandmother, came to all my plays on Sunday afternoon.

"I'm a little deaf," she would tell the usher so that he would put her in the first row. This was an old lady's coquetry. She would never have said, "I don't see so well," because that was the truth. It was easier to say, "I'm a little deaf," without being ashamed, since that was not true.

At the end of each act she got up and blew me kisses, murmuring, "My treasure." Then I could see her through the hole in the curtain whispering to all her neighbors the very thing I had forbidden: "You know, that's my grandson." She said it with the same pride as she had said at the Comédie Française for such a long time: "You know, Georges Berr, that's my brother."

Every Thursday I went to have lunch with her. She waited on the balcony for me, and leaped for the door when I rang, crying, "Don't worry, I'll get it!" She didn't want anyone else to welcome me before she did. If I went to wash my hands, she begged: "Don't be too long, we have so little time together"; and if the telephone rang, she shouted, "Oh! wouldn't you know it! They won't leave us alone for two minutes, they're all jealous of us!"

The other days of the week did not interest her. She lived only for Thursday. Every evening except Thursday she religiously wrote on her calendar: "I'm bored."

2

"Don't Smile, You Idiot!"

~~~~~~~~~~~~~~~~~~~~~~~~~~

"A child will be born from our encounter tonight: Hercules."

On the stage of the Comédie des Champs-Elysées, Jupiter was taking leave of Alcmene.

"Poor little girl," sighed Alcmene, who clearly hadn't read Homer.

"It will be a boy!" thundered Jupiter.

No presentiment or hope suggested to me at that moment that I would be playing the very same part some twenty years later. I was hypnotized, spellbound by the incantations filtering from the stage . . .

After the curtain fell, I tiptoed through the wings between hanging ropes and pulleys to meet Louis Jouvet. He was playing Mercury in "Amphitryon 38" by Giraudoux. He had directed the play. He was also the producer and the manager of his theater, la Comédie des Champs-Elysées.

Everything about him was blue: blue cape, blue helmet, blue eyes. He had an ironic smile which was tempered by a certain tenderness. Without giving me the chance to introduce myself, he guessed I was an aspiring young actor:

"What are you working on now?"

"Romeo and Juliet."

"Why not? And what do you think of Romeo?"

I was stumped. The speech I'd practiced about my esteem and admiration for him, my desire to become a member of his company, suddenly fell to pieces. I hadn't thought he would skip all conventional formulas of politeness and ask me point-blank what I thought of Romeo. I couldn't answer. I was riveted to the blue eyes of Jouvet and I wanted to cry. He went on:

"I see . . . You don't think much of Romeo. It doesn't matter, my boy, not at all. I might be able to use you somehow. Come back and see me tomorrow."

The next day, he offered me a three-year contract.

How much I liked him already! Twenty years later, I would still be calling him "Monsieur Jouvet" and he would still be calling me "my Jean-Pierre," boxing my ears and treating me like a kid.

We started rehearsals of a revival of *Knock*, his perennial success. He cast me in the part of a mute peasant. In the wings, a gaunt, secretive, nearsighted fellow wandered to and fro. He was writing plays no one cared to read. Jouvet was using him to run errands. His name was Jean Anouilh.

Knock enjoyed its usual success. I must have been eloquent in my speechless part, for one of the critics wrote of me: "How lucky he is to be seventeen, to be gifted, and to have Louis Jouvet as a mentor."

One lovely afternoon, I was strolling along the Champs-Elysées with a head full of fantasies, confidence, and hope for the future. I ran into a friend. "Instead of walking around with your finger in your nose, you should be running over to Cocteau's on rue Vignon. He's been trying to find you for a week."

Cocteau! For us apprentice actors, he was not only an author but a figure of legend. *Les Enfants Terribles*, *Orphée*, Nijinsky, Diaghilev, Picasso, Stravinsky . . . we weren't sure how all these magic names and titles fitted together, but we did know that they all gravitated around a single name, even more mysterious, and charged with magic: *Cocteau*.

I arrived at his apartment, a somber curiosity shop full of odds and ends: pencil sketches, plaster masks, photos pinned to fragments of red velvet, gothic chairs, old postcards. Marcel Khill, a young Moroccan fellow who was Cocteau's secretary, led me into his room. When my eyes were accustomed to the darkness of his smoky lair, I discovered Cocteau sitting in bed looking like a withered pharaoh. His burning eyes and bony profile seemed drawn (even here Cocteau was twenty years ahead of his time) by Bernard Buffet. Before I could utter a word, he declared, "You will be my Oedipus."

"But you don't even know me . . ."

"You will be my Oedipus."

I had heard that Jouvet was going to produce *La Machine Infernale* (*The Infernal Machine*) at the Comédie des Champs-Elysées. But he hadn't breathed a word of it to me. He was thinking of giving Oedipus to Charles Boyer, or even to Serge Lifar. But Cocteau swept away all my apprehensions. He scribbled out a letter which he asked me to deliver to Jouvet:

"Jean-Pierre is the one. Look at him closely. Listen to him carefully. Without thinking about who he 'was.' Don't forget that I'm seeing and hearing him for the first time without past prejudices. He has the youth, the command, the wildness, the arrogance, the moonstruck quality, the fury, etc. You know how I hate to impose myself on a director and of course the final decision is yours. But if you agree, we would have an actor trained by you. Once the part is cast you'll see how simple everything is. In short, give him a chance! Don't abandon him to the filthy movies which are destroying the theater for us. And don't let me down."

In February we began to rehearse. Jouvet had reserved the practically silent role of the messenger in the last act for himself.

It's impossible to remember the long rehearsals of *La Machine Infernale* without emotion. I can't look at that violet poster without being saddened by the fact that eight of my friends listed on it are now dead: Jouvet, Cocteau, Christian Bérard, Romain Bouquet, Jane Lory, Le Vigan, Pierre Renoir, and Marcel Khill, who was killed at the beginning of the war.

There were four months of rehearsals. Jouvet, consumed by doubts, would bend over a row of seats, scrutinizing us, tormenting us. When he didn't get what he wanted from an actor, Jouvet bullied him and attacked his ego until he was stung to the quick, until he reared like a bewildered horse, and charged the lines of the text with newly discovered energy, with new rage. But Jouvet was also unusually willing to take the risk of being contradicted, and was constantly asking us for our opinions. Maybe this is a quality of all true leaders, a knowledge of the human heart which Saint-Exupéry refers to when he writes: "Make your subordinates feel that you need them, and not that they need you."

I was not in the first act of *La Machine Infernale*. In the second act I wandered across a tilted stage under an eerie neon light. Lost in my thoughts, I collided suddenly with the Sphinx. Although, in this play, she has the outward form of a young girl, she is nonetheless accustomed to devouring the young men of Thebes, who cannot answer her riddle:

"What animal walks on four legs in the morning, two legs in the afternoon, and three legs in the evening?"

Oedipus, like all the others, tries desperately to think of the answer. But the Sphinx is in love for the first time, and sacrifices her own life by whispering to him, "It's man."

Intoxicated by his triumph, Oedipus cries: "I've vanquished the unclean beast! I'll be king!" For Queen Jocasta has promised her crown and her hand to the man who overcomes the Sphinx.

Poor Oedipus! He didn't know that he would end up as a parricide and would commit incest.

Bébé Bérard, a bearded, tender ogre and a painter of genius who was making his debut as a set designer in *La Machine Infernale*, had littered my path with bones supposed to represent the remains of the Sphinx's victims. Each evening before the second act began, I pushed them aside so that I wouldn't stumble over them. And each evening, Bébé darted out to replace them just before my entrance. The struggle to arrange the bones began as soon as the stage manager had signaled the end of the intermission.

During the rehearsals Jouvet had bullied and tortured me. As I made my exit on opening night, after the encounter with the Sphinx, the applause was frenetic. Jouvet was in the wings, checking the lights. I stationed myself in front of him and waited for a compliment. He pretended not to see me. I couldn't understand. As the applause continued, I stood there gasping for breath, hoping for a word. He persisted in ignoring my presence. When I couldn't stand it any longer, I grabbed his arm and shouted: "Well?"

Finally, he looked at me and answered calmly. "Well, my boy, just try to repeat consciously every night what you did unconsciously tonight."

Between the third and the last act, there was a costume change. I barely had the time to glue on a beard and age myself twenty years. It was Jouvet who helped me put on my make-up. It was also he who poured the hemoglobin on my cheeks before Oedipus came back on stage with his eyes gouged out.

The opening night was a triumph. Forgetting my costume, my beard, my punctured eyes, the blood which flowed down my cheeks, the tragedy we had just played, and the audience's emotion, I bowed, smiling with all my teeth.

"Don't smile, you idiot," hissed Jouvet.

Cocteau spent his evenings in our dressing rooms, spewing out long monologues:

"You know, people think you actually write a play. But I've never written a line. It's all dictated to me. *La Machine Infernale* was dictated to me in one night. How could anyone possibly change a line of it? It's one substance; if you tear away a piece the whole thread will unwind. Me? I'm just taking orders. . . . But who from? I'm a poet who obeys orders from his night, just like Picasso is a poet of . . . of what? You know what it is: you write a play, the actors play another, and the public hears a third. All success is a misunderstanding . . . I'll have to write a play that we can all go off and do together. I'll put in a role for Simone Simon. She'll be accompanied by a little black boy who'll be her interpreter. Simone will blurt out: "Boudou, boudou." The little black boy will explain: "Mademoiselle wishes to say: 'I love you' . . ."

"There aren't any actors left. An actor isn't supposed to eat. Or wash. An actor is supposed to learn to have tears without crying. Most actresses only want to play pixies now. But there's no such thing as a pixie . . . A table has to have four legs . . . People are monstrous. Only the young love me . . . They see my plays twenty times, thirty times . . . There are only a thousand people who have seen *La Machine* but they are the same ones who come back every night . . ."

It was true. *La Machine* attracted fanatics. Violent arguments broke out in the theater. The students fought for us, as they had fought, a hundred years earlier, for Victor Hugo at the premiere of *Hernani*.

At the closing of *La Machine Infernale*, Cocteau began to write *Les Chevaliers de la Table Ronde* (*The Knights of the Round Table*) for Jouvet, Lucienne Bogaert, and myself. Jouvet was supposed to play Merlin the Enchanter, Bogaert the Queen, and I, Sir Galahad.

Unfortunately, three years went by before Cocteau found a theater for his work. Jouvet didn't want to produce it. Bogaert was no longer interested, and I was under contract to a German film company. Jean Marais, who was supposed to be my understudy, inherited my role.

But the paths of Cocteau and myself were to cross several times more in years to come.

During the performances of *La Machine Infernale*, I got my first big break in films.

Lac aux Dames was supposed to be for Johnny Weismuller, glorious Tarzan at the height of his muscularity, but Hollywood wouldn't loan him out; and Marc Allégret, the director, began searching for a young French lead. I was among the hundreds of actors or athletes that he interviewed. I went to his studio on rue Vaneau, where I found him with two other men whom he didn't bother to introduce. After a few moments of conversation they asked me to undress so that they could judge whether I was built well enough to play the part of the champion swimmer. Intimidated, confused, and without the least notion of what I was supposed to do, I stood there in my underwear, eyed by three strangers: Marc Allégret, Phillip de Rothschild, the producer, and André Gide. They didn't seem to be especially impressed by my musculature, but Gide suggested that maybe a trainer would be able to build me up a little. I did a test with Simone Simon, along with ten other candidates. Simone, who had a great influence over Marc Allégret, pushed my candidacy. I went through a second test and finally got the part.

But there was no question of resting on my laurels. I left for Cannes with a gym teacher who had me run, swim, hoist barbells, throw the javelin, jump, and box from sunrise to sundown. From sundown to sunrise he kept close watch at my door—an unnecessary precaution since I was exhausted anyway. Finally we left for Austria to film on location. In an attempt at chivalry, I offered my pullman berth to the script girl who didn't have one of her own. She was a plump girl who answered to the picturesque name of Corky. Who could have guessed that as Françoise Giroud she would become the editor-in-chief of *L'Express* and a member of Giscard's cabinet?

The lake where we were shooting, although much too cold for my taste, was very beautiful. Simone Simon, who had the natural, delicate charm of a wildflower, seemed put into this world just to play the pure and perverse ingenues of Colette. With her freckled face and turned-up nose she offered the camera a kind of intimate sincerity touched with mischief that swept away all of the cinematic conventions of the period. We rolled in the hay, clambered up trees, swam in the immaculate waters of the lake. The lovely Rosine Deréan played my other girlfriend. Colette had written the dialogue and Georges Auric had composed the music. Marc Allégret had put the most tender and the most secret parts of himself into the film. *Lac aux Dames* was a resounding success.

Like so many actors, I've become used to hearing this refrain: "You really lucked out from the start. You began your career in Cocteau's *La Machine Infernale* and in the hit movie *Lac aux Dames.*"

It's true that I was lucky. Chance plays an important role in all professions, and particularly in ours, where success depends upon imponderable factors; but the public always associates an actor's beginnings with a hit, for the simple reason that he is only noticed after the purgatory of bit parts and walk-ons.

How many productions did I succeed in sneaking into before *La Machine Infernale?* An endless succession of shabby tours, auditions, understudying actors who never got sick . . . Like all my colleagues, I knew long months of hope and despair. I can see myself again shivering on a lawn at La Malmaison, dressed as a shepherd (in front of the very house which I would buy twenty years later); or playing a goateed and bewigged notary in *l'Ecole des Maris* at Becon-les-Bruyeres; or as a bowlegged beggar in *The Poor of Assisi* at the Oedenkoven Theatre (don't ask me where the hell that is, because I have no idea).

Even Jouvet, after having granted me the principal role in *La Machine Infernale*, offered me only paltry parts for a long time afterwards, because he believed that one must learn the hard way too.

I did six films before *Lac aux Dames*. *Jean de la lune* was the first. Expecting that it would fizzle, Jean Choux had entrusted the direction to his assistant. In my scene I'm asleep on a train on the knees of Madeleine Renaud, who regrets having left her husband for me. She jumps out of the train at Laroche-Migennes, abandoning me to my childish dreams . . .

Echec et Mat (*Checkmate*) was next. There was a young prop man in the crew who never brought us what we needed. Apparently he had better things to do. His name was Charles Trenet.

Then, *Faut-il Les Marier?*, filmed in Vienna with Annie Ondra, the wife of Max Schmeling. He was very jealous and since I was no Joe Louis I was careful not to overdo our love scenes. I wasn't allowed to finish the film because I'd forgotten one small detail when I'd signed for it: my military service. The Austrian police took me to the border and handed me over to the French police. Pink with shame, I was taken to the Army Service Corps at Versailles.

Then, as soon as my duties were over, I filmed something

3

From Madame de Maintenon to Bernstein's Pig

At that time, in the late '30s, Henri Bernstein was the most formidable, the most frenetic, the most thunderous, the most aristocratic, the most arrogant, the most vehement, the most tyrannical of contemporary French authors. He was an inspired prophet who was also the owner of the temple, for the Théâtre du Gymnase belonged to him, and he directed his own plays there.

Bernstein's exceptional vigor was not limited to the domain of the theater. He attached great importance to his feminine conquests, which were many and varied. He wasn't young or handsome, but when he had chosen to appropriate (and I use the word conservatively) some ravishing creature, he conducted his siege with such relentless persuasiveness, such passion, such an avalanche of flowers and telegrams, that he always arrived at his goal.

A well-known ingénue once confessed to me that she was called to Bernstein's apartment to be interviewed for a part. She found him completely naked in his drawing room and, before any introduction, he asked her to go down on her knees and pay him some special and rather intimate homage. When the innocent young actress told me that story, she blushed, and added: "I did it, of course . . . but still . . ."

He also imposed a despotic control over actors. Among others, Claude Dauphin and I were to become his victims, alternately succumbing to and rebelling against his tyranny.

Claude, whom I had met at a café called the Univers, where students and teachers of the Conservatoire rubbed elbows, was not only an exquisite actor but the vanguard of a new school. Instead of the cape, cigarette, and savoir-faire of a matinee idol, Claude had a thin face that wasn't made up, a quavering voice, and hair that was always falling over his eyes.

There are friendships which happen and others which you seek out. I wanted to be Claude's friend. Madame de Maintenon helped me out.

One Sunday on the way back from Chartres, we stopped in front of the chateau of Mme. de Maintenon. As we stood admiring it silently, I came out with some comment that produced gales of laughter.

It was then that I noticed a mischievous glint in Claude's eyes. It was a kind of brotherly complicity which seemed to say, "Isn't it great that we both think the same things are funny, or touching? From now on a wink will be enough for us to understand each other."

In the spring of 1936, Bernstein offered us both a part in a play which he hadn't written yet. But in order to accept it, I had to forego all film contracts for a year or more, since Bernstein didn't allow anybody who was acting in one of his plays to do a film at the same time. I told Bernstein that I would be more than happy to make this sacrifice if the role was worth the trouble, but that I didn't see why he needed me, since he already had Claude under contract. Bernstein answered that he had reserved roles of equal value for the two of us, and cited the enticing example of Pierre Blanchar and Charles Boyer in *Melo*. I signed an agreement with the usual clause providing a forfeit of 300,000 francs in case of breach of contract—which cut short my movie career and put me at the mercy of Bernstein.

Three months later, the night before the reading of the play, Bernstein called me.

"My dear boy, I miss you so much," he said, to my great surprise. "Let's have a simple little dinner together at my place."

Flattered, I spent an unusual evening at his home, completely taken in by his charm. Bernstein was lyrical, dazzling, and kept relentlessly filling my glass. At midnight I wanted to leave but he kept insisting, "Drink, drink some more."

Soon my spirits began to flag. Why had he covertly signaled his latest concubine to leave us alone? He was mumbling disjointed statements whose meaning I couldn't quite figure out.

"My dear, I have created a sublime role for you . . . When I think that for a miserable three hundred thousand francs you could abandon me, I can't sleep anymore. Dear, dear Jean-Pierre, for whom I've just written the role of his life . . ."

I left, dimly aware of signing a paper which he had pushed in front of me.

The next day was the reading. We gathered around the "master," who was seated under his own portrait by Manet.

First act: My role was short.

Second act: My role was unsympathetic.

Third act: My role was nonexistent.

Bernstein stopped to recover his breath. Sensing my disappointment, he whispered into my ear: "The sugar is at the end."

Fourth act: No sugar.

Fifth act: The sugar is hard to swallow.

A few hours later I went back to see Bernstein. He received me with: "If it's to ask my permission to do a film, the answer is no."

"I don't want to do your play."

Being hit on the head with his Manet portrait couldn't have brought a ruder shock. He swooned, choked, tore his hair, and barely had enough strength to call his secretary to the rescue . . .

"Do you know what this little worm has just had the nerve to say to me?"

"?"

"He says he doesn't want to do my play! Never, do you hear, *never* has even Sarah Bernhardt had the gall to . . ."

"But it's not gall. On the contrary, I'm saying with great respect . . ."

"You can take your respect and shove it!"

". . . that I have the deepest admiration for your work . . ."

"The hell with your admiration!"

". . . but this part has nothing to do with what you promised me, or with the sacrifice I've had to make for it!"

In the secretary's icy look I could read: "You've really done it this time. It'll take a month to calm him down."

"In any case," bellowed Bernstein, "you can begin by giving me six hundred thousand francs and then . . ."

"Three hundred thousand."

"No, *six hundred thousand*. Last night you signed a paper that doubled the breach of contract clause. Maybe you drank too much to remember."

Since I was unable to cough up 600,000 francs for Bernstein, I had to do *Le Coeur*. Rehearsals began—directed with such mastery!—by a Bernstein become charming once again. No director could break in an actor like he could, or make a text come alive by silences, variations in rhythm, and tiny, instinctive gestures. He could simplify the most melodramatic sentence by suggesting that we pause, sigh, contemplate our fingernails, or touch the arm of a chair. He had a horror of anything facile or conventional, of anything which produced hackneyed readings. He asked us to overreach these usual interpretations with unexpected or unusual inflections.

On opening night I received several gifts, two of which brought me particular pleasure. One was a little poem that Louise de Vilmorin had hidden, for my benefit, in a bouquet of wildflowers:

> J'te vois rêveur et j'te vois beau
> Quand j'te vois beau, je suis rêveuse
> Quand t'es rêveur, je suis peureuse
> Quand t'es les deux, tout est nouveau.

The other gift was more concrete. It was a live pig. Pieps, the young daughter of Granowsky, my director for *Tarass Bulba*, had sent me this strange gift to bring me luck.

Bernstein turned pale when he saw it. My piglet had metamorphosed into a wild boar and was charging him. He screamed and shouted for the police, convinced that the unchained beast would devour him whole, or at least trample him underfoot. To the pig, however, he was merely an obstacle. It butted him out of the way and galloped backstage like a true ham. It ended up under the skirts of an actress who entrusted it to my dresser to make pork chops out of it.

We were called on stage. We said "Merde" to each other. That's the French way to wish 'Good luck" or "Break a leg." As tradition requires, Bernstein grabbed a huge wooden cane from the stage manager and pounded on the floor nine times, then more slowly three times. The curtain rose.

The play began with a scene between Hélène Perdrière and me. It was a scene of intimate, bashful confessions. I admitted to her that I loved her, although she was the wife of my best friend. For six weeks we had been rehearsing in a low key, exchanging sighs and murmurs.

But that night the honking taxis, clumsy usherettes, program vendors unloading their trash, slamming doors, banging seats, and stepped-on feet provided an annoying accompaniment to our love duet, all but drowning it out. Bernstein was making desperate signals to us from the wings. Finally, we had to shout like maniacs, which made the scene meaningless, since the whole play depended upon the husband being in the next room and not hearing a word of my confession. The only possible way we could have saved the play at that point was by improvising some lines about his hearing problem.

At midnight, Bernstein called me on stage and congratulated me. Then he asked me if I thought that my scene in the fifth act was necessary.

"Yes, I do."

"Well, I don't."

"If you cut it, I warn you, I'll be sick tomorrow," I shouted.

"I wouldn't think of cutting your scene, my boy," he said, embracing me.

To tell the truth, I hated playing that scene. I could never manage to enter with tears streaming down my face, and I had to resort to ammonia. I'd always disliked that kind of subterfuge.

The next morning my father woke me up. "Now just listen to me calmly," he said. "Bernstein telephoned me at dawn. He's offering you a compromise. He'll cut your scene in the fifth act—now stop hollering and listen to me!—and give you permission to make a film in exchange. If you agree, go and have lunch with him."

Bernstein was very amusing during luncheon that day, imitating the people who had complimented him at the stage door the night before. (He always stood at the stage door after every performance, waiting to shake hands like the groom at a wedding reception.) There was the colleague who had said to him: "My dear, with actors like that . . . !"; there was the actor who had said: "Dauphin is good, of course, but with lines like that . . ." Then there was some idiot who'd blurted out: "So what have you been up to?"; and the unknown man who had whispered in his ear: "My dear, you're not going to believe me, but I was so overwhelmed by the end of the third act that I leaned over toward my wife and said: 'Oh!' Those were my very words!"

Before we parted, I asked Bernstein to write our new arrangement into the contract.

"You mean you don't trust me?" he asked, in an injured tone of voice.

We parted the best of friends, even though he had exploited me and cast me for the part by using strategy that would have embarrassed Machiavelli. I don't know anybody who could have resisted the old man when he took the trouble to turn on his reserve of charm, humor, and persuasiveness.

Embellished by many uncontrollable bursts of laughter, the performances of *Le Coeur* continued until the summer of 1936. Then Bernstein granted us a month of rest. I convinced Claude that real vacations could only be taken on an island where the surrounding sea provided a barrier to newspapers, mail, the telephone, and other pains in the ass associated with civilized life. I also convinced Blanche Montel and Rosine Deréan to come with us. We left for Majorca.

One morning we were strolling along the shore at Formentor when we fell into a trance before a low, white house peering at us through a jungle of cactus and trees. It was a Mediterranean paradise of ordered luxuriance and savage grace . . . Two peasants signaled us to enter. They offered us wine in a shady room decorated with rare earthenware plates.

"Who does this *casita* belong to?" I asked, trembling with desire.

"The Señor Ramires."

"You think he would rent it to us?'

"Si . . . si."

The same evening we moved in.

Rosine started rearranging things in the middle of the night. The rare earthenware belonging to Señor Ramires was smashed to pieces. For no particular reason she found it necessary to move the beds into the kitchen, the kitchen things onto the patio, and the patio furniture into the bedroom. Claude and I staggered around under the weight of buffets, sofas, and plaster saints, shuttling between an annoyed Blanche and a Rosine gone wild. Dawn found us collapsed in the midst of bits of crockery, broken furniture, and beheaded saints.

Sometimes we left our little *casita* to become acquainted with the inhabitants of Formentor. We encountered a blonde British actress who, followed by a black woman, walked the sands seductively, waiting impatiently to be recognized by a parasol pine or a palm tree. Our next-door neighbor was a fat American woman who lived in Paris on Saint-Germain-des-Prés and had been wounded by a series of Left Bank love affairs. In front of our house, a dark boy, with hair as curly as a Greek shepherd's, was being pursued by a loose girl who wore a charcoal sack for a dress and lived on the beach. For this charming and motley society we decided to throw a cocktail party on our terrace. Our glasses were soon full of mosquitoes.

"Another mosquito cocktail?" asked Claude, ever the gentleman.

Just then, a bomb exploded on a hillside, too close for comfort.

"Quesaco?" we asked our two servants.

"Bah . . . un poco de revolucion."

The Greek shepherd had profited from this interruption by having a quickie under the cactus plant with the British star, who wrongly surmised that someone had finally recognized her.

Poco or not, I had to leave my friends and return to France to shoot *La Porte du large*.

I arrived in Paris during the hullabaloo of the 14th of July. No one here suspected that the "poco de revolucion" was the beginning of the Spanish Civil War. In the months that followed, while I was shooting my film in Bretagne, my friends were waiting to be repatriated from Formentor in the midst of daily bombardments.

Meanwhile we were filming the exteriors for *La Porte du large* in Brest. We were living at the top of a street of brothels in the quite respectable Hotel de la Poste. It was a peaceful establishment, maintained by two timid old ladies; and since their usual clients were a few traveling salesmen, two or three priests, and some retired naval officers, the arrival of a film company caused quite a stir.

There in Brest we had been handed our scenarios and Victor Francen and I had become indignant when we discovered that our roles were considerably different from the way they had been described to us. They had been cut down to the benefit of Roland Toutain, a young actor-acrobat, who was now, in fact, the hero of the story. Not only had he been given the comic, fanciful scenes, as had been expected, but also the love scenes, which I had thought were for me, and also the scenes of heroism, which were Victor's hunting grounds. Roland Toutain had even been granted the privilege of saving a plane in danger and becoming blind in the course of it.

Victor and I discussed our strategy and decided to send two

letters of complaint to our producer, asking him to accept our resignations.

When our director Marcel Lherbier learned that Victor and I didn't want to do the film, he tried to arrange matters by offering to put out Victor's eyes (I mean in the film). Victor was thrilled. But Mary Marquet maintained that her husband's female fans wouldn't be able to stand seeing him blinded. Besides, *she* couldn't get used to it either. Lherbier's suggestion went quickly into the wastebasket.

Then someone suggested making Victor one-eyed. This had been more or less fashionable ever since the days of Nelson. Now the fans would still have one eye, and the bandage over the other would lend a note of heroism.

We began shooting.

Eve Francis, a hoarse tragedienne who had specialized in the works of Claudel, was hired to rehearse the actors. She had got it into her head at the start to try to transform Roland into a dramatic actor. Pinning him into a corner, she provoked him, hypnotized him, tried everything to get the right reaction. Finally, weeping herself, she begged: "Cry, Roland, think of that admiral that you respect who's lost his right eye. Cry! Think of his wife, think of his son, think of his *right eye* . . ."

Roland burst out laughing.

There was another scuffle between Marcel Lherbier and myself over the subject of beef stew. In a scene between the admiral and his son, Victor was supposed to ask me, "How's the food at school?" and I was supposed to answer, "Good."

I asked Lherbier to add, "Except for the beef stew." Why? I really don't know. Lherbier refused. I kept insisting.

"I'd feel a lot more comfortable with the beef stew. Somehow I just can't answer 'Good.' It's so terse."

"But 'beef stew' sounds so stupid!"

"Why? What's wrong with beef stew?"

"What's good about it? I forbid you to mention beef stew."

"It's a free country. I'll talk about beef stew if I want to."

Finally, the producer decided that we would shoot the scene twice, one time with the beef stew and one time without it.

4

Where the Hell Is Honduras?

Drôle de Drame marks a turning point in the history of French cinema. It was France's first attempt to produce the kind of screwball comedy at which the Americans excelled. We had had our comedians, of course, but they were only offered military farces or slapstick.

Louis Jouvet as the clergyman, Jean-Louis Barrault as the tender assassin, and Michel Simon as the innocent botanist created profound characters, types as defined as Harlequin, Pierrot, or Scapin. I played a milk delivery boy obsessed with criminology. In a droll costume of beige top hat, striped shirt, rubber gloves, purple satin apron, and linen pants, I marched through the film crying: "M-i-i-i-ilk! . . . M-i-i-i-i-ilk."

The publicity man had had the bright idea of decorating the façade of the Colisée, where *Drôle de Drame* was playing, with blown-up photos of our reviews. Naturally, he tried to choose the most flattering excerpts for each of us. Thousands of pedestrians walking down the Champs-Elysées every day past the Colisée saw the following words posted under my photo: "Miracle of miracles! Jean-Pierre Aumont is almost believable!"

At that time *Drôle de Drame* wasn't a big success. But ten years later, after the war, it made an extraordinary comeback. I suppose Jacques Prévert's humor was ahead of its time in 1937.

In July Rosine and Claude decided to get married. It was like a wedding in an operetta with the provincial accent of the mayor, the choir of young girls, and the village of Roquebrune-sur-Argens perched on top of a hill. Rosine was wearing a blue dress that matched her eyes and Claude was all in white with an unbelievable little hat that looked like a child's. Only four of us were there. Blanche was Rosine's maid of honor and I was Claude's best man. I'd stocked up with several boxes of candies which I threw at the children of the village after the ceremony. Blanche remarked that I should have been throwing rice instead. I was crushed.

On the way to Saint-Tropez, where we had established our headquarters, we noticed a little elf with his cape floating out behind him, wavering uncertainly in the center of the road, as lines of startled drivers veered around him. As we drew closer we recognized Paul Géraldy, a poet friend of ours. Seemingly unconscious of the fact that he was holding up the flow of traffic, he signaled our car to stop. Then he peered anxiously inside and, over the sound of the angry honking coming from behind, shouted, "Do you think that the cinema is going to take the place of the theater?"

"Yes, and my ass, too, shithead!" bellowed the angry driver in back of us.

Our friend invited us to dinner for the following day, at his estate at Beauvallon.

"Come at sunset, there are mauves and shades of pink that you wouldn't believe."

Unfolding his wings, he glided away.

Night had long since fallen when we arrived at his home. We dined to the chirping of crickets by candlelight.

"Lower the shade a bit," sang the poet, keeping time to his most famous verse with a raised fork on which dangled a piece of veal. Rosine was dozing; at times Claude or I would give her a sharp kick under the table. She would wake up with a start, venture at random, "But really, poems like yours will never disappear," and go back to sleep.

At Saint-Tropez reigned Colette. Or, rather, Madame Colette, as we all called her with respect and admiration, for she was, since George Sand, the most renowned woman writer of the French language. *Gigi*, her most popular work, shows only a superficial aspect of her talent. There was more depth and a more brilliant style in such novels as *Chéri* or *La Naissance du Jour*. She was also famous for her repartees. Once, looking at her best friend on her deathbed, she sighed: "Poor Marguerite! She certainly wasn't made to be a corpse!" To her sixteen-year-old daughter, Bel Gazou, she said: "You've arrived at an age to make a complete ass of yourself. At least do it with enthusiasm."

I went to see her at her vine-covered estate of "La Treille Muscate." Having read with rapture every one of her novels, I had imagined some kind of ethereal creature lying on a sofa like the dying Elizabeth Browning, in *The Barrets of Wimpole Street*. How wrong I was! I found myself facing a strong and stout woman, talking in a hoarse voice with the rugged accent of Burgundy, enjoying everything in life to the utmost, whether food, or sports, or arts, or love.

After a day spent in helping her dig holes in her garden, she invited me to stay for dinner. It was an overwhelmingly hot day. I asked her if I could take a shower.

"Get undressed and stand over here," she ordered; "my plants need water."

There was no way to say no to Colette. I had to stand, naked, in the center of her bougainvillaea, and let her sprinkle me with her watering can.

Walking through the rich forests which bordered the deserted beaches of Saint-Tropez, I bumped into a couple of poachers: Madeleine Renaud and Jean-Louis Barrault. They were living in a tent, sheltering their pantheistic romance in the depths of the woods. A year earlier, I had known Madeleine to be a confirmed city-dweller, dividing her time between the Comédie Française, the film studios, and the education of her son. But the miracle of love had transformed her into an anarchist girl scout, trapping rabbits and fish by her lover's side.

I left Saint-Tropez with regret. I had signed to go to Algeria to make *S.O.S. Sahara*.

Our female star, Martha Labarr, had the turned up nose and prominent cheekbones of Marlene Dietrich. She accentuated this resemblance as much as she could. Since Marlene had worn several miles of veiling in *The Garden of Allah*, my co-star, who was playing a woman lost in the desert, did the same, whether it fitted in with the scenes in the script or not. She appeared every day for shooting in feathers and rose gauze, and her attempt at imitating the Dietrich style made her look more like Theda Bara.

While we were in Munich to film the interior sequences of *S.O.S. Sahara*, Hitler invaded Austria. One afternoon my attention was attracted to a large mob in the street. Hitler had returned from Vienna and was parading through Munich, standing up in an open car with his arm outstretched and eyes fixed. The onlookers bowed down and murmured what seemed like a prayer. There was no cry, no acclamation, but rather a kind of mystic trance, much more terrifying in a different way.

The war was coming—you could almost feel it in the air. In our hearts we knew that Munich had only been a brief respite.

Once again I did a picture with Anabella and Louis Jouvet: *Hôtel du Nord*. How strange it was for me to be co-starring with the man who had taught me everything I knew.

Afterwards, I went to Denmark and Sweden with Blanche. Happy vagabonds that we were . . . these were the last days of peace and pleasure. On returning to Paris on the fourteenth of July, I saw Marlene Dietrich singing on the steps of the Opera: "Lorsque tout est fini . . ." ("When it's all over") Little did we know how right she was.

I managed to eke out a few more days of vacation in the south at Juan-les-Pins, where the Charleston alternated with the Booms-a-daisy. The bandleader, dressed like Hitler, taunted the saxophonist, disguised as Mussolini. Women allowed themselves to be hoisted over shoulders with their feet in the air, revealing their thighs and their bellies, transformed by the heat, the noise, the music, and the insanity of the time into revelers without wills of their own.

It was like a cannibal celebration or a black mass. Everyone was greedy for the last moments of a disintegrating world.

Maybe these orgies were, after all, only bewildered prayers.

I received my mobilization papers at Cavalaire. I hardly suspected that I would disembark five years later at this exact place for the liberation of France. Ignorant as we were at the time, it was impossible to imagine our country vanquished.

I was assigned to the 3rd Armored Division, which didn't exist yet. While awaiting its formation I acted as assistant to Jean Giraudoux at the Ministry of Information. Feeling less at ease in the "phony war" than on the sunny slopes of Troy, he directed the Ministry of Information with a sluggish indifference.

At the end of a month I left him. With an official embrace he said to me, "You have rendered a great service." For a Minister of Information he seemed very poorly informed!

It was at Reims that I joined my regiment. At that time the "phony war" had reached a deceptive hiatus. Paris was trying its hand at appearing militant.

WE WILL WIN BECAUSE WE ARE THE STRONGEST, said the posters. Cocteau proposed: WE WILL WIN BECAUSE WE ARE THE WEAKEST!, to which Jouvet countered: WE WILL WIN BECAUSE THEY ARE THE BIGGEST ASSHOLES!

On May 8, 1940, I received a telegram telling me that my mother was on her deathbed. I obtained permission to be with her during her last hours. She had a heart disease which in those days was incurable.

Although weakened and emaciated, fighting for her breath, she hadn't lost any of her eccentric geniality. The night before she died she said to the doctor who was examining her, "Let's face it, doctor, you don't give a damn whether I live or die."

And as the poor man protested, she added, smiling, "Don't worry about it. If you were dying I wouldn't give a damn either."

I tried to comfort her. I swore to her that the war would soon be over, that she would get better, that we would all go to the South together for her convalescence. She smiled, but she didn't believe me.

On May 13 the Germans, who had invaded Luxembourg,

Holland, and Belgium, seized control of the airfield at The Hague. My mother could no longer breathe. She took a last look, full of love, at my father, my brother, and myself. Then she murmured, "What a pity. We were so happy . . ." and it was over.

On May 15 the Germans were at Antwerp and at Abbeville. Since my furlough was up, I had to leave my father and my brother to their grief and rejoin my unit. The 3rd Armored Division was no longer stationed at Reims. The army had started its retreat, a disorganized effort, verging on panic, with a few soldiers carrying on trying to stem the German advance. A laughable attempt. We were engulfed and pushed toward the south as if by a tornado.

In the villages we passed through, the houses were plundered, the furniture overturned, the linen scattered, and photos, letters, books soiled and trampled. The German planes rained bombs on us as we huddled together in ditches. Children screamed, women sobbed, soldiers ran in all directions. Bullets spurted everywhere. From the door of a farmhouse an old woman howled: "What's happening? I want to know what's happening . . ."

Clambering through that hell over the hoods of cars or the running boards of trucks which were advancing in slow motion, I tried to locate the rest of my unit. I could hear fragments of sentences coming from a radio. General Weygand was giving his last orders of the day: "The enemy will soon be at the end of his powers. Just hold on."

Idiots! We were beaten, but good!

Not far from Toulouse, eight hundred kilometers from Reims, where I had left them, I found some of my comrades. They had changed so much in the last few days that I had trouble recognizing them. They were starving and in shock, incapable of understanding what had happened. Some were still shaken by convulsions. Others had disappeared, been killed, or taken prisoner.

I was alive, on account of the death of my mother. It was as if she had chosen to die on the thirteenth of May to protect me. Ever since that day, all the important events of my life have occurred on the thirteenth, including the birth of my first son. It's as if my mother wished to let me know that she is still watching over me.

Then Pétain called for an armistice. "I have asked our adversaries [they were no longer our enemies] to meet with me in honor and dignity." France was divided in two, with the northern half and the Atlantic coast under German rule, and a smaller section remaining—for the time being—unoccupied. We were demobilized at Toulouse. On the Place Lafayette, as circular as a carousel, the survivors wandered round and round . . .

On June 18, a man spoke from London: "We have lost a battle, we haven't lost the war . . ." What kind of bull was he giving us? "Immense forces haven't entered the action yet . . ." Oh, really? What were they waiting for? Where had they been fifteen days ago when we needed them? No one quite caught the name of this pathetic dreamer . . . La Gaulle? Begaule?

At that time Vichy seemed—how naive we were then!—to be a haven in the debacle. I went there to meet my father. Autumn seemed overladen with our defeat. A long period of shock began—the dregs of the struggle.

We strolled around the hot springs of Vichy without hope, like the victims of some incurable disease caught in an endless pilgrimage. To Jean Luchaire, who had already started to collaborate, Jouvet said with a premonitory smile, "You will be hanged, my dear friend."

Cocteau remarked: "Either we didn't have enough faith or we didn't have enough bad faith to win this war."

Gide was forbidden to lecture. They held him responsible for our defeat. When he asked me, "What are your plans?" I answered: "To live." An ambitious answer in those days.

From La Charité-sur-Loire, where he had been fighting, Claude wrote me: "Cheers, Jeantou. There's not much left for us to do, now that everything has collapsed. Let's drink to the health of the good old days, 'casitas' and innocent laughter; it's all over now. At least we had it once; that's better than nothing."

Little by little, like a man who has undergone a serious operation, we were getting used to our new lives. I went to meet Claude at Cannes, where many actors had gathered. We all decided to give some performances in the unoccupied zone, which we referred to—and rightly so—as "the pre-occupied zone."

Those actors who didn't want to or couldn't go back to Paris dragged their grief and their makeup into all sorts of unlikely places: outdoor theaters, circuses, town halls, garages, barns, or creaking bandstands. Sometimes we were lucky enough to perform in real eighteenth-century theaters, marvels of architecture and proportion.

A town crier would announce on the square that that evening Claude Dauphin, Danielle Darrieux, or myself was going to appear in such and such a comedy, not on film but in the flesh.

I had chosen to act in *Trois et Une*, a comedy by Denys Amiel. At the end of the performances, Robert Lynen, who was playing my younger brother, would mysteriously disappear. He was a sensitive and introspective twenty-year-old who had become famous as a child actor.

We used to tease him when he refused to reveal the whereabouts of his private rendezvous. We didn't know that he was actually meeting a group of the Resistance of which he was already a member.

Poor Robert. Not long afterwards he was arrested, sent off to Germany, and brought before a firing squad. We were told that before he was shot, he had even won the admiration of his executioners.

I'll never forget how he looked on the night before Christmas, 1940, when we were playing at Perpignan. It was very cold. Robert was marching along with a pack on his back, looking like a boy scout. After the performance we got together for a frugal Christmas eve supper and began reciting passages from *Phaedra* and *Britannicus*.

Robert was entranced. Right then and there he decided to learn the classics. Nothing seemed more urgent to him. The tragic fate which lay in wait for him, the risks he was already taking, everything that he knew or could foresee—all this was nothing compared to the immediate necessity of learning some scenes from *Phaedra* and *Britannicus* before the night train departed for Beziers. Today there aren't many of us left who were there as he walked out of the restaurant for the station, with a sailor's bag over his shoulder and his teeth chattering, keeping himself warm with some verses from *Phaedra:*

> Dans le fond des forêts votre image me suit.
> Les lumières du jour, les ombres de la nuit,
> Tout retrace à mes yeux les charmes que j'évite . . .*

Or perhaps with another confession of Hippolytus which would have described him so well:

> Le jour n'est pas plus pur que le fond de mon coeur.†

The last performance of *Trois et Une* took place at Antibes. Among the people who came to congratulate us was a man of about thirty who introduced himself to me as the consul of Honduras.

What strange forces control our lives? Some days later I was lunching at the home of some friends and the subject of autograph hunters came up. Without attaching any particular importance to it, I told them that the consul of Honduras had come backstage to ask us to sign his program. I saw my friends grow pale. They shouted: "And you didn't ask him for a visa?"

"A visa for where?"

"For Honduras!"

"Where the hell is Honduras?"

"It's in America, you jerk!"

At that time, leaving for the States was every young actor's

---

* Your image haunts me in the forest's depth,
  The light of day, the dark of night,
  All trace again before my eyes the charms that I avoid . . .

† The very light of day is not more pure than my heart's core.

dream. But you had to have a visa. And, to get a visa you needed a contract.

At my friends' insistence, I went looking for the consul. I found him, by chance, in a street in Cannes. His name—may God keep him—was Mauricio Rosal. He gave me a visa for Honduras, with the right to spend a week in New York in transit.

A few days later there was a boat leaving from Portugal.

When I arrived in Lisbon, I couldn't believe my eyes. Such an abundance of food, wealth, everything we no longer had! Beautiful cars gliding down the avenues. Cheeses displayed in shop windows, light golden in color. The street stalls buckled under mounds of butter, fish, or fruit. How beautiful it all was! At least the hardships we were enduring had given us back the gift of wonder.

At the end of July, I embarked on the *Nyassa*. Lisbon disappeared in the setting sun. Dolphins swam in the estuary of the Tagus. Soon we had overtaken a small barge filled with hay.

It was black as night as we entered the ocean. A woman threw a bunch of flowers over the handrail into the dark water. The lights of Estoril came into view, the last glittering extremity of Europe.

Gazing at the wake of the boat, I mulled over my memories. A sentence from one of my films brought tears to my eyes: "You always say: 'There goes another boat, leaving.' There are also those which return . . ."

Would I ever return?

5

NEW YORK, KATHARINE CORNELL, AND GREGORY PECK

"Get a move on! We're arriving. New York!"

I spring from my berth and rush to the bow of the ship. It's dawn. I can barely make out a few points of light on the approaching shore.

Starting all over again in a new country is like drinking from the Fountain of Youth. I feel energetic and light, as if I were sixteen once more.

We glide past the Statue of Liberty. At its foot lies Ellis Island. There is a strange inconsistency between this statue, holding out a beacon for all the peoples of the earth, and this island, where immigrants are screened and sometimes refused. All of us feel frightened, and somehow guilty; are we going to make it?

Before long a welter of concrete and steel bursts from the fog, a jagged mass in the form of a ship's prow, sprouting towers and cubes.

"New York, I'm ready for you . . ."

The taxi driver seems friendly. He slows down as we pass the gray *Normandie* which is moored to its dock. There is a French sailor on the deck fifty feet above my head who looks as lost and isolated as I am.

Times Square. Next to the billboards, the uninterrupted flow of pedestrians is an army of ants. A giant mouth vaunting the virtues of Camel cigarettes sends jets of steam toward a polluted sky. It is 10 A.M. The flashing marquees of the movie houses are crammed one against the other. There is something invigorating about all this squalor. It is anonymous, uncaring, perhaps even hostile. But it grows . . . and it grows . . . it's alive.

The only person I know in New York is Henri Bernstein. A valet in white gloves meets me at the door to his Waldorf-Astoria apartment. The walls are covered with the pictures he has managed to save: a Toulouse-Lautrec, a Courbet, some elegant drawings by Constantin Guys, and his own portrait, as a child in a sailor suit, by Manet.

"Come in, come in, *mon cher*. What *are* you waiting for?" The voice is just as hoarse, the tone as pompous as ever.

When I step into the room, there's no one there.

"I'm in the bathroom, where else? Come in."

I find him, lounging in a bathtub full of suds. Before I have a chance to tell him how glad I am to see him, he stands up suddenly out of the bubbles and throws his arms wide to expose the gargantuan mass of his seventy years. "Take a close look. Do you think my body's still good enough for the beaches?"

It has been two years since we've seen each other. In the meantime war has broken out. Poland, Belgium, Holland, Denmark, and France have been invaded. Millions of people, including some of our friends, have been killed, taken prisoner, or deported. He doesn't ask me for any news; he doesn't want to know by what miracle I have ended up in New York. He just wants to know if he could still cut a figure on the beaches.

I assure him that few physiques have preserved such majesty.

"You're not just saying that to make me feel good?"

Compared to him, I declare with hand on heart, the Apollo of Belvedere is a puny runt.

Reassured, he climbs out of his bath and drapes himself in a large towel like a toga. He is as gigantic and imposing as Notre Dame with its spires and arches and gargoyles—especially its gargoyles.

While admiring himself in the mirror he asks me (finally!) how I've been able to leave France. "Through sheer luck, I met . . ." He doesn't let me continue. In any case, he wouldn't have heard.

"Your arrival couldn't have occurred at a better time, dear boy. I'm in the process of writing a play for Katharine Cornell . . . I see by the bovine expression on your face that you've never heard of her."

"I just got here . . ."

"She's merely the greatest actress in America, that's all. You can tell Sarah Bernhardt and Helen Hayes to start packing. She can play *any*thing. She has the brow of an intellectual, the eyes of a saint, and the mouth of a whore. I don't know anybody in France who compares. Anyway, there aren't any actresses in France . . . even less actors . . . B. is a genius at loafing, without genius. F. can only play emperors or thugs, he's limited. Charles Boyer? He won't do Thursday matinees. You call that an actor? Did I tell you that Kit's husband—yes, she lets me call her Kit . . . I'm quite a ladies' man over here—is the director and the producer? Well, dear boy, he is. I've made things easier by writing this play directly in English . . . I was helped by a secretary who happens to have nice little buns . . . By the way, do you speak English? You should start. Everybody speaks English in this country, there's nothing we can do about it. Where were we? . . . oh, yes, in this play—it's the best I've ever written—there's an absolutely sublime role for you. Kit and Guthrie are having dinner with me this evening. Come over at nine o'clock for coffee . . . and learn English by then . . ."

At nine on the dot, showered, closely shaven, and dressed to the teeth, I arrived at his apartment with my heart pounding. Looking more Olympian than ever, Bernstein introduced me to Kit Cornell and Guthrie McClintic.

Miss Cornell was in the process of eating, or should I say

devouring. Voraciously. Voluptuously. At forty there was more of the peasant about her than of the actress. Nothing affected or artificial; but something warm and robust, like the scent of hay. Her handshake was solid, she had a clear and hearty laugh, and she looked you straight in the eye when she talked. I liked her immediately.

Her husband, on the other hand, wore a fixed, ironic smile that was anything but pleasant. He looked me over pityingly from head to toe with an expression that seemed to say, "So this is what Bernstein has been raving about for the last three hours? Nothing to write home about . . ."

He asked me if I spoke English.

"Not much," I said, in English, rather satisfied with my answer.

"Just the same, you do know a few words, don't you?"

"I know 'akimbo.' "

To illustrate I put my hands on my hips. There was a horrible silence. McClintic looked at me as if I were retarded. Bernstein began chewing his nails. Kit burst out laughing; but it was a laugh full of tenderness. In an attempt to recover from this faux pas, and to prove to them that I did know some English, I launched into a stammering tirade about the extent of their popularity with the French.

Bernstein, seeing that I had gone too far in my efforts at flattery and thinking that the less they heard from me the better, stood up.

"My dear boy, leave us alone now, will you? I'll call you tomorrow. By the way, where are you living?"

"At the Paramount Hotel."

Once again there was a long silence. Bernstein stared at me as if I had gone mad. He couldn't imagine anyone living anywhere but at the Waldorf, and certainly not at the Paramount, which was on the West Side. Kit couldn't have cared less about it, happy as she was with her camembert. McClintic threw me another of his caustic looks.

Not knowing what to do, I murmured, "It's . . . central."

"Oh! that . . . ," said McClintic, "that it is."

Laconically he let some cigarette ashes fall on the rug.

I left them and drifted around in the hallway for a while, incapable of finding the elevator.

All of the next day, a Wednesday, I waited in vain for the telephone to ring. Pacing about in my room like a caged animal, I repeated over and over again to myself that, after all, I was no beginner, I'd proven myself already, I'd made a name for myself in Europe, they could take that part and shove it . . . In other moments I admitted that I was a complete unknown in this new world and would have to start all over again.

How on earth could I have been stupid enough to say I was living at the Paramount? I could have said I was staying with friends. A phone number would have been enough . . . And why had I uttered the word 'akimbo'? I'd learned in school that it meant "hands on hips" . . . but maybe it meant something else over here . . . maybe it meant "fuck you," or something . . .

Thursday I decided that it was against my dignity to wait any longer. I took a stroll down Fifth Avenue, where I mistook Rockefeller Center for St. Patrick's Cathedral. To my great surprise I also discovered Simone Simon standing in front of Cartier's window, looking at her own reflection. She invited me to go to Westport with her that same evening. Annabella and Tyrone Power, husband and wife at the time, were opening there in *Liliom*.

When we got to Westport several journalists pounced on Simone and asked her if I were her new lover. Such audacity astounded me, but Simone seemed used to it. She answered with the most charming smile: "We're old friends."

Annabella and Tyrone Power were an incredibly handsome couple. How they loved each other! And how I envied them for being on a stage . . . Acting was like opium to me, and I needed it badly.

It wasn't until the following Monday that my telephone rang. Without saying hello—but I was used to that—Bernstein thundered:

"I got you two hundred a week. I was an idiot, I could have gotten more. They want you at any price. Just between us, *mon cher*, I can't get over it. You acted like a simpleton the other night . . . well, one shouldn't try to understand. Go see Gert Macy right away. She's the manager of their company. Do you know her sister Louise? You don't know anybody, do you? Well, she happens to be Harry Hopkins' wife. Tell Gert that you know her very well . . ."

"But I've never even seen her!"

"I'm telling you to pretend that you're best friends. That'll cinch the contract. Don't laugh, dear boy, it's essential . . ."

On the twenty-eighth floor of a Times Square building, the profile of Gert Macy was silhouetted against a view of the *Normandie* anchored in port. Sitting very upright in her tweed suit, shielded by dark glasses, Miss Macy said, "How wonderful that you're a friend of my sister! She's coming over tonight. Please have dinner with us. I know she'll be thrilled to see you again."

The following day I met Saint-Exupéry, whom I had known slightly in Paris. Under a rough and awkward veneer he had the naive heart of the Little Prince. As soon as he knew that I was going to stay in New York, he offered me his penthouse. "I'm leaving for California tonight. Take the keys and make yourself at home as long as you like . . ."

It was a duplex with a terrace that had a view of the whole island of Manhattan, stretched out like a long ship between the Hudson and East rivers.

Bernstein read me his play, the story of a sculptress, Rose Burke, in love with a fifty-year-old businessman and a young Frenchman at the same time. I had only two scenes, but they were essential to the plot and the part would be fun. For the rest of the play—five endless acts—I fought against falling asleep. It's true that I didn't understand a lot of what Bernstein was reading me, but he took no notice of that, delighting in each word and grunting with pleasure every three lines or so.

After such a hectic week, I still had to go to Honduras to exchange my temporary visa for a permanent one which would give me the right to work in the United States. As we took off for Central America, I was treated to a bird's-eye view of New York at midnight. A web of shimmering dots merged into a volcano crater: Times Square at night.

Who would have thought eighteen months before when I was crawling from ditch to ditch with the bombs raining down on me that I would be spending the first of October in Tegucigalpa, capital of Honduras!

A tropical sun overwhelms the town enclosed by seven gloomy green mountains. There is something African in the whiteness of its houses, the abject poverty of its street urchins, and the clouds of dust. From age five to thirty, all of the men are in uniform, either as schoolboys or as soldiers. Overripe melons and giant bananas, the provisions of the day, glide by on the heads of the women. At eight o'clock the whole town (a mixture of Spanish and Mayan with the reddish color and cheekbones of Indians) gathers in the market place. The church has been decorated like a music hall, with red streamers and lighted crosses . . . The voice of the priest is drowned in the blare of a military band set up in the church courtyard. The beggars are discreet here, but the country has an atmosphere of poverty, despite the silver mines so numerous that up until recently they were still shoeing their horses with silver.

The next morning I got my visa. On the thirteenth of October I officially entered the United States at Miami. The immigration officer asked me if I approved of polygamy. I must have said the right thing, because he let me through and wished me good luck.

As soon as I got back to New York I started working.

I had a month before the *Rose Burke* rehearsals to forget the English I had learned at school and replace it with the English spoken in this country. There was often not much similarity between the two. I had to try not to be confused when I heard "thanks" instead of "thank you." I had to get used to "can't" in place of "cannot." On Broadway, "tonight" was spelled "tonite."

I found another hotel called the Mayflower which would, it seemed to me, cause less of a stir at the mention of its address.

My first night there the telephone rang at 4 A.M. It was—who else at that hour?—Bernstein.

"Hello, little one, did I wake you? It couldn't matter less. I'm taking you to Washington tomorrow. Kit Cornell is doing a trifle by Shaw, *The Doctor's Dilemma*, or something like that. Why she wants to prostitute herself in the provinces instead of concentrating on the role I wrote for her is a mystery. Maybe she needs the money, but, after all—what can I do about it? I want you to study her carefully and tell me what you think of her . . . in all frankness. What train? You're crazy . . . Nobody takes the train in this country; I don't even know if there are any . . . There's a perfectly sublime airplane that goes from New York to Washington in five minutes . . . You must be dead drunk, Jean-Pierre—again! . . . I assure you, you worry me sometimes . . ."

The next morning I dropped by his hotel to pick him up. When we climbed into a taxi, I heard him tell the driver to take us to the train station. "But I thought we were taking an airplane," I ventured timidly.

"Don't be absurd, dear boy! Nobody takes a plane in this country. I don't even know if there are any. Everybody takes the train. There are some absolutely divine ones with air conditioning which only take a half hour. Why do you want to risk our lives in a plane? You're talking nonsense again, my boy. I thought you were more sophisticated than that . . ."

Washington. The curtain rises, and Bernstein repeats his instructions. "I want your sincere and brutal opinion of her. If you think she's bad, which is highly possible, just tell me right out. Be blunt. Nothing in the world can force me to give my play—the best thing I've ever written—to that woman . . ."

Kit Cornell makes her entrance. Applause. I feel Bernstein's nails sinking into my forearm.

"She's divine, isn't she? . . . What an actress! . . . (she hasn't said a word) . . . But why in the name of heaven does she waste her time with such nonsense?"

Back in New York, David Selznick, the mighty producer of *Gone with the Wind*, peers down the length of his cigar at me. I feel like a horse at a county fair having his teeth inspected. He is a formidable man, untidy, arrogant, talkative. He sits with his feet on the table. I am offered a contract of two hundred dollars a week. On Berstein's advice, I tell him I don't want to sign anything before the premiere of *Rose Burke.*

On December seventh, I am lunching at a restaurant with a friend when the radio announces that the Japanese have bombed Pearl Harbor. Hundreds dead. Several battleships sunk. Everyone around me continues to eat. Not the slightest reaction. Then shouts and screams all of a sudden. "What's happened?" I ask. "Has Roosevelt declared war?"

"Oh, no," my friend answers, "it's the results of the football game . . ."

San Francisco. The streets are vertical. Invisible cables entrusted with hoisting the trolleys to the tops of the hills make a noise like crickets. Kit has invited me for Christmas. I have received some cards signed "with love" from people I hardly know. In France, in those days, you wrote your own message on blank cards. The custom here is for everybody to send prefabricated messages containing one of the twenty formulas of prayer or good wishes to those whom he hardly knows. I have applied myself conscientiously to this task.

"How far along are you with those slobbering Christmas cards?" asks Bernstein.

We begin to rehearse. He's in a rotten temper because for the first time in his life he's not directing his own play.

At three in the morning the telephone rings. "Hello, dear boy, did I wake you? Our rehearsal has plunged me into the most abysmal depression. *You're* better than I would have thought. You use the arms of the chair a lot and you act a little like some sultan. But I suppose that's all right for here . . . B. looks like a cadaver. He's sinister. He always gives the impression of just having returned from a funeral, especially in his moments of great gaiety . . . That little item who plays the nurse—I'd love to lay her—but she thinks she's St. Bernadette or something. The play is a pure marvel—I'm being objective, of course—but it's like a peacock who refuses to show its tail. What do you think of it? Is it better than *Le Coeur?* Yes, how nice of you to say so. Still, *Le Coeur was* a divine play. You don't know a thing . . . You seem to be making some headway with Kit. Just remember, you're going to have to choose. Kit won't give you the time of day if you have a fling with the nurse. In your place I wouldn't hesitate. To be the lover of the greatest American actress is a feather in your cap . . . You know, in the end, they always do exactly what I want. I've always wanted B . . . and I got him. He's an excellent actor, full of charm. And that woman, Cornell, she's marvelous! Conventional, but marvelous. I don't know what it is she does with her hands, her thighs, her belly, she puts sex into everything . . . What did you say? She has an inferiority complex? Maybe she has a complex but the inferiority belongs to McClintic. Just between you and me, what do they really think about my play? Do they realize it's a masterpiece? What did Kit tell you today? . . . Nothing? . . . And B? . . . Nothing? Why it's insane . . . The war? What are you talking about? This play is absolute gold. In a hundred years they won't have to change a comma of it . . . Where was I? Oh! yes . . . during Kit's three pages of monologue, I want you to play with your shoelace instead of looking at her all the time. The left one. That will signify that you're listening to her but that you don't agree with what she's saying. I'm happy we're opening in San Francisco. It's the cultural center of this country, you know. A city of great prestige . . . Three weeks here, and then New York . . ."

One day I arrived late for rehearsal. Imagine my distress when I saw someone else rehearsing in my place. He was a tall thin guy, dark and handsome, like a young Gary Cooper painted by El Greco. By all appearances I had lost the part to him. Kit noticed me standing stock still at the back of the room.

"Hurry up, Jean-Pierre, you're late. We asked your understudy to stand in for you just to save time."

She introduced me to him. His name was Gregory Peck.

Without sharing Bernstein's contempt for Guthrie Mc-

Clintic, I did find his direction a little strange. He placed his wife in the center of the stage for the entire play, lit by a rose spotlight to which she had exclusive rights, and he directed the movements of the rest of us so that we'd never pass between her and the rose spotlight. Whenever Kit had a line, we had to stand absolutely still.

When McClintic discovered me playing with my shoe-lace—as Bernstein had asked me to do—he had a fit. Never in the history of the American theater had an actor who was not the star of the show dared to meddle with his shoelace. I think Gregory Peck almost inherited my role again that day, but Kit pleaded in my behalf and I was pardoned. After that, the word "shoelaces" was banned from all conversation.

Gert Macy had forgiven me for my white lie about her sister, and we became good friends. One day, however, we began talking about Berstein's relationship with the girl who played the nurse.

"Do you think he fucks her?" I asked.

Gert became pale and had to be helped into an armchair. Then she leaped up and slapped me. "Jean-Pierre, you must never, but NEVER, use that word," she panted.

"Okay."

How was I to know? For a foreigner, one word is as good as another. He may not be aware of the nuances or taboos that have become attached to it. I apologized profusely, and asked her what I should have said instead.

Gert thought deeply for a moment. "You should have said, 'Does he screw her?' "

Every morning while we learned our lines, Kit and I strolled through the Presidio, a walk along the bay lined with eucalyptus trees. Contrary to the insinuations of Bernstein, there wasn't anything going on between us other than a very warm affection. One day when we were talking about Gregory Peck I said to her, "Since you have your own company, you should put him under contract. Otherwise Hollywood will snatch him right out from under your nose and you'll never see him again . . ."

She laughed. "Poor Greg! I like him a lot but he'll never make a film in his life. One of his ears is larger than the other."

On opening night, I received a number of telegrams, most of them from people I didn't know. There was also one from Greg:

"Don't pronounce 'model' like 'muddle' and you'll be the darling of America."

Everything went well. There were sixteen curtain calls. The audience laughed at all my lines. Both my exits were applauded. There were scouts from all the Hollywood studios in the audience.

After supper, Bernstein dragged me into the deserted streets at three in the morning to wait for the first papers. We sat down in a cafeteria to read them. They were glorious for Kit and for me but bad for the play.

"Poorly constructed, stupidly motivated . . . Miss Cornell is handicapped by her playwright . . . For Jean-Pierre Aumont, it's a triumph . . . With what talent he listens to the endless tirades of his partner . . ." (That was an allusion to the scene in which I'd stopped touching my shoelaces.)

Bernstein threw the paper on the floor and swept me out. "Let's face it, it's a flop. Sixteen polite curtain calls won't change anything . . . It was so stupid to open a work like this in San Francisco. If we had opened right on Broadway we would have had the greatest hit in the last hundred years . . . But San Francisco, it's Timbuktu! . . . nobody knows where it is . . . As for your own success, of course I'm thrilled, but it's a mystery. Let's be honest. You can't speak a word of English. You learned your lines phonetically, which is nice, but you don't understand half of what you're saying. And the audience doesn't understand the other half . . ."

"Maybe it's good for actors not to understand everything they're saying. You're the one who likes unusual readings."

"But the *audience* . . ."

"Maybe the audience would rather imagine, dream, than understand every word . . ."

"Whatever the case, your fortune's made. And you owe it all to me . . . I want you to know that I'm pleased because I like you a lot and you deserve it, but can I ask you one favor in return?"

"Whatever you want."

"The nurse."

"What?"

"Please, dear boy, give her to me . . . After your reception tonight, you'll be able to screw any girl you want in this one-horse town. It's a regular nest of rich heiresses. I strongly advise you to marry one . . . but the little item who plays the nurse . . . I think I should warn you: she's stewing in gonorrhea . . . At my age you aren't that particular anymore . . . And, of course, I'll be able to help her with her role, she needs it badly . . . I'm asking you, little one, let me have her. It's an old man who's begging you . . ."

I was having lovely dreams (and the nurse to whom I wasn't at all attracted played no part in them) when I was suddenly awakened by a furious call from the stage manager. Everybody was waiting for me to rehearse. I didn't understand.

"Rehearse what? We opened last night." How was I to know that before opening in New York rehearsals were supposed to continue every day, even for months.

In spite of this extra work, which I found dull and even detrimental, my days in San Francisco were happy. Bernstein got over his bad reviews in the arms of the nurse. All of the Hollywood studios had offered me screen tests, but I still scoffed at Hollywood. The only thing that interested me was to play *Rose Burke* in New York. Gregory Peck and I had become friends. He was married to a plump and vivacious blonde, a Finnish girl who worked as Kit's hairdresser.

One night Greg and I were on our way to the theater. It was snowing. I slipped on the ice, twisted my ankle, and lay on the pavement without being able to move for several minutes. Later Greg confessed what had passed through his mind during this short interval: "Here's the opportunity of my career. Jean-Pierre won't be able to play tonight. I'll get a chance at his role, then I can prove to Miss Cornell that I have talent . . . If Jean-Pierre can't walk for several days I'll call my agent. He'll get some Hollywood producers to come . . ."

Then he added, with a twinkle in his eyes, "When I realized that I still didn't know the part well enough to pull it off, I picked up Jean-Pierre and helped him into the drugstore. His ankle was bandaged and I never played in *Rose Burke* . . ."

Seattle, Milwaukee, Chicago, Columbus, Toronto . . . Everywhere the reviews were bad for Bernstein, courteous for Kit, and lyrical for me . . .

I should have been worried, but I wasn't. In those days I took success for granted and naively thought it was normal to be admired. Why on earth shouldn't everyone love me?

Toronto was our last stop before New York, our dream, especially mine, since I was getting my first chance to play on Broadway. My career in this country depended upon it.

At the end of the show I glanced at the call-board. My knees gave out when I saw the closing notice posted there.

I was shattered. Bursting into Kit's dressing room, I shouted at her, "Aren't we going to play New York?"

"No."

"But why?"

I'll never forget the expression on her face. She looked at me with a mixture of pride, remorse, and tenderness, and tried to smile. "You really want to know why, Jean-Pierre? It's because you steal the show; and I can't afford it."

I was so thunderstruck I couldn't think of anything to say. It was true that my reviews were better than hers, but I had thought that the reasons were obvious to everyone. I was a new face and Americans love to make discoveries; and then, my French accent added a certain romantic flavor to Bernstein's rather conventional text. Above all, my role was short and to the point, indispensable to the action.

Kit's part went on interminably. She was on stage for all five acts. This seems flattering to an actress at first but always ends in catastrophe. She hadn't lost any of the radiance which had enchanted her audiences in *Saint Joan* and *Candida. Rose Burke* simply suffered from the comparison. No actor can save a bad role. She was no exception.

In spite of my disillusionment and despair I couldn't help

admiring Kit for the way she answered me. After all, she was the producer of this show, the wife of the director, the greatest American actress. And who was I? A total unknown.

To my insolent question she could have answered: "That's not your affair, really . . ." or, "Speak to the manager." She could easily have used the excuse of the play getting bad reviews everywhere, or could have lied and said that no theater was free in New York. She could have avoided the question entirely or left some false hope for the future.

But Kit was too sincere to dodge embarrassing questions or to get out of them by subterfuge. I've admired and respected her for that honesty ever since.

6

HOLLYWOOD

I came back to New York in low spirits, as unknown as when I
had left it full of hope some months earlier. Then I remembered
the offers from Hollywood.

As strange as it seems to me today, I was in no great hurry
to get there. Philip Merivale, who had played the fifty-year-old
industrialist in *Rose Burke*, offered me his car, and I decided to
see something of the United States on the way.

I convinced my friend Jean Schlumberger to go with me.
Johnny was the Benvenuto Cellini of the New World, having
designed gold ropes and clanking diamonds for royal necks as
diverse as those of the Queen of Yugoslavia and the Duchess of
Windsor. We couldn't have been less alike. I was as outgoing as
he was reserved.

Driving across Texas, we found ourselves in the middle of
the most absolute desert imaginable. There wasn't a shack or a
cowboy in sight. During one of our stops, I was just about to
relieve myself on the side of a cactus when Johnny paled.

"You're not going to do *that?*"

"But there's not a soul around for three hundred miles."

"It's the principle of the thing. You are a French citizen and you represent your country wherever you are. Zip up your pants."

We were so irritated by each other that we ate at different tables all along the route. The waitresses were a little surprised when they saw us leaving in the same car.

In Arizona we were stopped for speeding and brought before the local magistrate, who wore a ten gallon hat and carried a pistol on his hip. To me he looked just as if he'd stepped out of some B western. Unfortunately, the judge interrogated us separately. He riddled me with questions in such an accent that I didn't understand a word of what he was saying. Thinking that it would be more polite to answer "yes" to all the questions, I talked myself into a pickle.

"Are yew a for'n spy?"

"Oh, yes, yes."

"Wuh yew sent heah t' try t' o'erthrow the guvn'ment?"

"Yes . . . yes, of course."

He threw me in the clink.

Though my companion's disposition was unimproved by this episode, he was still too well-mannered to reprimand me. He decided not to speak another word for the rest of the trip.

Finally, after three weeks of travel, the last one without exchanging one word, we reached the border of California. In gigantic capital letters the word "HOLLYWOODLAND" stood out against the bank of a cliff.

The air is invigorating here, the light raw and cruel, a light for young people. All along Sunset Boulevard, which stretches for twenty-five miles from Los Angeles to the ocean, newly built, clean, white cottages seem to have sprung up overnight among the well-behaved palms on manicured lawns. In Hollywood, Beverly Hills, Santa Monica, it's the scrubbed appearance of the plants, houses, and streets which wins the newcomer over.

We stopped at Grauman's Chinese Theater, where the feet and hands of Jean Harlow, Mary Pickford, Maurice Chevalier—even the profile of Barrymore—are imprinted in cement. One walks with respect across these famous molds, these slabs which are like tombstones: "Douglas Fairbanks, May 18, 1920." The apex of his career or the date of his death? I wondered.

I left my luggage at the Garden of Allah and went out to look around. It was 8 P.M. There were endless lines of cars, glistening like greyhounds, but not a pedestrian in sight. Soon a traffic cop pulled up next to me.

"Having trouble, buddy?"

In his mind that could be the only reason I was walking.

That same evening, Johnny (we were reconciled) got me invited to dinner at Norma Shearer's. Knowing how pleased I'd be, she seated me next to Charlie Chaplin.

"Are you an actor?" he said.

"I thought so until now, but sitting next to you I'm afraid to admit it."

He laughed and began talking in spurts. Though his hair was gray, he had the same candid eyes of the silent screen Charlie. According to Malraux, I told him, a certain tribe of Arabs considered him a god.

"Do you know, there's a city in Japan," he said, "where right in the middle of the public square there's a statue of a little man with a cane on a pedestal . . . it's me!"

He laughed again and poked me in the ribs like a businessman at a convention who thinks he's just told a good one. After dinner our hostess showed *Woman of the Year*, Spencer Tracy's and Katharine Hepburn's latest film, which had yet to be released.

I went to see my agents. There were two of them. One was Charlie Feldman, who would become a brilliant producer, and the other was Ralph Blum, famous for two reasons: He was married to Carmel Myers (the immortal fiancée of *Ben Hur*), and he had a cellar full of precious wines. Arriving at his house for dinner, I noticed with acute disappointment that these superbly dated bottles were there to be seen, not drunk. For him his cellar was a museum. You died of thirst while walking past those dusty labels with the magic names. He was your guide. He positioned you at the best angle to admire a Sauterne as if it were a Rembrandt, and one obviously didn't drink a Rembrandt.

After a dinner without wine, he told us with the smile of a true voluptuary that he had saved a special treat. He showed Katharine Hepburn's and Spencer Tracy's latest film, *Woman of the Year*.

On the social level I was launched. A young Frenchman who wasn't bad looking, who owned a dinner jacket and could babble a few words in English, was received with open arms in those days. Even today, anything new has widespread credit at first. I've always found Americans generous and hospitable at the beginning. Initially, it isn't difficult to please them, but making it last is another story. When the novelty has worn off and a new face steps into the ranks—especially if it's another European one—the limelight shifts.

I had often heard that Hollywood was rigidly stratified. Every Saturday there were the ten-thousand-dollar-a-week parties where nobody who made under eight thousand was invited. Then there were the five-thousand-dollar parties, the two-thousand-dollar parties, etc. This may have been true at the time, but never for me, being French.

I spent the next day at Jack Warner's. His wife, Ann, a dark, oriental-looking beauty, took me by the hands and asked me if I were Capricorn or Taurus. Before I had a chance to answer, she exclaimed, "I know, I know . . ."

After dinner Ann and Jack (everybody calls you by your first name right away) took us into a room where I could admire, among other pieces, a marvelous Picasso. Suddenly the Picasso turned and disappeared, giving way to a screen.

"Get ready," said Ann. "I've chosen a special film for you. It's Spencer Tracy's and Katharine Hepburn's latest film together, *Woman of the Year*."

The following day, I was invited to dinner at Joan Crawford's. Everything about her seemed immense: her eyes, her mouth, her shoulders, her greeting. Half of Hollywood happened to be there that evening: a shy and secretive fellow named Glenn Ford; Clark Gable, with the smile and waggish eyes that were his unchanging trademarks; Johnny Weissmuller, who, puffy with sleep, hardly uttered more than the lines he had learned for Tarzan; Fred Astaire, looking like a tap-dancing Voltaire; Jackie Coogan, no longer "The Kid"; and Mary Pickford, no longer "Little Lord Fauntleroy." I felt as if I were walking through Madame Tussaud's wax museum, with the wax melting a little bit.

Among those living sculptures, one ray of light stood out: Judy Garland, the Piaf of the New World. All the misery of mankind seemed to float in her eyes.

On a sofa sat the loveliest creature: Gene Tierney. I was trying to flirt with her when Charles Boyer took me aside:

"Watch your step, she's a married woman. It simply isn't done here."

What a strange country!

"Jean-Pierre," whispered Joan Crawford, "I've looked all over for the film that would please you more than any other, and I think I've found it."

"Woman of the Year"?

"Yes . . . yes . . . isn't that wonderful! . . . How did you guess?"

I spent the next four days at the homes of my French friends, where I wouldn't have to worry about anyone showing me *Woman of the Year.* First at Charles Boyer's, to whom much honor was due. He had created a welcoming center for the French of California. In his home he had judiciously and lovingly compiled an abundant library of French books. Playing the roles of judge, ambassador, priest, and philosophy teacher all at once, he received with patience all of his countrymen who came to him in order to plead their case and demand justice. At his home I met Kisling, Jean Renoir, and René Clair. There was also Dalio, who had played the European butler, or maitre d', in more Hollywood films than I can remember.

Meanwhile, my agents were becoming restless. Among all the studios that had offered me a screen test, they had chosen MGM, thinking that it was the company with the most prestige. They sent out a man from their agency named Bill to follow me around like a watchdog and scrutinize my behavior like a Jewish mother. He called me every day to tell me what tie to wear, what kind of cologne to put on, and what girl I could go out with. He was furious because Louella Parsons had reported I'd gone dancing with a certain Rosalyne Loomis, who he thought was unworthy of me. He told me to buy an Oldsmobile, advised me to stop at red lights, and took me to a businessman who would handle my appointments (nonexistent at the time) and pay my bills.

We decided that I should do my screen test in one of the *Rose Burke* scenes. George Cukor would direct it, which was a great honor. He was Joan Crawford's and Greta Garbo's director, the best that Metro had to offer.

Two days after the screen test, Lilian Burns called me into her office. She was a warm, intense little woman who looked after the hiring of new actors and put the beginners to work.

"Jean-Pierre," she said immediately, "your screen test is a disaster. It's badly played and badly directed. I should tell you to go to another studio or pack your bags, but I've been able to convince Mr. Mayer to give you a second chance. You're going to do exactly as I tell you. You'll learn a scene from *Liliom* and George Sidney will direct it."

"Miss Burns, that's a waste of time," I answered. "If I was no good in a scene that I've played successfully fifty times, directed by the best director in your studio, I'll be worse in a scene that I don't know, directed by a nobody."

Her brow clouded over imperceptibly and she murmured, "*Liliom* is the perfect role for you, and George Sidney is not a nobody."

How was I to know that he was her husband?

So, I made my second screen test with *Liliom*. At the end of it, George Sidney kept the camera running to judge my spontaneity by asking me a few questions.

The first question was, "What's your name?"

"You know very well what it is," I answered.

"Cut!" he yelled.

"What's wrong?"

"I don't want anyone to think you're *temperamental.*"

My answer, which he thought would appear impertinent, was excised from the footage.

That was it. I received a seven-year contract starting at two thousand dollars a week. Two thousand wasn't bad, considering I'd been making two hundred a month before, but I wondered why it had to be for seven years, since I had no intention of rotting away that long among these palm trees.

With infinite patience my agent explained: All the big studios followed the same policy. It took them two or three years to make an actor a star and they couldn't take the risk of being dropped once he became famous.

"Go see Louis B. Mayer," he added. "He's waiting for you."

Mayer turned out to be a chubby little man with glasses on a chain and the dimpled hands of a cardinal. I found him in his office, sitting between a map of the world and two flags. Behind him, like some gigantic crest, was a window which commanded a view of the grounds adjoining the studio. An Alpine village melting into the Chicago underworld and, next to that, a Norwegian fjord ending suddenly in a Polish ghetto. Some Hindu temples were hanging over the Place de la Concorde while Niagara Falls emptied into the Great Wall of China. I even caught sight of a cowboy riding across Texas and stopping abruptly in front of the Eiffel Tower . . .

In this carboard universe the only real edifice was a narrow little shop which sold gravestones. MGM had offered a fortune to its owner to sell out, but all in vain. Louis B. Mayer had finally met his match.

Every morning, when L.B.M. made his entrance at Metro-Goldwyn-Mayer through crowds of genuflecting courtiers, he had to pass in front of the gravestone shop, an insolent reminder of the limits of power.

I walked toward the horseshoe-shaped desk and the little man who could make his empire tremble. He was lost in shadow between the United States flag and the flag of California.

"Don't sit over there, young fellow. Come close to me, near

the foot of this map of the world. It's placed here to remind us all how insignificant we really are. Come, come closer. Don't be impressed by my legend. I'm a man just like everybody else . . . a little better, perhaps, but a *very* little, and if God chose me for this post, it was because he wanted a man who's just like everybody else . . ."

Satisfied by this beginning, and by my deferential silence, he continued to talk about God, then about himself, then about God and himself. At times he seemed to confuse himself with God and God with himself so smoothly that I lost track of whom he was talking about. I was all the more confused because of his tone of voice, which was unctuous and monotonous, like a priest's. He was crying. Then I was crying, too. Finally, he held out his pen for me to sign the contract.

"Use my pen, young fellow. It will bring you luck. And keep it as a souvenir of this moment."

I fell on my knees and signed. I felt as if I were taking vows to enter a monastery where I would serve Louis B. Mayer in sackcloth and hairshirt for seven faithful years.

He made a sign, somewhere between a dismissal and a benediction, and I left the Presence, walking backwards and bowing all the way to the door.

That same evening I had dinner at Hedy Lamarr's. Framed by mountains, her wooden house evoked her native Austria. There on her terrace, which seemed to float over the canyon, she appeared, dressed in red, her black hair flowing. She was a vision of sensuality, with the nose upturned just enough to keep her from being too beautiful.

During dinner she pressed one of her knees, the lovelier of the two, against mine . . .

The following week, we were engaged.

I gave her a diamond ring and told my father, who had arrived in the States, to fly out to meet his future daughter-in-law. The marriage had been planned for the beginning of July.

But, beautiful as she was, the moodiness of the Austrian star began to worry me. One evening, when we were driving back from a concert, I braked a little too quickly. Hedy became hysterical, claiming that I had purposely tried to throw her against the windshield because I was jealous of her beauty . . .

The day my father arrived, I went to meet him at the airport. Realizing that his arrival in some way made my engagement official, I was suddenly seized with panic.

"You take care of her," I said with cowardice unbefitting a gentleman, "I've had enough." I jumped on the first plane for San Francisco, leaving the poor man standing there with his mouth open.

In San Francisco I spent a wonderful, solitary weekend. I discovered that I wasn't at all bored with my own company, and that I wasn't yet mature enough to handle a Tyrolian temptress already three times divorced and nursing in her personality all the complexes and insecurities of our old Europe.

I returned to Hollywood. Hedy threw our ring in my face; then she picked it up and walked out.

Twenty years later I saw her again in Portofino. In the meantime she had been married and divorced several times again, but she'd preserved a lot more esteem and tenderness for me than for those who had married her.

While my romance with Hedy was going on, I had started filming *Assignment in Brittany*. It was one of the big productions of the year, and MGM had destined Robert Taylor for the principal role. But Louis B. Mayer liked me a lot. The fact that my first screen test had been bad and that he had ordered them to do a second prompted him to consider me as his protegé, his personal discovery . . .

I was assigned an English teacher—a Russian, of course—a Dr. Mitchneck, who was ordered never to leave me, in or out of the studio. A veteran, Jack Conway, was chosen to direct the film but became ill before long and was replaced by a newcomer who was under contract to MGM. His name was Jules Dassin.

The reviews of *Assignment in Brittany* were excellent for me. Everybody congratulated me as if I had invented the electric lightbulb: "How happy and proud you ought to be." Perhaps I should have been, but I wasn't. In other circumstances such a success would have filled my heart with joy; but today? Happy, without love? Proud? When the whole world was one big blood-bath and I was living it up in Hollywood?

Several days after the release of *Assignment in Brittany* Cole Porter gave his annual party. His hilltop Bel Air estate that evening was like a fairyland. Tables set up around the pool offered a view of multicolored mountains and rolling lawns, sloping gradually into the pit of Los Angeles, which was glowing with lights like some starry sky stretched beneath our feet.

Everyone who mattered was there. And, because I was French, and because my film had just come out, because my brief engagement had attracted other women who wanted to get married, I was often the center of attraction.

I was seated between Gene Tierney and Lana Turner. The caviar followed the foie gras. Violins played waltzes . . . There was an atmosphere of pleasure, well-being, romance . . .

What was it, then, that was turning my stomach into a tight knot? I got up and left.

In the surrounding hills, I ran through the wind. I couldn't stand this endless parade of wealth any longer, this assembly line of rich foods and entertainment, these women who were too well-dressed, I couldn't keep raking in money for smiling in front of a camera while so many of my friends and countrymen were either dead, hunted, deported, or without food. As for my contract and my newfound success, at that moment I didn't give a good goddamn for them. I ran back to my car and returned to the hotel. There I gave the porter a telegram.

"Captain de Manziarly. Free French Forces. New York. Have decided to join the Free French Forces."

I went up to my room and slept like a log.

7

The Cross of Lorraine

When I announced to L. B. Mayer that I had just joined the Free French Forces without consulting him, he wasn't quite as cordial as he had been during the interview in which he spoke about God. This time the talk no longer centered around heaven but around the sums that Metro had expended to promote my image and make my first film a success. The fact that he had already put my second film, *A Thousand Shall Fall*, on the drawing boards added fuel to his fury.

I assured him that the war would soon be over, and that I would come back intact; I even said that I would profit from this interruption in my career by improving my English. Mr. Mayer grew pale. "Whatever you do, don't do that! Your accent is your main asset. I'd rather see you come back without a leg than without your accent!"

We separated with a sticky embrace. I wasn't aware at the time that he was already scheming to get me back so that I could make that next film before my departure for the war.

I went to New York and presented myself to Captain Sacha de Manziarly of the delegation of Free French Forces. He was a friendly, outgoing man who had lost a leg in the First World

War at the age of seventeen. Although the wound had given him constant pain ever since, he never complained about it. The captain was more than happy to accept my request for enlistment, but asked me to wait until he could arrange the necessary papers for my passage to North Africa.

At the end of a week he called. "Your departure for Algeria is delayed. I'm putting you on a special assignment for three months. Go back to Hollywood."

"I just came from there! I didn't join the Free French Forces only to go back!"

"MGM has sent us a remarkable script. A war film about some prisoners who escape to join DeGaulle. It's called *The Cross of Lorraine*, and it's all to the glory of the Grand Charles. God knows our general needs to take care of his propaganda in this country! Between those who believe in Pétain and those who support Giraud he's not in a very good situation here. I talked about your case to our representative in Washington. He agrees that it's important for you to make this film, so, don't worry, the war won't be over in three months . . ."

That Louis B. Mayer was certainly a sly one! He had had the cunning idea to rebaptise *A Thousand Shall Fall* and call it *The Cross of Lorraine*. That way my military superiors would be sure to want me to do it. The scenario, which I had read already, dealt with life in prison camps. These men, like all other prisoners, naturally wanted to escape. Mayer had merely added the notion that, if successful, their goal would be to join DeGaulle. I left again for Hollywood and immediately began filming *The Cross of Lorraine*.

I was staying at the home of my costar, Gene Kelly. It was the first time that he'd ever abandoned his tap shoes to play a dramatic role. He was an obstinate fellow, headstrong and hardworking—Irish, in other words. And charming, too, when he wanted to be.

The filming (Tay Garnett was the director) was more difficult for me than for Gene. The Free French Forces delegation had asked me to supervise the production closely, being careful to let nothing pass that wasn't authentic in regard to France and useful to DeGaulle's propaganda.

Every time I asked for a change we had to stop working and consult the scenarist, the dialoguist, the assistant producer, and L. B. Mayer himself. Obviously, MGM and I brought different attitudes to the making of this film. I was doing it to serve the cause of the Free French Forces and all they wanted was for me to make another film. After all, what were the Free French Forces to these faraway Americans of Hollywood other than a shadowy delusion, the fantasy of a handful of fanatics under the spell of a temperamental general?

Fortunately, I was saved by a Gaullist colonel on leave, Dr. André Lichwitz. Expecting a mixture of George Washington and Julius Caesar, I found myself face to face with Casanova. The fact that he was a good-looking, elegant charmer hadn't prevented him from fighting heroically in Libya. He set about the business of seducing stars and starlets as soon as he arrived.

He was pleased by his reception in Hollywood and began playing the role of technical consultant for my film to the hilt. He was more preoccupied with film and theater than with the Resistance, with DeGaulle, or with the hell of Bir-Hakeim from which he had just come. There was a surprising contrast between my civilian friends, who talked constantly about the war in an attempt to compensate for the fact that they weren't participating, and this soldier, who had just come from it and was trying to forget it during his short leave.

One evening, as I was waiting for someone at the Beverly Wilshire, the most radiant apparition emerged from the elevator. Covered with gold and topaz like some Byzantine idol, hair floating on royal shoulders, Maria Montez crossed the lobby and disappeared into the street. How beautiful she was!

As soon as I could get friends to introduce us, I invited her to dinner. In those days she was the queen of technicolor enchantment, having just achieved success in those innocent and outlandish screen epics *Arabian Nights* and *Ali Baba and the Forty Thieves*. Knowing these films, I'd expected the same studied languor which she displayed on screen. Instead, I found her

spontaneous, direct, and childlike, warbling the tale of her no-
madic life in an adorable Spanish accent: Born in Santo Domingo, where her father was consul general of Spain, brought
up in a convent in the Canaries, married for eighteen days to an
Irishman who was naive enough to think he could lock her up in
some frosty castle. Then Maria had whirled through London,
New York, and San Francisco like a cyclone before settling in
Hollywood, where her beauty and personality soon made her
one of the most popular new stars.

To say that between us it was love at first sight would be an
understatement. From that day on, I spent every evening at her
place. It was a strange house. You didn't answer the telephone
or read the mail; the doors were always open. Diamonds were
left around in ashtrays. *Lives of the Saints* lay between two issues
of movie magazines. An astrologer, a physical culture expert, a
priest, a Chinese cook, and two Hungarian masseurs were part
of the furnishings. During her massage sessions Maria granted
audiences.

After eight days of partying, André Lichwitz went to rejoin
his unit in North Africa. He promised to take me with him to
the first Free French Division which was moving from Libya to
Tunisia.

"You know," I told him, "I won't be able to call you by
your first name anymore. You're a colonel and I'm a sergeant."

"Don't be an ass. If I get you into our Division, it's to have a
friend there . . . to talk about film and theater. Besides, I've
written a play I want to read to you. You can do it when the
war's over. Now, before you join our unit I want you to memo-
rize this officer's manual. You'll stop at Washington; I'll inform
General Bethouart and you'll take the officers' exam."

The desire to marry Maria had been brewing in me for several weeks. One day, while her faithful Hungarian massaged
her, I heard myself saying, "Let's get married on the thirteenth."

The words had hardly come out of my mouth when I realized my presumption. What could I, who was leaving for the

war in a few days, have to offer Maria, other than loneliness, anguish, and the uncertainty of my return?

I heard her pick up the telephone and say, "Jean-Pierre wants to get married on the thirteenth. Where is Venus? Is Saturn in the third house? . . . after five o'clock?"

She hung up and turned toward me. "That will be okay, Jean-Pierre, if it's after five o'clock."

Later I asked Maria if she were surprised by my decision.

"Not at all. I knew we were getting married in July."

"How did you know that?"

"Oh, come now, it was written in the stars!"

On the thirteenth of July we were married. The same morning Charles Boyer went with us to a jeweler, where I bought the ring and Maria got me a gold identification bracelet. She went into a corner so that she could have a surprise message engraved on the inside for me. Charles, who had been looking over her shoulder, shrieked: "Shakespeare . . . You're going to marry Shakespeare!"

At the wedding Janine Crispin and Charles Boyer acted as best man and maid of honor. As a painter friend of ours, Frederic Sprague, played "The Wedding March" on the organ, Maria slowly descended the staircase, draped from head to toe in rose tulle, followed by her astrologer, her gardener, and the two Hungarian masseurs who held her train.

The following week I went over to MGM to say goodbye to my friends. Just as I was leaving the studio, an electrician ran up to me and whispered, "I'll pray for you, Jean-Pierre."

Maria only had a few free days before she was supposed to start making *Gypsy Wildcat*. Nevertheless, she managed to get her studio to let her go with me to New York, where I would board a cargo ship for North Africa. We stopped at Washington so that I could settle two affairs. First of all, I had to pass my officers' exam. I'd studied the manual that André Lichwitz had given me. Everything went well until the presiding officer, a colonel, asked me about bazookas. Not knowing much about the particulars of that weapon, I replied: "Colonel, if I'd known you were going to ask me that question, I'd certainly have studied it."

My answer was good enough to earn me the rank of second lieutenant.

My other mission was more difficult. For two years I had been in contact with Louis Jouvet, who was touring South America with his troupe. After two very successful seasons in Brazil, Argentina, Chile, and Peru, he now wanted to do some performances in the United States. Several of us, including Renoir and Charles Boyer, were trying to get him into this country, but the FBI wanted one of us to appear for an interview. Since I was going to Washington, and in the hopes that my departure for the war would speak favorably in his behalf, I was chosen to plead Jouvet's case.

I found myself at the Department of Justice, in front of a commission of about ten members: agents from the FBI, the OSS, Army Intelligence, Navy Intelligence, the State Department, and others.

They overwhelmed me with questions: "Who did Jouvet vote for in 1936? What would Jouvet do if the Germans were threatening to kill his children unless he consented to blow up some factories in America? What do you think of DeGaulle, Pétain, Giraud, Maurice Chevalier? Will France become communist? Does the Resistance really exist?" And so on.

Despite my efforts the commission refused Jouvet his visa. The reason? His troupe was too large. How could they ever be sure that some spy hadn't slipped into it? Jouvet had to stay in South America until the end of the war.

There was nothing else to do but to sit around in New York waiting for departure orders. Maria had to return to Hollywood, where they were waiting for her with *Gypsy Wildcat*. I accompanied her to the station. She burst into tears behind the window glass of her coach. I didn't hold up that well, either . . .

As I walked back to the hotel in low spirits, I was attacked by a group of hysterical young admirers on Fifth Avenue. They pulled and shoved me, attempting to rip the buttons off my uniform. I tried to escape but they were becoming more numerous and more aggressive. One of them grabbed my military cap.

Their cheers and screams soared through Central Park, attracting the guests of the Hotel Pierre to their windows. Finally, the police arrived and dispersed my fans, asking me not to go out on the streets again without a police escort. Diving into a taxi, I had myself driven to Woolworth's to do my last shopping. Suddenly, the same screaming horde began to charge the store. "How did you know I was here?" I asked one of them.

"Your cab driver. He came back to Fifth Avenue and told us that the French General was at Woolworth's."

When I left, I was entrusted by MGM with a print of *The Cross of Lorraine* to take to General DeGaulle. Bernstein had also handed me several copies of a pamphlet that he had written called "Joan of Arc and DeGaulle."

"Give these to some influential people in North Africa, dear boy. It's up to you to decide who . . . I'll leave it to your discretion . . ."

I called Maria for a last goodbye. She cried. Suddenly I was crying too.

Through her tears, she said:

"I've made a decision, Jean-Pierre. If San Antonio doesn't stop this war within a year, I'm not going to speak to him anymore."

Poor San Antonio! When I first met Maria she used to pray to him all the time. Little by little she stopped praying and started bargaining with the little wooden statue. "If you arrange things with my studio so I can go to New York with Jean-Pierre, I won't do anything bad for three days." Then she began giving orders. "Send me a good cook by tomorrow morning, San Antonio!"

Now she was using threats, if I understood her right!

8

"It Takes Twenty Years to Make a Man."

There are long pauses in the course of wars, long hours of loneliness and bitter tedium between actions. While my friends were playing soccer or football, I preferred to jot down my memories of the free and easy past and to keep a kind of journal on the events of the present.

My intention here is not to publish the complete journal of my experiences during my eighteen months with the 1st Free French Division; many accounts of the war, more authoritative than mine, have already been published. But by some stroke of fortune I encountered some famous people (such as Malraux or DeGaulle) and took part in events (such as the liberation of Rome or the disembarkement in Provence) which I wrote down on the spur of the moment and which I present here in excerpt.

October 1943. Liberty Ship. We sleep thirty at the bottom of a dirty hold, one on top of the other in tiers of fixed hammocks. And this is a luxury. Five hundred men and noncommissioned officers are packed into a place reserved for the baggage. There's no room on the deck encumbered by trucks, munitions, and life-rafts. There are two salt-water showers. Fresh water has been rationed.

Several of the civilians speak French. They seem to be destined for some administrative function at the time of the liberation. Among them are three philosophy professors. Thinking of the starving people of Europe, a G.I. mutters: "Poor bastards! They ask for food and we send them philosophers."

I give French lessons to twenty-five soldiers who haven't the slightest notion of the language. I begin with: "I am, *je suis.*" Two of them get discouraged: "Oh, that's too tough . . ." The others ask me to teach them only what's absolutely necessary: "Hey, baby, how about a fuck? . . ."

We've been zigzazzing across the Atlantic for three weeks, trying to evade the submarines. Sometimes at midnight, in the wind and rain, a few pals and I go up to the deserted deck and gropingly concoct a Coca-Cola cocktail with 90 percent alcohol stolen from the infirmary. The taste is abominable, but it really packs a wallop.

It is during one of these midnight parties that a stout English soldier begins talking to me. Although I can't make out his features in the dark, it is obvious that he is intelligent, alert, and witty. All night long we talk about France and its literature, especially about theater. He seems to know all our plays by heart, from *Andromaque* to *La Plume de ma Tante.* The name of this learned elephant? Peter Ustinov.

At last the straits of Gibralter are outlined in relief by the rising sun. For Peter and me this is a landmark, a symbol, but to the young G.I.'s rolling dice on the deck it's just another rock. Most of them don't even glance up.

Oran. Along the pier in gigantic letters: A SINGLE GOAL, VICTORY, GENERAL GIRAUD.* The wharf is full of American and English soldiers, French sailors, Italian prisoners who smoke more than they work, and Arabs to whom my comrades throw cigarettes. At the receiving center I am assigned a dormitory bed (all the hotels have been requisitioned). I walk into the city. At a crossroads there is a signpost: "New York

---

* Giraud was a French General whom Roosevelt was backing in opposition to DeGaulle.

6000 miles; Rome 900 miles." At the post office where I have gone to send Maria a telegram, I am told to go back and get my own sheet of paper. None to be found. Finally, I have to stop an American soldier and ask him for some.

Departing for Algiers. The train is chock-full. On it are some boys who have just arrived from France. Once in Algeria, they become the prey of French recruiting agents who whisper: "Join DeGaulle, you'll be the first to land in France . . ." Or, "Go with Giraud, you'll be better paid . . ." Like those hotel porters before the war who waylayed prospective clients at the railroad station: "Go to the Excelsior, the food's great." Or, "At the Terminus Hotel the view is pure heaven . . ."

I meet the editor of one of the big Algerian dailies who was known to be "a bit of a collaborator." Nonchalantly he suggests: "Why don't you go see Giraud's private secretary instead of reporting to the Gaullists . . . it's so much better! What are you, a lieutenant? That's ridiculous. He'll make you a captain. Do you want me to call him? . . ."

His wife points to my Cross of Lorraine and whispers: "You don't still believe in that parrot-roost, do you? Be careful, it's not looked upon too favorably around here."

Henri Bonnet, Under-Secretary of Information, offers me a post which would entail supervising the film studios in France and eliminating collaborators after the liberation of our country. I don't think I'd make a very good organizer—or judge. I can't really see myself deciding whether to condemn X or Y to death. I tell him that I prefer a purely military assignment.

The dung heap of Algiers hardly pleased me. I was in a hurry to join Lichwitz and the 1st Free French Division in Tunisia, but I had to wait to become officially assigned to that unit.

I met Saint-Exupéry again. Two days before he left for his last mission we walked the deserted streets of Algiers the whole night. He was horrified by the war, disgusted by politics, but he had lied about his age so that he could continue to fly. At times he stopped walking to gaze up into the sky.

DeGaulle saw *The Cross of Lorraine* and wrote to thank me

for having shown in a beautiful film the active participation of all the French in the Resistance, under the sign of the Cross of Lorraine. "It's important that this silent and bloody war be brought to the attention of our faithful friends, especially those in the United States."

Edouard Corniglion-Molinier, who was my producer for *Drôle de Drame*, had become a colonel. He had toured the world, been honored in some places and thrown in prison in others. When he finally got to Cairo he found two telegrams waiting for him. One appointed Colonel Corniglion to a post in London. The other named Colonel Molinier Commander of the Free French Air Forces in the desert. He chose Molinier's post and took command of the squadrons "Alsace" and "Lorraine."

One day DeGaulle came to inspect his aviators as they were on leave and getting laid in Cairo. Panic! Out of desperation Corniglion-Molinier asked some of the Australians who were camped nearby to dress up in French uniforms for the inspection. They agreed; but when DeGaulle asked a few questions they didn't answer. None of them could speak a word of French.

"What's wrong with your men? Can't they talk?"

"I think, sir," answered Corniglion-Molinier, "they are overwhelmed by the emotion of seeing you."

In November, 1943, I am finally assigned to the 1st Free French Division, which made history at Bir-Hakeim and El Alamein, giving the Allies their first complete victories.

At the end of the campaign in Libya, General Brosset took command of that Division. His headquarters in Tunisia is in an olive grove facing the Mediterranean between Nabeul and Hammamet.

General Brosset has the charm and natural authority of men who are sure of their strength and their seductive powers. His blue eyes, full of irony and kindness, are like a sailor's. With giant strides the general leads me to a tent where fifty officers are celebrating the Indochinese New Year with a Vietnamese meal. Cambodians are serving us little plates of various dishes which the others taste tentatively and Brosset devours in handfuls with the appetite of Henry VIII.

The great adventure begins today, April 13, 1944. From Bizerte in Tunisia, we are shipping for Italy.

Soon we have cleared the Strait of Messina. It's like seeing the face of an old friend—the little seaport towns, white houses with red tile roofs, grouped around the church, the lazy boats lined up on the sand, and the cemetery bristling with cypresses. Italy, tender Italy, the sight of you is always enough to reconcile us with the Italians . . . In the village of Alba Nuova where we are camping, thirty kilometers to the north of Naples, the inhabitants are friendly, almost too friendly in fact. They are all antifascists! Everyone adores France. They are even willing to forgive us for the tenth of June, 1940, when they stabbed us in the back. Mussolini? They never heard of him. Those soldiers who gave their lives for him in the Alps or in Libya will have to content themselves with the wreaths which have been placed on their graves.

A socialist-communist committee has been set up. The priest of the village goes there to smoke his pipe and the Italians have placed a photo of DeGaulle between Matteoti, Karl Marx, and Stalin.

May 11. Departure for the front. The zero hour for the Infantry is tonight at 11.

One of our communications officers has stepped on a mine and his body hasn't been retrieved. He was carrying all the plans and operational maps.

Now it's a question of penetrating the Gustav line, which is defended by twenty-five German divisions.

May 15. Sant'Ambrogio, Sant-Apollinare, San Giorgio have been taken. A German captain has been captured. I drive him to the prison camp at Sessa. He claims to be certain of the victory of Germany.

"What about the Russians?"

"Poof!" (a disgusted face)

"Don't you find that they're gaining ground?"

"It's because we want to shorten our lines."

He adds: "If we lose the war, Bolshevism will devastate Europe. And the French won't be strong enough to stop it. We'll win because we know why we're fighting."

"Don't you think we know why we're fighting?" I shout at him.

As I'm getting back into my jeep I feel two arms encircling me. They belong to Marlene Dietrich. In a linen uniform with her blonde hair tucked into a cap, she has been going from camp to camp, from hospital to hospital entertaining the American troops. I ask her to come and sing for us and she agrees.

She climbs into my jeep. Night falls. I take a wrong turn. We're lost somewhere near Cassino in a no-man's land bordering on enemy territory. Being made prisoner isn't a very agreeable prospect for me, though I envision it daily; but to be responsible for Marlene's capture . . .

In the eyes of the Germans she is a renegade who serves against them on behalf of the American army. They wouldn't hesitate to shoot her. Under the veneer of her legendary image, Marlene Dietrich is a strong and courageous woman. There are no tears. No panic. In deciding to go sing on the field of battle she knew the risks she was taking and assumed them courageously, without bragging and without regrets . . .

By doubling around we make it back to our lines, but it is too late for her to meet Brosset. Too bad for both of them. They seemed made for each other.

May 20. Cassino has finally fallen to the English and the Polish. Although we are only eight kilometers away, we don't find out about it until the papers and radio have spread the news around the world. Every soldier is preoccupied with his own sector and couldn't care less about anything that happens outside of that square mile.

Cassino. The place has ceased to exist. Not even ruins; just scattered rocks and holes filled with stagnant water. The burned out trees lend something tragic and desperate now to the countryside of Italy. A Canadian sergeant begins explaining the siege of the last four months to me: "You see, we occupied the post office over there, and the Germans were holed up here, in the Grand Hotel of the Roses . . ." he makes gestures like a blind man, indicating nothing but empty spaces.

May 22. Well, the guys were right. "Le Grand Charles" won't ever let us down. Ten days after the start of the offensive, he comes to inspect the troops, see the wounded, and pin on some decorations. Accompanied by Generals Juin, DeLattre, and Bethouart, General DeGaulle makes a short speech. What an impressive face he has—emaciated, exhausted, with the unrelenting gleam of a vision in his eyes. He always seems to see further ahead in space and time than anyone else.

"All of you play an essential role in the great campaign of '44 which is just beginning. Gentlemen, it is my profound honor to salute you."

He shakes our hands, glances at the map, and rides away in a jeep.

May 24. I have been detailed as a liaison officer to the 757th U.S. Tank Battalion. We have to attack Pontecorvo.

I keep in touch with two American captains via walkie-talkie. Piper and Zipper are their code names; mine is Hop.

"What's in front of us?"

"Half a company of tank destroyers," I answer.

"That's not enough. We need the Infantry. What's at our right?"

"The Liri River, and then the Canadians."

"And to our left?"

"The 3rd Infantry."

"That'll do. But we have to have the Infantry in front of us."

"The soldiers can march alongside the tanks," I say.

"No. In front."

Piper and Zipper are obstinate. They were taught in their Texas boot camp that the Infantry is supposed to precede the tanks and they aren't going to do it differently now.

I climb into the gun turret of my Sherman. In front of me is half a company of tank-destroyers, behind me a company of medium-sized tanks commanded by Piper and Zipper.

Bivouac in the southwest of Pontecorvo.

Piper has just divided up his K rations with me. He complains about the French jokes made against the Americans, the American jokes against the English, the English ones about the Australians, and so forth.

I answer: "Each company thinks it's better than the other company, each army thinks it's better than the other army. It doesn't do anyone any harm; it even creates a healthy sense of competition."

Someone says to Piper: "You always take a village faster than our troops because you mow down everything in sight as you pass through. You'll raze an entire city just to keep from losing one man."

"Maybe you should understand," retorts Piper, looking him straight in the eye; "a city can be rebuilt in a matter of months, it takes two minutes to make a shell; but it takes twenty years to make a man."

Cannons, mortar, *nebelwerfer*, machine-guns haven't stopped firing on us. A shot has grazed my neck without wounding me. I spend the night sleeping under my tank. Next to me is the corpse of a Senegalese, eyes fixed, teeth exposed. Neither the presence of death, nor the heavy noise of the landing of rockets, nor the smooth whistle of their trajectory can disturb my sleep.

Departure at dawn. A strong concentration of enemy anti-tank weapons is reported. The Krauts are sending an S.S. regiment to block the route to Frosinone. We're expecting heavy losses. Two tank destroyers have just been set on fire.

We advance to the front lines. Each embankment, each trench, each thicket masks a surprise. A blazing fire forces us to stop at the side of Mount Leucio.

The wounded and the prisoners are brought back. One of them—nineteen years old and wounded in the head—asks me for water.

"Ich habe kein wasser zeit gestern gehabt. . . ."

I want to give him some but the marines are opposed to it.

"Don't do that, lieutenant. They don't give any to us. Bastards, all of them. Now it's their turn."

Perhaps, but the boy lying at my feet isn't responsible for all that.

At the end of the day we go off to reconnoiter Mount Leucio. We have taken control of the valley of the Liri. This scuffling of tanks, men, jeeps, planes—all of this hullabaloo—has the air of a game, but what a stupid game.

On Mount Leucio we become the target of the enemy artillery on the far bank of the Liri. A shell falls six yards away from me. I'm surprised to discover that, just as in 1940, I'm less frightened than I thought I would be. It's always the same story: when I imagine what it's going to be like I'm scared to death, but when I'm actually in the thick of it I'm not nearly as frightened.

All the same, whenever that whistling pierces your eardrums and you feel that the shell is going to hit, that it's meant for you, you end up flat on your belly trying to dig a hole in the ground. How large and vulnerable I feel at such times! How I wish I could shrivel up and disappear.

But as soon as the shell has burst, your strength and confidence return. You feel a little ashamed. Then you pick yourself up off the ground, shrug your shoulders, and begin thumbing your nose at that invisible artillery . . . until the whistling starts all over again.

The link-up between the Americans who landed at Anzio and the bulk of the Fifth Army took place yesterday in the Pontine Marshes. Pontecorvo has finally fallen under the twin efforts of the Polish forces and our marines. The bridge over the Liri, which connects the southern part of the city to the northern part, is gutted like the bridge at Avignon. Some marines are taking target practice at a photo of Victor Emmanuel.

Every evening we have to organize anti-rape patrols. The Senegalese and quite a few legionnaires have been attacking any peasant woman in sight, young or old. If any of the other soldiers try to interfere or defend the screaming Italians they meet with a volley of bullets. It's a serious problem and it bodes ill for the French girls once we get to France.

But not all of the women are totally unwilling. An old Ital-

ian woman, seeing some infantrymen making off with her donkey, cries out heroically: "You can have me, but don't take my
donkey!"

June 4, 1944. Rome was liberated this morning.

We parade down Piazza Venezia and along the Corso del
Impero. The crowd is delirious with enthusiasm; they stop the
jeeps and trucks, embrace the soldiers, throw them flowers,
offer them wine, call General Mark Clark *Il Liberatore.*

Little girls in school uniforms patiently lined up along the
Corso, with their hair tied up in ribbons and their satchels at
their sides, toss bouquets to us.

*I must admit that I had no inkling as I marched down Piazza
Venezia that one of these little girls would become my wife twelve years
later.*

*But, when my sons were still little boys and I was telling them the
story of the liberation of Rome, I said to them: "When your mother saw
me march by with hundreds of other soldiers she pointed her finger at me
and said to her sister: 'That's the one I'm going to marry.'"*

June 6. The Vatican. More marble stairways than I can
count, and saluting guards with halberds, who wear yellow-
striped costumes designed by Michelangelo. Finally we come to
a large red rectangular hall. Fifty war correspondents are waiting silently. Against one of the walls is the gold throne and the
papal tiara ornamented with the keys of Saint Peter. Suddenly a
white silhouette enters the red, hushed chamber, followed by
florid, ornately dressed attendants. Everyone falls to his knees.
Looking as long and white as a church taper, the Holy Father
commences to speak.

Little by little, the correspondents draw nearer, tentatively
at first, then more and more boldly. Some climb up the steps of
the throne. Others lie under the nose of His Holiness in order to
get a better picture. The cameras are whirring. The cham-
berlains and cardinals have fallen into a panic. With sweeping
gestures they attempt to make the cameramen understand their

sacrilege. Even the Pope himself, though he continues to speak, nervously signals the crowd to move back. It's hard to hear what he's saying. Not that I am very far from him, but all of my senses are focused in contemplation of his face. Finally he appeases the surging mob of reporters with a dramatic sign of the cross. Arms outstretched, face raised trance-like toward heaven, looking suddenly very large and erect, he becomes a white cross.

Now everyone forms a line. Pius XII distributes to each a likeness of himself and a miniature rosary.

"Where are you from?" he asks in English.

"From New York, Holy Father."

He passes to another. "Where are you from?"

"From Ohio. Do you drink champagne, Holy Father?"

Tearing himself away from these disrespectful signs of curiosity, the Holy Father retires. At the door he blesses us one more time.

The Excelsior Bar. Everybody hugs each other, buys a few drinks, runs from group to group, sings, picks up girls, loses them, forgets about them, finds them again . . . The marines are ordering some poor, trembling Italian men to put their jackets and ties back on. At midnight I find myself—God knows how—with an Englishman and an American at the home of a repenting Italian.

"We're cowards."

"Hey, no, you're not . . ."

"You ought to spit in our faces . . ."

"Some other day. Drink . . ."

Another, less repentant, tells us the story of the German occupation.

"The people were really admirable . . . admirable. An old man pointed in the direction of the Tiber when some Germans asked him how to get to the train station. *Un poco* time lost, *un poco di benzina* lost . . . we kept them going around in circles like that . . . As for me, do you know what I did for the *Resistenza?*"

"What did you do?"

"I hid."

June 8. It's really a good feeling for a Frenchman to be able to march through Rome exactly four years to the day after France was stabbed in the back by Mussolini. In a long line our division crosses the city to resume the march on Florence.

The Corso is crammed with Americans now. One of them has tied a live goose to the front of his jeep, no doubt in homage to those geese that saved the Capitol, so the legend goes, by warning its defenders with their cries. The walls are crowded with posters for and against the King.

"Who chased out Mussolini? It was the King," say the posters of the monarchists.

"Who upheld Mussolini for twenty years? It was the King," parry the Communists.

Other posters proclaim the sacrifice of 360 hostages shot by the Germans. These 360 victims are flaunted as proof of the Italian contribution to the Allied cause.

June 10. We move into the front lines again in an attempt to liberate Siena. At Viterbo Commander Amyot d'Inville stepped on a mine, and was blown to bits. The news comes as a real shock for all of us, but we try not to show it.

"He was one of the best," says Tournier.

"He was a symbol of free France," says Mangin. "I wouldn't give two cents for the hide of any Kraut who falls into the hands of our marines today."

The route is cluttered with dead horses and burning tanks. Through the heat and nauseating odor, through the dust which gets into your nostrils and mouth, the slow column of foot soldiers advances. The spectacle of these dirty, struggling, sweating men weighed down by packs in the midst of Shermans and bulldozers is revolting. War becomes more mechanized every day but the infantryman's lot remains the same.

Tournier, who narrowly escaped death by some miracle, says: "Now I have proof of the existence of God." But the other guy, who died next to him, did he too have proof of the existence of God?

June 19. This time it's Colonel Laurent de Champrosay, an early hero of the war, organizer and commander of our artillery, who has been killed by a mine.

For the second time in ten days, death has sprung a de-layed-action trap and deprived the Division of one of its ir-replaceable leaders.

It's raining now. The war takes on a desperate aspect.

The mortars, the bombs, the machine-gun bullets, the mines—they're all just part of the war—but the rain . . . We are suddenly struck by a feeling of injustice, a feeling that the Good Lord has turned against us.

June 20. A morning departure. The bulldozers precede us, filling up the bomb craters that we have to cross. It's a matter of taking a detour around Radicofani, key to the plain of Tuscany.

Revolvers in hand, we enter a farmyard that has been pointed out as a nest of enemy resistance. One of the Americans bends over to pick up a pen. "Don't touch it!" a sergeant bellows.

How many guys have lost an arm since we've been in Italy because they picked up a pen or a bar of chocolate or soap which was mined? The Krauts will stuff a goddamned mine into any-thing—the carcasses of animals, even the corpses of their own soldiers.

Smith, the American lieutenant who was commanding the tank "Pin-up Girl," has just been wounded. I fill in for him and we advance a few more miles without a hitch. Suddenly a bar-rage of enemy artillery falls on us from all sides. A green snake winds across the field.

"Watch out! German patrol."

With the machine-gun mounted on my tank, I fire a few shots at them. Some figures fall down. Others raise their arms and surrender. Some disappear like rabbits. I turn my prisoners over to Lieutenant Tournier and rush by jeep to the general's headquarters, where the chief of staff is waiting for my report.

This time the bastards are aiming at me for sure. It's a question of barreling along fast enough to pass between the bullets. Two Senegalese are howling in a ditch. They have been wounded in the shoulder. I load them into my jeep and take them to the first-aid station. Then I jam the accelerator to the floor and roar off down a road full of holes, once again crouching under a storm of enemy fire.

July 23. For us, the Italian campaign is finished. It will have cost the Division 700 dead and 2,000 wounded. We have come down again from Radicofani. Then, by way of Rome and Alba-Nuova, we have reached Tarento, which is in the southern part of the boot. It's a burning desert. Our only problem now is that we have to ship out on L.S.T.'s—but for where? France or Yugoslavia? And each man wonders: If it's France, will I be in the first group to land? It's a prayer that quickly becomes an obsession. General Brosset has called for me. He is sending me as a liaison officer to the 3rd American Division.

"They'll land first," he tells me. "We'll follow twelve hours later. I thought you might enjoy a seat in the first row. Take my car and go straight to Naples. I'll join you tomorrow and introduce you to General O'Daniel."

July 26. The 3rd American Division is camping in an olive grove at Pozzuoli. Brosset presents me to O'Daniel, then takes me to swim in a creek at the bottom of Pausilippe.

We are two friends on a lark. Such vitality! . . . such health! . . . Brosset amuses himself by swimming under water and staying there as long as possible. He makes fun of me because I don't know how to do it.

9

The Liberation of France

~~~~~~~~~~~~~~~~~~~~~~~~~~~~~~~~

August 8, 1944. Embarking on an L.S.T. at sunset, we group ourselves in the center of the Bay of Naples and a convoy forms.

At the moment when we are starting out in long lines toward Cape Mysene, a launch comes bouncing across the waves. In the rear of it are some officers in white. A man in the front, bareheaded and wearing civilian clothes: it's Churchill. Leaning against the wind, he gives us the V for Victory sign. The men rush to the rails: "Winnie! it's Winnie, the old man himself! Good show, Winnie! Good show . . ."

They are all moved. Down deep they feel that he has come flashing through that bay with arms outstretched just to give each one of them his benediction.

August 13. We are really going to disembark in France! They've confirmed it at the briefing. We'll land at Cavalaire, the 36th Division at Sainte-Maxime and the 45th at Saint-Raphael. Commando raid on the Hyères Islands and Cape Nègre. I ask General Shepperd to let me disembark with the first elements of the Division.

"I know what that means to you," he says. "I'll see what I can do."

That evening the lists are posted. I am not included in the first boats. At midnight I wake up and add my name to the list.

August 15, 6 o'clock. A red rim on the horizon: you can hear the cannons. "Here we go," sighs Lieutenant King. Piercing the night, radar waves bring back to the watchroom the outline of the coast in miniature. A whitish trail on the dial of the radar is the first image that I will have of France.

6:20. The loudspeaker announces an imminent raid by enemy planes.

6:30. The chaplain says Mass.

7:00. It's daylight. I can make out Cape Lardier. The crew works the winches to put the landing craft into the water. The naval artillery begins firing. English bombers gleam in the rays of the rising sun.

7:20. I climb into the bow of my landing craft. It begins riding the waves with a rocking movement. Now it's easy to make out the beach and its border of pine trees, but a thick white smoke masks Cavalaire. Artillery salvos. The ramp clangs down and we wade into the water up to our shoulders. We reach a road across from the Hotel Pardigon by means of a lane which has been cut through the pines. One of our tanks has just finished burning up. Everything is calm and quiet. The men work methodically, nobody seems in a hurry. A group of German prisoners passes by, and for the first time I experience a feeling of hatred. In Italy the Germans were our opponents; but here, on this beautiful roadway, they are thieves.

It is my duty to locate the available itineraries and draw up a list for the Intelligence Section while my comrades are disembarking tonight. In addition, I have to try to contact as many members of the local Resistance as possible.

11:00. I arrive at General O'Daniel's headquarters. The password for today: "Free France." His headquarters are in a farm, at the border of La Croix-Valmer.

On the way, a young woman, her husband, and a little boy accost me. "Did you expect the landing?" I ask them.

"Eh! Peuchere!, bombs have been dropping on our heads for eight days, you'd have to be a simpleton not to expect it!"

2:00. The engineers have detonated the underwater mines, sending up immense geysers of sand and water. The L.S.T.'s dock alongside floating pontoons. A lone plane drops a few bombs on the beach. We take cover in a grove of pine trees.

4:00. The maquisards that I have been able to contact haven't been much use to me. I go back to my headquarters. My peasant friends are in animated discussion about some Americans who have pinched all their wine.

"We offer it with pleasure, but they want it all. It's not reasonable . . ."

"Didn't they at least bring some whiskey?" asks the husband.

A young woman with made-up face comes down the road dragging some bundles behind her and cursing.

"Eh!, that's the local slut! She slept with a German officer."

"Didn't anyone shave her head?"

"It'll just grow back. No, it would be a better idea to tattoo the word 'whore' on both her cheeks!"

I am the first French soldier to arrive in Cogolin. An excited crowd quickly gathers around my jeep. The women embrace me, squeeze my hand, jostle me. "Well, well, you certainly didn't come too soon! We've been waiting so long."

Some are laughing, some crying. I ask a fat matron who is standing off to one side by herself, "And what about you, Ma'am, are you happy to see us?"

She puffs out her pendulous bosom and sighs:

"Oh! putaing!" *

As night falls, one of the maquisards finds me. He gives me some information on the German troops in the region.

The boy's name is Jacques Jadel. He has just spent three months in prison and traveled seventy kilometers on foot in three days.

"Go to sleep."

"No, no. It's so good to be able to speak freely. I've waited so long for this moment."

* "You bet your ass!"

In the darkness, he begins to talk: "After I left prison I tried to locate my commander. He'd been killed and in his place there were two men who couldn't stand each other. It's kind of sad, you know."

His faint, bitter smile is like a cry in the quiet night.

"The French militiamen were atrocious, more cruel, more sadistic than the Germans. As soon as they arrested you (it was always by denunciation, you know, my wife's best friend turned me in because she was sleeping with a militiaman)—as soon as they arrested you, they forced you to rat on your pals. If you refused, they started torturing you. They put one guy's head in a paper press until his skull cracked; they tore out people's fingernails. *Frenchmen* did this, you understand, *Frenchmen*. I had more luck. I argued with them and they suggested I enter the militia. When I refused they turned me over to the Gestapo. It was almost a deliverance." The same tiny, bitter smile.

"And what about Pètain?" I ask him.

"Pètain." He shrugs his shoulders. "We don't wish him any harm. Do you know what they ought to do with him now? They ought to give him a job as a janitor in a public bath."

Midnight. My comrades from our division have begun landing. Some of them are lively and joyous, others silent with emotion. They stare into the night at the France they have been dreaming about for so long. Others are singing—with such irony—"Maréchal, here we are!"

August 16. Slept two hours in a ditch. At dawn I go to Saint-Tropez.

Some maquisards and American parachutists are fraternizing under the plane trees. The harbor is off limits; it hasn't been demined yet.

Everyone gathers at the Café de la Renaissance. Last night, some Americans parachuted onto the peninsula. A French boy whistled the Marseillaise so that they could locate him in the dark. The Americans asked him if they had actually reached Le Muy.

"No, this is Saint-Tropez . . ."

"Oh well, let's go to sleep."

And the whole battalion of paratroopers went to sleep fifty kilometers from its destination, guarded by a young patriot.

August 23. Paris has been liberated! . . . Paris has been liberated! . . . We are drunk with the incredible news! . . . But we don't have time to celebrate. We must liberate La Garde and La Crau. My God, we've lost so many men. Tournier, who arrived from Indochina to reconquer France, has been killed in his tank at the gates of Toulon.

At 6:00 General Brosset and I are entering a still-occupied Toulon. A column of German tanks comes at us. We have just enough time to make an about-face.

August 26. Marseille, the edge of the city: not a living thing in sight—empty streets, empty windows. Suddenly the air is full of angry bullets. Some militiaman who knows that all is lost is firing haphazardly.

A car roars by at eighty miles an hour, machine-gun at its window. There is an atmosphere of civil war, of nightmare. My mission is to contact the 3rd Division, but where it can be found is beyond me. Perhaps it's at the railroad station. My brother François (who has been attached to our division) and I drive down an empty avenue, turn onto an empty square, and mount the ramp of the station, also empty. This isn't the light emptiness of peaceful nights nor the sunny emptiness of the siesta hour, but rather a hostile emptiness, the emptiness of a trap. At the top of the great flight of stairs we turn right and suddenly I have the presentiment that something bad is going to happen. Just as I'm about to mention it to François, a shower of bullets nails our jeep in place. Opposite us, only thirty feet away, is a German blockhouse which is firing at us from above. The air is so thick with bullets that the shots seem to be coming from everywhere. François slides under the jeep. I shield myself behind a kiosk. The bullets pursue me. My pants are soaked with blood. They must have got me in the leg. I run down the side stairway, still surrounded by bullets. Now I'm in the street. Where should I go for help? Who should I look for, who should

I avoid? There are traitors who wear the armband of the Cross of Lorraine. How will I know? Maybe the 3rd Division really *is* at the station, or quite possibly it's the collaborators. I run toward the Terminus Hotel: French soldiers! I'm saved!

A car takes me to the hospital. The x-ray shows that I have a piece of 88 shrapnel in my knee. Luckily the joint hasn't been affected and I can still walk. There is more shrapnel in the left leg but it hasn't done much harm. I'm in a hurry to get back to the division. I won't let them operate on me at Marseille— Marseille frightens me today.

August 27. They operated on me under general anesthetic, and everything went well. As I want no part of the ordeal of evacuation into North Africa, I have had myself transported to the home of the V.'s at Sanary. The father is in jail for collaboration. The mother and the daughter are most happy to redeem his conduct by taking care of me.

September. Still limping, I rejoin the division at Lyon. All the bridges have been blown up with the exception of the two most ancient, which were constructed by the Romans and which seem to flout all attempts at dynamiting. The other bridges are hanging in the water, cut in two. The firing is still going on on all sides, just like at Marseille. But life is not interrupted here. A deserted square is repeopled as soon as the machine-guns are quiet.

General Brosset, who has just received his third star, drives up the steps of the town hall in his jeep, signaling his trailer to follow. The people of Lyon can't believe their eyes. My unit parades through Place Bellecour mingling with the maquisards.

Our marines, in retribution, have been looting the homes and businesses of the important families of Lyon. Barberot has raked in 180,000 francs in two days plus a few more miles of silk to make scarves for his marines. It's possible to be a courageous fighter and remain a dandy, I guess.

The upper middle class girls are happy to give themselves to these romantic victors. They want to follow them to the front. The marines have a lot of trouble getting rid of them.

On the thirteenth day of each month the beneficent presence of my mother continues to manifest itself. This thirteenth of September the General has announced three pieces of good news to me:

1. I have been named first lieutenant.
2. He has obtained the Legion of Honor for me.
3. He has chosen me to serve as his aide-de-camp.

We have been forced to stop at Nuits-Saint-Georges because we ran out of gasoline. Our division consumes fifty thousand liters a day and we haven't a drop left. Our rapid advance is the cause of it: we were supposed to be only at Avignon; but we're already four hundred miles ahead at Dijon; we could have gone farther if we had had more gas.

Eve Curie, the daughter of Mme. Curie, has been attached to our headquarters. At mess she adds the restrained, sober radiance of her personality to our conversations, enlarging the subjects and offering fresh insights. Her foremost concern, however, is to function as a soldier.

Someone says that Churchill doesn't like DeGaulle. "Ah!" cries Eve, suddenly passionate, "in 1940 I saw Churchill in love with DeGaulle, in love. . . ."

André Malraux commands a half-brigade of Resistance fighters. I am flabbergasted to find him in the uniform of a colonel.

"Well, what did you expect, a corporal?"

"No, but it seems funny for you to have any rank at all."

He laughs. He takes in everything around him with piercing, restless glances, and then retreats into himself to ruminate on them. He deplores the dissolution of the Resistance and its absorption into the army. The landing in France has put an end to the epic of the Resistance.

Free French fighters and members of the Resistance, used to being outside the law and living trapped in forests or hemmed into oases—Bir Hakeim or le Vercors—feel a little lost today. I'm not even sure that the Free French share a common spirit. I think that they were united by a common surge of honor at a critical moment in the history of France, but beyond that, their aspirations and ideals are as diverse as possible.

Paris, November 27. I have just driven General Brosset's trailer to the Invalides. I left it there in the cold gray twilight of the courtyard guarded by two Senegalese holding the battalion flag. The general! I repeat these two words over and over to myself, as if they had lost their meaning! The general!

For one whole month I did not leave his side for a second. Every morning we drove into the icy cold of the Vosges, me wrapped in my hood and the general in his shorts, as usual—driving his jeep by himself. His driver would climb into the back seat and I would climb into the front beside him. In the early hours of the morning we would barrel down the road singing whatever came into our heads. *Sambre et Meuse, You Won't Take Alsace and Lorraine*, or old songs like *Fanchon*. But there was one song that the General loved best of all. It was a gypsy air, a sad, haunting, feverish melody with a refrain like this:

"You'll never meet a man

Who's lived a life like mine . . ."

That's the way I'll always remember him: young and full of joy on a road in the Vosges, cleaving the cold air with his bare chest and singing in a voice that had become hoarse from shouting, but singing so warmly, so happily!

"You'll never meet a man

Who's lived a life like mine . . ."

To get more quickly from one brigade to another, we crossed no-man's land—but not without some apprehension. The pines often hid snipers; snow and trees made ambushes easy; the three stars on the general's cap and on his jeep were a good target; and we were singing at the top of our lungs. Pico stood braced against the spare tire holding a machine gun, ready to shoot. I loaded my revolver and kept it on my knee.

"Be careful with that," said the General. "It can go off by itself. I'm always afraid of those things. I wouldn't want to die that way."

Death. He spoke of it often, but without any terror.

"They won't get me. They're too stupid."

I knocked on wood and we began singing again.

He had been hit by an exploding shell and wounded lightly

in the chest six weeks earlier. But he refused to admit that there was anything wrong with him. When he saw his name on the register at Spears hospital, he made an indignant scene and threatened to tear off his bandage if they didn't erase it immediately. He couldn't admit that he wasn't invulnerable.

Sometimes the jeep got stuck in the snow. Then Brosset would climb down and push it out of the rut by brute force.

"Gee, what a guy!" an American soldier had shouted with enthusiasm after seeing him one morning bare-legged in the snow freeing the jeep with one shove of his shoulder. The compliment had thrilled the General.

He was never tired, never cold. Gifted with exceptional strength and health, he was profoundly happy. Happy about his four children, happy about his body and his reflexes, happy to be commanding such a fine unit, happy to know that his men loved him. On the evening of a victory he wrote proudly to his wife: "I'll never be a real general, but my Division is a real Division."

After his death General DeGaulle said of him: "He has shown continual proof of his courage, unselfishness, and loyalty." He added. "His final hour was one of triumph, since he led you to one of the most glorious victories of this war. Brosset has fallen on soil reconquered by you under his command. I'm sure that this is the way he would have wanted to die . . ."

General Brosset died on November 20. The nineteenth, we took the Buick which he was so proud of and which only went out on grand occasions. We were going to corps headquarters to get last instructions for the next day's attack involving several Allied armies.

By this time Leclerc had already taken Baccarat, and Bethouart had attacked Montbeliard from the south. We were scheduled to get into the fray the following day. Two kilometers before L'Isle-sur-le-Doubs the General, as usual, took a blind corner on the inside and collided headlong at sixty miles an hour with an American truck. The Buick was smashed but we got out of it with a few scratches.

November 20, a Monday, we left about 7:00. The General

was beaming. We started across the River Rahin on a bridge which had just been put up by the engineering corps. Below us three soldiers were sitting in a jeep wedged in the middle of the river. They were surrounded by water right up to the seats. They had wanted to go through before the Bailey Bridge was ready and had been surprised by the depth of the river. It took a crane to get them out. We had forded this river ourselves the day before. I remarked to the General how much the water had risen.

We sped toward Plancher-Bas. At a turn in the road we discovered that another bridge over the Rahin had been mined. We had to stop so that the engineers could clean up the middle of the bridge to make room for the tanks.

I see it all again; the three of us, the General, the driver, and myself, walking to that very place where Brosset would find death some hours later.

Now it was raining in torrents. The General sent me to Champagney to contact headquarters by radio. When I came back, he was driving another jeep.

"Where's yours?" I asked him.

"In a ditch," he answered quickly, as if that was the usual place for it.

At Auxelles, thirty prisoners were standing by the side of the road. Brosset glanced at them. Pico took the opportunity to lift a couple of watches. There was heavy enemy fire.

The pace of the three combat teams accelerated. We were really making good time. How happy the General was!

"We'll be in Giromagny this evening!" he kept repeating.

We started out again full speed ahead toward Champagney to get in touch with the chief of staff. A toppled pylon blocked half the road, and a wire had twisted itself around the axle of the jeep. We had to stop.

A good angel was trying to slow Brosset down. But he wanted to go faster, faster. Never had he seemed so impetuous, so impatient. Several times he shouted out, "This is the life!"

He didn't want to wait for Pico to unwind the wire, so we stopped a third jeep. He jumped in and took the wheel; the new driver climbed in next to him, and I got into the back seat.

"Why are you laughing?" he asked me.

"Because your face is covered with dirt."

"That's what's so wonderful about it all! At this very moment we're struggling through the mud; and tonight I'll be in my trailer, with my lovely chrysanthemums."

I shook off a strange feeling.

The driver, a sergeant whom I didn't know, warned him, "Be careful, General, this jeep pulls to the left when you brake."

He didn't answer. In a moment we were off like an arrow. When we reached the bridge where we had stopped that morning, we were going about seventy miles an hour.

"Watch out," I cried, "that bridge is mined!"

The general braked, the jeep skidded and flipped into the water . . .

The rest is like a nightmare; some parts are very vivid, others are vague . . . I see myself trapped under the jeep and the rushing water, trying desperately to pull myself free without success. My breath is giving out. "Just hold on and don't breathe, you're going to black out; but someone will save us, they will, they have to . . ." Just as I am beginning to suffocate I notice that my feet have come free. I slide backwards between the bars supporting the roof of the jeep and surge to the surface, gasping for air. The current tugs at me, but I feel strong hands hoisting me onto a barge.

"Where is the General?" I cry.

I hear some men answer, "Don't worry, everything's fine."

Soon I realized that they were lying. The driver was bleeding by the edge of the road but the General was nowhere in sight. Men from the engineering corps were probing the water in a haphazard search for him. Before long they managed to attach a cable to the fender of the jeep. Now it emerged. For one second I saw the General sitting stiff and immobile behind the wheel. Then the body began rocking back and forth and was carried away by the current.

Further down the river other engineers had formed a chain and succeeded in getting hold of his body. Then the current wrenched it away again and it disappeared.

The offensive continued. We had taken Giromagny and

progressed beyond it. Stani Mangin had gone ahead to break the news to his sister, Madame Brosset. Colonel Garbay, who had taken over the command of the Division, decided that the funeral services would be held on the twenty-third regardless of whether Madame Brosset was able to attend. The attack had to continue, and this priority overshadowed even the respect which was due to our dead leader.

In the chapel at Spears Hospital I bent over the body of the General. He looked just as we had known him in life: noble and strong. There were wounds in the forehead and the neck. He had probably been killed as the car fell into the river. How the driver had escaped only with a split lip and I with only a broken wrist remains a mystery.

The plans for the funeral went into effect. Fortunately, General de Lattre arrived an hour late just as the mass was beginning and just as Madame Brosset was entering the church. Her brother hadn't found her. She had been traveling on her way to the General's quarters, and had stopped when she saw the crowd gathered around the church.

I felt myself walk toward her as if in a bad dream. Above all, I feared that Mme. Brosset would unconsciously blame me for being alive. As soon as she saw me, however, she held out her arms.

The burial was delayed because the bridge which led to the cemetery had been carried away by the same torrent. The rain hadn't let up for three days.

I accompanied Mme. Brosset to the place where the accident had taken place. The river seemed so shallow; the bank so low . . .

Afterwards we drove the General to the military cemetery at Villersexel. We drove at fifteen miles an hour through the rain from Lure to Villersexel. During this long trip, I couldn't help smiling when I thought of what the General's reflections on this tedious pace would have been.

The service at the cemetery was very short. Only Garbay and a few officers were there, plus a guard of honor and Father Hirleman. While they lowered the coffin into the ground they sounded the bugle call for the dead. That was all.

December. This morning I found myself alone with the chief of staff, Saint-Hilier, and it took all my self-control not to sink into a real depression. Saint-Hilier sensed it. He spoke about the grim realities of war with a tenderness of which I hadn't suspected him capable.

When I reproached myself for being alive when the General was dead, he said to me: "When we were evacuated from Bir-Hakeim we had to clear a path for ourselves across a minefield and get the hell out, abandoning our friends on the sand. We just had to let them die. It's the law of war. And they called us heroes . . ."

Paris. A month of convalescence. My wrist is in a cast and the wound in my knee has reopened. Claude Dauphin has asked me to act with him in *Une grande fille toute simple* by André Roussin. The opening night will be a benefit for our two divisions. I will rehearse for two weeks and give fifteen performances. Then another actor will take over for me when I leave.

The thrill of climbing back on a stage momentarily erases all of the fatigue and confusion which I've been feeling. Neither Claude nor I have played Paris for six years.

After the first performance we walked on stage in uniform to conduct an auction; we were met by a torrent of applause. Claude was crying. I felt empty.

January 5, 1945. Claude has done something very touching. During the intermission he explained to the audience, unbeknownst to me, that this was my last performance and that I was leaving for the front.

"When I give the signal, we'll all wish Jean-Pierre good luck."

At the last curtain call, I gazed out at the red, packed auditorium. Suddenly I saw the whole audience rise in one motion and shout something that I couldn't make out. At first I thought there was a fire; then finally I understood what they were saying: "*Bonne chance*, Jean-Pierre."

January. The villages of Alsace. Swollen with rocks, turrets, and steeples, stuffed with storks' nests; vineyard trellises pierce the snow-covered slopes of the Vosges. Moroccan troops in somber robes warm themselves around a blaze in the public square. The right to pillage is a part of their contract with the Army. When in France they are given extra pay in compensation; but the *pleasure* of stealing cannot be replaced.

The Germans are enlarging their bridgehead at Colmar. Our division has retreated to the left bank of the Ill and has succeeded in slowing the attack. Leclerc sends these words to General Garbay: "Bravo, old fellow! We liberated Strasbourg, but we would have lost it again without your boys."

January 23. Tomorrow morning we are going to launch an offensive. Our mission is to reach the Rhine at Bardolsheim, cut the pocket of Alsace in two, and clean up the northern half.

January 27. Illkeusern. Firing on all sides. I'm beginning to like this business less and less. Less here than in the Vosges, less in the Vosges than in the south, less in the south than in Italy . . . Maybe my wounds and the accident have made me more realistic. As long as nothing happens to you, you think you're invulnerable to bullets. They're for the other guy. But a wound, light as it may be, forces you to look at things a little more realistically. That's when real courage is revealed, a courage which shows itself in the face of danger.

The fresh cadavers are piled into a truck one on top of the other, like so much garbage. Some of them still have their eyes open. The hands stiffen the quickest. The hair seems to stay alive.

I think of the mothers who will receive this telegram: "Soldier X died courageously for his country."

A compassionate captain will write them later that their son was killed by a shot in the heart, that he died without suffering while attacking an enemy position to liberate a portion of France.

She won't know, thank God, that he wasn't attacking an enemy position, that the shot didn't touch his heart, that he wasn't heroic. Or rather, that he was even more heroic—tired, cursing the cold, the command, the rust on his machine-gun, the monotony of K rations, his sergeant's ugly face, his leaky boots . . . She'll never know that he wasn't in the act of liberating a part of France, but that he was sacrificed for a diversionary tactic, or by error, or merely for a prestige victory. She'll never know that that same evening, the colonel of his brigade (as kind a man as ever lived) will clap his hands and declare: "Only eighty dead? Great!"

No, and she won't know either that her son has been thrown like a dog into a cartload of cadavers and that the only funeral service he has received from the chaplain are these words to the gravedigger: "Hurry up."

February 10. Three weeks ago when everything seemed lost and the Germans were advancing toward Strasbourg, General de Monsabert, no longer knowing where to turn for help, climbed up to the monastery at Sainte-Odile to pray. He promised the saint a thanksgiving service if she would lead us to victory.

Today he has kept his word. Everyone has gathered at the very heart of Alsace for a simple Te Deum. The flag has been placed on the altar.

Afterwards we went to Colmar, where de Gaulle reviewed the troops. The Division was decorated with the Croix de Guerre. Some young Alsacian girls in native costumes were applauding. Their bonnets looked like large black poppies.

De Gaulle has brought Mauriac and Aragon with him. Claude Guy, his aide-de-camp, tells me that the impression de Gaulle gives of not noticing or being interested in what's happening around him, even at the most important moments, is misleading. Actually, the General is gifted with an astounding memory, sees everything, and has a lively sense of humor which would surprise even those who think they know him well.

March 7. The Americans have crossed the Rhine at Remagen. Our Division has been sent to rest. Finally! But our relief mingles with our regret at not being able to participate in the final assault.

Germany? There it is behind that river, an easy prey. Since

we won't have the chance to invade it, I at least want to contemplate it.

Leaving Strasbourg, it's necessary to march three or four kilometers through a deserted countryside to reach the Rhine.

Some outposts are manned by Moroccan troops.

"Get down, lieutenant, the Krauts can see you from that tower. They're going to shoot at you."

I just want to take one good look. At my feet, the Rhine, yellowish and slow; to the right, the iron bridge of Kehl, cut in two. Opposite me is Germany: a series of blockhouses, and the first houses of Kehl, green and sad.

I return slowly to Strasbourg, then continue in a jeep with Blonblon, my driver toward Dambach. Gradually the night envelops us. This departure from Alsace is the end of an important chapter in my life. And I hate anything that ends.

God knows, war is horrible. God knows, I'm not particularly sensitive to the beauties, rigors, and duties of military life. Nevertheless, I already feel sad about leaving the Division. Not for any particular friend there. In spite of what they say, the war doesn't very often lead to profound friendships. It's our Division as a whole that I'll be missing. It has its own life, its own soul and charm. Every night in December when I was acting at the Ambassadeurs Theater I would think of the Division and realize how much I missed it. When I got back to the Division I didn't think about the Ambassadeurs Theater at all, even though the play I had been in was still going on. I am the first to be surprised by it, but that's how it was.

This nostalgia for an active, dangerous, unpredictable life will probably haunt most of the men who fought. A monotonous, punctual existence full of family responsibilities and daily worries is going to weigh heavily on them. Only now do I understand why the oldtimers who talked about 1914–18 referred to it with a wistful sigh: "Those were the good old days."

I'm driving my jeep down the Strasbourg-Dambach road, straight and shiny as a rail. To the right and left the countryside has become a series of marshes. Night comes slowly, slowly. Blonblon, my driver, is humming a vague tune. I think of the eighteen months which I have just spent, the fullest and richest days of my life.

And all the men I've met, lived with, or seen die inspire me with a feeling of . . . of respect. Yes, respect. Respect for my companions, whose courage is tempered with so much compassion and modesty—and very often with humor. Respect for these American and Canadian soldiers who have died on the Rhine. Young farmers from Minnesota or Nova Scotia, cowboys from Texas, workers from Portland or Brooklyn, their farm or village hasn't been bombed; their father or wife hasn't been deported; their country wasn't invaded. For a cause that is not evident to them and which doesn't affect them directly, they are fighting in a country they don't know. Respect—for the English working under bombs in London, sleeping under bombs, living under bombs, and ignoring them. Simply because it isn't good manners to complain, they have chosen not to mention the existence of Hitler and the fact they themselves have been moving around for five years in a nightmare of "blood, sweat, and tears."

In the approaching darkness, only the skeletons of the trees are now visible. The villages are empty. Long yellow streaks remain among the black clouds. The soft, sad twilight and dappled water make me feel like crying. All along the road crucifixes stretch their wooden arms toward a sky rayed with gold.

Blonblon whistles "Lili Marlene."

PART TWO

10

HONEYMOON IN PARIS

When the war was over, I came back to New York. Maria was there waiting for me. After two weeks we took the train to Hollywood. On the platform of the station my three little sisters-in-law fretted impatiently: Adita, Consuelo, and Lucita (ages eighteen, seventeen, and sixteen). They had arrived from Santo Domingo during my absence. I didn't know them yet. Maria, who adored them, had given me the most flattering description of them. But that was nothing compared to the superlative flights of fancy she had used to describe me.

During eighteen months of separation (a separation coming so quickly after our marriage) her heart and overactive imagination had transformed me slowly into a superman, a hero combining the virtues of Caesar and Romeo, of Bayard and Apollo. When, after seeing my photo my three sisters-in-law didn't manifest enough enthusiasm, Maria cried: "Every photograph is a betrayal. A Greek God, I tell you, I've married a Greek God."

Maria got off the train first, and when I climbed down after taking care of our bags, the three girls were dashing around in every direction and ignoring me completely. "What are you looking for?" Maria shouted to them. "The Greek God," they answered, "where is the Greek God?"

"He's right here," replied Maria with a trembling voice, pointing to the wan and peaked specimen of a soldier I had become.

Speechless with disappointment and disbelief, my three sisters-in-law attempted a half-hearted curtsy.

The three sisters-in-law and the baby we were hoping for made Maria's house seem too small. We discovered a larger one with which we fell in love immediately. It had an Italian-style façade and a large front lawn. The back yard was a jungle of orange and lemon trees, rose bushes, and avocados.

People never seem to appreciate their blessings. The slightest problem overwhelms us with sadness or bitterness; we are singularly unconscious of our happiness, perhaps because we consider it our due. It has to be lost to be perceived. Later, I realized that the years spent in that house were among the most beautiful in my life. It's there that Lucita, then Consuelo were married, there that Maria-Christine grew up, there that we lived the richest hours of our love.

"Action . . . action . . ." On certain days a shivering and lank figure appeared at our home bearing the honorable title of Astrologer. With the gesture of a prophet he would expel Dr. Mitchneck, who was supposed to replace our Spanish and French accents with his Russian one, and Dr. Saxer, who was there for the purpose of teaching us gymnastics to the music of Brahms. Pushing aside these specialists of the vocal cords and muscles, our astrologer would cry: "Action, action . . ." and disappear. No one had any idea what kind of action he was talking about.

We were expecting a child and it was determined that a caesarean would be necessary. Maria had chosen the date of February thirteenth to please me, but our astrologer, whom I was beginning to find a bit cumbersome, declared that the stars were more favorable on the fourteenth. The fourteenth was chosen for the delivery.

Maria was sure that we would have a son. I started looking

for a first name. Lucita shrugged her shoulders. "Your son! . . . Your son! . . . for the moment it's at most your fetus!"

After several false alarms, Maria began to get impatient. "Poor boy," she lamented, "he really wants out. If we wait any longer he'll suffer from claustrophobia all his life."

Finally, at the predicted time, we drove Maria to the hospital.

She was half-conscious and murmured some verses by the Countess de Noailles:

> Je suis encore avec les anges sur l'échelle.
> Je ne peux pas venir si vite auprès de vous,
>   Mais je chancelle . . .*

Charles Boyer, who had already been my best man at our marriage, and who would be the godfather of our son, accompanied us.

At nine in the morning a nurse announced: "It's a girl."

I could see my daughter behind a glass window. The nurses were powdering three babies and rolling them on a table the way a baker kneads dough; two of them were red, grimacing, and shapeless; the third was fresh and beautiful. I prayed for it to be my daughter. It was. Because of the caesarean she had come into the world without any trouble and already had sleek, clean skin, a small turned up nose like her mother's, beautiful chestnut hair, and blonde eyebrows. . .

Charles was panic-striken at the idea that the babies could get mixed up in the nursery, but I already knew that there was no danger of my confusing my daughter with another.

In the meantime, I had been making *Heartbeat* with Ginger Rogers and Adolphe Menjou. Sam Wood, the director, seemed unsure of himself and shot every scene over and over.

From these miles of celluloid the editor somehow managed to piece together an agreeable film. Surrounded by pink flood-

---

* I am still with the angels on the ladder.
  I can't join you so quickly,
  But I falter . . .

lights, Ginger Rogers gave an effective performance. She was a very courteous co-worker. If my tie was askew she didn't tell me, but called the assistant instead and said: "Would you mind warning Mr. Aumont that his tie isn't straight." Adolphe Menjou, who had a mustache and eyebrows like commas, had assumed a one-man battle against Communism long before Senator McCarthy. At a time when we had hardly won the battle against fascism, Menjou—also an Adolphe!—was drawing up lists of suspects while putting the finishing touches on his makeup.

As soon as this bit of fluff was completed, Metro loaned me to another studio.

This studio was Universal, where Maria was the reigning queen. However, it was not with her that they intended me to work but with Yvonne de Carlo, whom they were trying to set up as a rival to Maria. At that time it was the policy of all the studios to create such opposition among their stars under contract. Thus, Debbie Reynolds was brought in to replace Judy Garland, Gregory Peck to oppose Clark Gable, Ava Gardner to supplant Lana Turner. If a star did poorly at the box office or became difficult, his replacement was right there waiting to take over.

I began filming *Scheherazade* with Yvonne de Carlo. It was the fictionalized (to say the least) story of Rimsky-Korsakov. According to the scenario, poor Rimsky, who didn't age a day during the film, must have composed all of his work in a week.

One morning, as I was playing a scene with Yvonne de Carlo, a tall, pale, thin boy appeared on the set. He had unruly hair and something of the child lingered in the way he looked at you. He was in the uniform of a parachutist, the same in which he was to die ten years later in Egypt.

He introduced himself as Jean Roy and told me that he had just been demobilized and wanted to write an article on me for *Cinemonde*. As soon as I'd met him I sensed that he was destined to become my best friend, and that he and Lucita had been made for each other. He was intelligent, quick, funny, and, above all, unconventional. He told several picturesque war stories which I was later to learn were deliberately less impressive than his actual exploits. That's how he was. Just for the pleasure of inventing an adventure story he launched into tall tales; but since he was honest and found boasting too easy, he always gave himself a role less flattering than it had been in reality. Contrary to most of us, his lies never won him any glory. They were simply an escape from reality.

That same evening I said to Lucita: "I've found your husband."

Maria spluttered, "Her husband? She's not even seventeen."

Lucita smiled faintly and said nothing.

The next day Jean arrived for dinner. He was never to move out.

Metro loaned me to a certain Nebenzal, a frenetic producer at United Artists, who had Maria and me make *Atlantis.*

The decors were a fantastic mishmash, including naugahyde doors which seemed to have come right out of the office of the frenetic producer rather than the mysterious palace of Antinea.

The first day of shooting, they hoisted me up onto a pair of shoes with three-inch heels. I asked why. They explained that Dennis O'Keefe, who played Morhange, was two inches taller than me.

"So?"

"So, you get top billing."

"I don't see the connection."

"It just wouldn't be right for you to look smaller."

"Good. Give me two-inch heels, not three."

"No, you're the star of this film. You should be at least an inch taller than everyone else."

Dromedaries arrived from a neighboring zoo. Alas, it was camels that we needed. A second hump was glued onto them with a lot of rubber cement. Since they looked a little shabby, a workman covered them with oil from a spray-gun to make their coats more lustrous.

We also had to play a scene with a leopard. In order to

prevent the beast from mauling us, he was given a large dose of tranquilizers. Then he had to live at our house for a few days until he became accustomed to us.

In spite of our frenetic producer, the three-inch heels, the bewildered camels, and the sleepy leopard, *Atlantis*, for some mysterious reason, didn't fare too badly.

One day a good friend of mine, the scenarist Salka Viertel, telephoned me and asked me to come to her place, urgently; she wouldn't tell me why. When I got there she whispered in my ear, "She's coming."

"Who?"

"She . . ." sighed Salka in awe, "She."

At that moment the door opened. Accompanied by two boxers, hair blowing in the wind, lean body molded by pullover and blue jeans, without an ounce of makeup, Greta Garbo made her entrance. After a few moments of silence she said, "I'm planning on doing George Sand. Would you like to play Alfred de Musset?"

Unfathomable, encircled by the two boxers, she disappeared in the sun and the wind. So did George Sand and Alfred de Musset.

I had always longed to meet her, and tried to learn about her through friends who worked with her. As soon as I mentioned her name, however, a religious terror seemed to seize them. They answered "She's okay." and changed the conversation.

I had gone to see her five times in *Camille*. She was both the dying courtesan and the ghost of that character, so much did her genius seem made of unreality. I found myself wondering if she actually existed. I still wonder.

In August Maria and I decided to finally go on our honeymoon. Entrusting Maria-Christine to Lucita and Jean, we flew off to Paris. As we approached my heart swelled. It was marvelous to be going back and to be going with Maria. We knew that there would be photographers there when we landed, but we didn't expect such a crowd. Maria, wearing a simple, tailored suit and no jewelry, seemed altogether different from the ornate siren whose image Universal had been promoting!

Spurning the Cadillac sent by Universal, we somehow squeezed into my brother's old Ford, whose motor was attached to the chassis with twine and whose doors were held shut with rubber bands.

First of all I wanted to show Maria the Place de la Concorde and the Champs-Elysées. A few days before in Los Angeles we had seen a film on the life of Wilson in which Marcel Dalio played the part of Clemenceau. As we passed the Grand Palais, Maria exclaimed: "Oh, look, a statue of Dalio."

This trip to Paris was exhilarating. Maria was the first American star to come to France since the war and, what's more, she was married to a Frenchman. This was enough to make her popular; but since she herself had fallen in love with Paris, it was no effort for her to feel absolutely happy there.

Later, when she acted in *L'Ile Heureuse* and it got bad reviews, Maria said wistfully, "I would so have loved to conquer Paris . . ." But during that trip in the summer of 1946 Maria, with a smile, had indeed conquered Paris.

In the euphoria of this vacation I nearly forgot that the war, the occupation, and the purge of the collaborators were still open wounds. Rosine Derean had returned from Ravensbruck disfigured. Her crime had been to hide allied aviators in the small castle that Claude Dauphin had given her when they got married. She had been denounced to the Nazis by her neighbors. We took Rosine out often to help her forget her long martyrdom. One evening the three of us ran into Corinne Luchaire in a nightclub. The woman who had been called "the Pompadour of the Third Reich" was wasted away by tuberculosis and looked more like a flayed animal than the ex-paramour of Ciano or Abetz. She came over to our table. I hugged her, since to me she was still the little girl that I had known when we made *Je t'attendrai* together. But Rosine couldn't forget what Corinne had represented during the occupation, or understand how she could be dancing in a nightclub when Jean Luchaire, her father, an enthusiastic collaborator, had just been shot. Rosine told Corinne she should be ashamed. They stood there, livid, trembling, two symbols: one of the Resistance and the other of the collaboration; one having escaped death by some miracle, and the other sliding toward it.

This trip included an encounter which, if it did not yield the fruits we had hoped for, was nevertheless bound to affect our destinies profoundly. At a press party given in her honor, Maria met Jean Cocteau. She was aware of the admiration I had for him and shared it. His work had moved her; the man fascinated her. Before he had even been introduced, Cocteau took Maria in his arms. Any barrier between the two was broken. We were friends, and quite naturally decided to make a film together.

Finding a producer wasn't hard. Decharme, who had never been particularly friendly toward me, was anxious now to have us under contract. I felt a secret delight in his suddenly obsequious behavior. Life has its reversals. It's enough to acknowledge them in passing with a wink of the eye.

We saw Cocteau often. Maria and he belonged to the same race. Both of them moved easily between the confines of the real and the unreal. Both of them were familiar with messages from the beyond, ghosts, and premonitions. From the moment of this first encounter not the slightest doubt remained: we were going to cancel our contracts with MGM and Universal and come to live in Paris as soon as we had finished our scheduled films.

II

COCTEAU AND
THE EMPEROR OF CHINA

On returning to Hollywood I could ascertain that Metro had
nothing planned for me. When they had hired me in 1942 I had
been their "protegé," but during my eighteen months of absence, they had fabricated some new stars, the surest being
Gregory Peck and Van Johnson. My French accent, which had
been my greatest asset, had suddenly become my greatest handi-
cap. All the same, my popularity with the fans hadn't suffered
in my absence. Whatever the case, it didn't really matter to me.

The most important thing was to get out of that feudal contract as quickly as possible and be able to do a film with Cocteau
and Maria in France. I waited for the day when the astrologer
said the stars showed the best aspects and asked for an interview
with Louis B. Mayer. I told him that I was homesick, that my
leaving wouldn't ruin his studio, and, quite simply, that I
wanted my contract annulled. This wasn't as easy as I thought it
would be. First he reproached me for abandoning MGM to join
the Free French Forces at the very moment when my popularity
was at its height; then he explained that loaning me out to other
studios brought a pretty good profit. I pleaded with him. He
looked at me with amazement: "You're not really going to tell

me that you'll earn more money by making a film in France than by remaining under contract with us, are you?"

"No, but it's not just a matter of money. I haven't worked in France for years. I'm homesick for Paris and this comeback in a film by Cocteau is very important to me."

He looked at me as if I were crazy and agreed to let me go—on condition that I turn over to MGM all the money United Artists was to pay me for *Atlantis*.

For Maria the problem was more delicate. She was still the Number 1 moneymaker at Universal, but her contract was about to expire. She had been offered a new one, for seven years, and with much better terms; but she had the right to refuse it. It was a big decision to make. She shared my wish to live in Paris; she was as thrilled as I by the idea of making Cocteau's film; and, as always, she wanted to please me. She refused the new contract.

Beyond the desire to make a film in France I had an almost physical need to play again on the stage in Paris. In '41 I had done my screen test for MGM in *Liliom*, and that character had haunted me ever since. I was acutely disappointed when I learned that they were going to do it in Paris, and that it was already cast.

In the midst of my melancholy I suddenly thought: "Since nobody will ever offer me the role of a bad guy, and since I'll probably be playing cleancut juveniles until I'm ninety, why not try to write myself a character similar to Liliom?"

I started a play entitled *The Serpent*. It wasn't really clear to me in what particular direction my serpent would spit its venom. I began with a scene in the last act, a violent, cynical scene in which the characters bared their souls to each other without my having the slightest notion of their motivation. Sitting at my desk my mind was a blank, but as soon as I went out for a ride or walked along the beach at Santa Monica, the ideas came to me. Obviously this method of constructing a play, or rather, writing it without having constructed it, is indefensible, but what can I do about it? Quite often one line gave me the idea for a scene.

After beginning it at Hollywood I continued *The Serpent*, which had become *The Emperor of China*, in the Grand Canyon—under the mocking glances of my brother and brother-in-law. Both of them laughed to see me at the bottom of a ravine or, later, in the Mormon temple in Salt Lake City scribbling a line on a little scrap of paper. They never imagined that the conglomeration of these lines would form a comedy which would be performed a short time later in Paris.

Marcel Herrand was the first person to read my play. He decided to produce it immediately at the Mathurins Theater. During the rehearsals in September, 1947, I made nonstop shuttles between London (where I was finishing a film) and Paris.

Sometimes I spent the weekend with Noel Coward at the foot of the white cliffs of Dover, enveloped in sea-wrack and mist. I told him the story of *The Emperor of China*.

"What a peculiar lad you are!" said he. "I feel sorry for Maria!"

I bristled. "You're not going to claim that you put yourself into all the characters you've created!"

"Oh, but yes, dear boy, every one of them."

Finally we left for Lille, where the play was tried out. It was an immediate success.

Nevertheless, Marcel asked me to cut a few lines which were too raw in the scene where Jean (the Emperor of China) makes fun of Yolande, his future mother-in-law, who has fallen in love with him and has come to hunt him out in his garret. I was amazed that Marcel Herrand could be shocked by a few brutal lines. He had produced plays which were a lot more daring! He explained to me that it was a question of tone. Since *The Emperor of China* was a light comedy up to the third act, this scene in quite another style came as a rude shock. He was right, but I was too stubborn to admit it. Every evening during the course of that scene there were some reproachful "oh's" from the audience but I kept it unchanged.

At that time I was so proud and surprised to have been capable of writing a play that I wouldn't accept any advice. It was worth more to me to have three acts full of faults that I could call entirely mine than to owe the least suggestion to anyone else. Thus, I even refused the generous advice of Jean Cocteau, about the last lines of the third act, determined as I was to go without any help, no matter how useful.

Cocteau understood my pride. Not only did he not bear me any grudge for it, but he wrote this foreword for the *Emperor of China:*

> Jean-Pierre Aumont has hit the nail on the head, with that special grace of his, by creating a character similar to those of Synge, but which is new in France and very characteristic of our times: a figure of myth, a liar, a teller of tall stories, an extortioner, whose charm casts a spell over his victims and over himself.
>
> We ought to congratulate the author so much the more for his creation since he does not at all resemble his hero. He invents, embellishes, amuses himself and entertains us with the charm of a child who plays at being a horse and becomes a horse. This entertainement will without a doubt one day be recognised as the portrait of the new generation.
>
> —Jean Cocteau

The Emperor of China opened in Paris November 3, 1947. On that day Claude Dauphin published a letter to me in *Paris-Presse:*

> My dear friend Jean-Pierre:
> When you were plastered with mud and sweat as you climbed the footpaths around Cassino on the lookout for any stone or bush which might prove fatal; when you found yourself, after four long years, among the sandy pines of Cavalair with the first American wave; when you lay on the platform at Marseille under a riddled jeep tending a thigh wound sticky with blood; when you tore yourself away with anger and despair from the torrent that engulfed your incomparable companion in arms, General Brosset, in the snowy Vosges; you could say to yourself: "No, I'm no longer afraid of anything." Admit, however, that when you are waiting trembling in the wings tonight, for the cue to enter, which comes

like the stroke of fate to betray or deliver you, admit that you will
be afraid. But you shouldn't be afraid, since you have created
something. It will be criticized and it will be praised. But now you
can mop your brow and say: 'This is what I have done, judge it,
but it is I who have done it.'

Claude was right. I wrote and I will write other plays. I've
acted in some and I will act in others. But that night, as I in-
terpreted my own text for the first time, offering the public fragments of dialogue which came from my deepest self, yes, that
was a sensation that I had never before experienced and would
never experience again.

Maria left for Hollywood to make *Tangiers* in a hurricane of
interviews, photos, champagne, tears, telephone calls, and
excess baggage charges. She was as happy for my success as if it
had been her own.

After she had gone, I went to see Cocteau. At first he had
imagined adapting Merimée's *La Venus d'Ille*, but he had changed
his mind and decided to write for us an *Orpheus* in which Maria
would play Death. For the part of Heurtebise, he asked me
what I thought of Jean Marais. I answered that it would be a
pleasure to work with Marais, for whom I had great esteem, but
we were too much alike. Young actors like Daniel Gelin or
Michel Auclair would create a more effective contrast to me.
After the 150th performance of my play I left Paris, entrusting
my role to Michel Auclair. I wanted to get back to Maria as soon
as possible.

In Hollywood I waited anxiously for news from Cocteau.
Finally we received the manuscript of *Orphée*. Maria and I were
enthusiastic. We considered it a new version of *Le Sang d'un Poete*
(*Blood of a Poet*). We were getting ready to go to Paris for the
shooting when a letter from Decharme arrived, informing us
that he found the film incomprehensible and offering us the
choice of several scenarios in its place.

We, however, felt ourselves bound to Cocteau, and rather

than shoot another film we tried, after having done everything in our power to convince Decharme, to find another producer.

We found one named André Paulvé. I sent him the manuscript. He wasn't captivated either by the strange beauty of *Orphée*.

Time passed. It became evident that we wouldn't be able to shoot *Orphée* that summer. Another producer proposed our making *Hans le Marin* (*Wicked City*) in France.

The moment we arrived in Paris I naturally rushed over to Cocteau's. At that time he was living at Milly and I went to spend the weekend. He showed me the sketches that Bébé Berard had designed for Maria in the role of Death. How beautiful they were! Then he explained sadly that no producer seemed to understand *Orphée* and that he would be reduced to producing it himself—later—with technicians and actors who would be willing to share the financial risks. I answered that Maria and I were with him and that we continued to have full confidence in him.

Then we heard nothing from Cocteau. A few weeks later, we read in a newspaper that he had decided to produce this same *Orphée* with Jean Marais and Maria Casares. I was shocked, hurt. Two years of waiting, the breaking of our Hollywood contracts, our loyalty to Cocteau: all that had led to this one notice in a newspaper.

Maria, who often made mountains out of molehills, always remained surprisingly calm and collected in the face of important events. She told me, "I won't like Cocteau any less for this." Then she added with a sigh, "But I would have loved to play Death."

To console her, I said, "You'll play other, more appealing characters, ones where you can be yourself, joyful and lovely and young."

Smiling sweetly, she answered, "But Death ought to be joyful and lovely and young."

12

MARIA

The Theater Guild of New York had bought the rights to *The Emperor of China* and chosen Philip Barry to adapt it in English.

My debut in the American theater couldn't have been more auspicious. Barry was the author of *Philadelphia Story*, among other successes, and at the time was a highly respected playwright. He began working. I had no news from him until one day, while on tour, I heard Maria screaming over the telephone. She had just received the adaptation of *The Emperor* and couldn't find words strong enough to describe her horror.

I thought that she was exaggerating, but once more she was right. I went to Barry's home in Florida to try to repair the damages. Of course he had emphasized the lighter aspects of the first two acts while at the same time toning down as much as he could all the strength and originality of the last act. As for his title, *My Name Is Aquilon*, I do not know to this day what that was supposed to mean. But alas! whether it was a question of the title or the changes he had made, it was impossible for me to suggest any compromises. Each time that I tried to convince him, he would answer with a superior smile: "You are a charming boy, but you don't know the American Public." Such logic was overwhelming.

In December we began rehearsing in New York. Lilli Palmer was my co-star. On January 5 we opened in New Haven. We received a warm response. In the evening we gathered to celebrate my birthday and Philip Barry bent toward Maria to ask her opinion of his adaptation. "Shit," answered Maria calmly. "But the production . . ." stammered Barry in a choked voice. "Shit." An embarrassed silence fell over the gathering. Someone timidly tried to save the evening: "Well, in any case, the scenery . . ." "Shit," continued Maria imperturbably.

The next morning we read the papers. The reviews were favorable for the play, reserved for Lilli, but flattering for me as an actor. Maria burst into tears. "This time we are screwed."

I had no idea what she was talking about.

"I know you," she said sadly; "if you had gotten bad reviews for your acting, you would have listened and refused to continue, but your vanity as an actor is going to outweigh your honesty as an author. You're committing a crime and I'll never forgive you for it. It's as if you were strangling our own child with your hands."

With these words, Maria left for Paris to film *Portrait of an Assassin*. The performances of my play followed their course from Boston to Philadelphia. Every day Barry arrived with new changes, each one worse than the last.

Finally the evening of the New York opening arrived. To my astonishment, Lilli Palmer softened her performance to three pitches below mine, in a register, tempo, and style which had nothing to do with our six weeks of rehearsal and our four weeks of previews. I was baffled, concluded that she must be sick, and tried to inject some extra force into the play to save it. Idiot that I was, I didn't realize that I was only undermining myself. The harder I tried to create some movement, the more restrained Lilli appeared to be.

I later discovered that Lilli, worried by the reserved reviews she had been getting outside of New York, had sent for a Teutonic acting coach from California, whom I referred to as Applestrudel. For a certain sum, this woman gave advice to many American actors. It was she who had taught Rex Harrison to look Siamese in *Anna and the King of Siam*. I ought to add that Lilli had offered the same tutoring to me, out of loyalty, but I had refused. I had written the play, and had been directed in that role by Marcel Herrand in Paris and Bob Saint-Clair in the United States. I felt that any intervention at this point would be more dangerous than advantageous for me.

Despite everything, the opening night seemed to end in success. Twelve curtain calls is a lot for New York. I called Maria in Paris to tell her the good news and then went to supper at Lilli's with a light heart.

Alas! at four o'clock in the morning, in a hostile Times Square, I sat down to read the reviews: Excellent for Lilli, abominable for the play. It was useless to read the other papers; the fate of our undertaking was sealed.

The failure of this adaptation of my play was a great blow to me. Like everyone else, my life had been a series of alternating successes and defeats, and I had accepted both with philosophy; but this time I was unjustly suffering the blame for a failure which wasn't my fault. I was wounded to the quick. I made up my mind not to return to Paris directly. First of all I realized that Maria had been only too right; and secondly, I naively believed that my friends would look on me as a leper, an outcast. Most important, I found it necessary to prove to myself that I was capable of writing another play, and I had to do it right away. Instead of taking the plane for Paris, I took off for Miami at dawn, the morning after the play terminated its brief run.

I began writing a scene which would later become the second act of *L'Ile Heureuse* (*The Happy Island*). In it, a film producer buys a scenario from an author and tells him that it will become a masterpiece on condition that the title, action, characters, style, general idea, episodes, and all the lines are changed. As a leitmotif I could hear the voice of Philip Barry: "You're charming, but you don't know the American public." Nourished by my disillusionment and indignation, the scene turned out well.

I kept writing, stopping at each of the little islands which form Key West. I added one scene to another without any link, a terrible habit that I couldn't seem to break. But I felt good. To hell with Philip Barry, to hell with the Guild, to hell with my flop. I wrote another scene which I later cut. It described a true episode in my life. One evening when Maria, in a very decolleté gown, was climbing into our old jalopy our black butler had said to us: "Here, take my Cadillac, please."

I called Maria in Paris. I realized that she was interpreting this sudden surge of pride which had made me flee New York to write a new play as indifference toward her. She couldn't understand why I hadn't leaped into the first plane to join her. That's what I decided to do.

Maria-Christine, who was three years old, was in New York with my father and his second wife, Anni, whom I loved like my own mother. I went to see them and to take my daughter back to join Maria in Paris.

Tender, funny, relaxed during the plane ride, my little girl watched over me. In a protective tone of voice, she kept saying: "Relax, take it easy." I tried to make her sleep but she refused.

"I don't want to close my eyes."

"Why?"

"They're too beautiful."

To someone who asked her: "Are you French or American?" she replied, "Neither. I'm a child."

When I got to Paris, Maria reproached me for my stay in Florida. I reproached her for not understanding the reasons. An evil spirit possessed me. The word "divorce" rose to my lips.

All night I wandered in the streets of Paris, ashamed of my stupidity, trembling at the thought of losing my reason for living. The next day, Maria and I found each other again. In the meantime the papers had published the news of our divorce. It didn't matter. We knew now that we belonged to each other. The truth was that in spite of our quarrels we were fiercely in love. This squall had been beneficial to us. The two last years we were to spend together would be the happiest of our lives. Our love was now more profound because we had nearly lost it.

Nicole Védrès, one of the few women directors in France, had decided to show on film the ten Frenchmen most typical of their generation. She had chosen Picasso, André Gide, Jean-Paul Sartre, Le Corbusier, and Jean Rostand among others. The film was called *La Vie Commence Demain*, and I was to interview these ten different personalities.

André Gide welcomed us into his apartment on rue Vaneau at seven o'clock in the morning. He had already been up for several hours reading a book by Simenon, who was his favorite author at the time.

At the age of eighty, Gide was erect and spare with a head sketched by Holbein. I asked him, as I always did, if he had any questions he would like me to put to him.

He answered with a demonic smile, articulating each syllable carefully: "I'd like you to ask me whether I intend to write a sequel to my journal."

Lights, camera, action. The film starts rolling.

"Mr. Gide, could you tell us if there will be a sequel to your journal?"

"An indiscreet question, young man, which I will not answer."

When I finished *L'Ile Heureuse*, I offered the main role to Maria. The character was a conventional Hollywood star. How I hate myself today for not having given Maria a deeper, more dramatic role.

The evening of the opening I was at Marseille, touring in another play, *L'Homme de Joie*. At midnight I called my wife. Things had gone badly. A power failure had kept the audience waiting an hour and a half between the first and second act. Then the show went on under dim, improvised lighting which lent a lugubrious tone to what should have been comedy.

I hardly slept that night. In the morning, the papers confirmed my nightmares. I walked sadly along the port with my friends. I could read in their looks: "What's Maria going to think! She'll never forgive you for this."

How little they knew her. An hour later I received the following telegram:

"Be happy and gay, my love, these little setbacks don't matter in the least."

After a brief return to Paris, I left again for Egypt to act in *L'homme de joie.*

We were supposed to open at the Royal Theater of Cairo on the first of February, but I was asked to arrive twenty-four hours earlier for a party which King Farouk was giving. An hour before take-off I went home to get my bags and found Maria in a state of extreme agitation. She had had a vision; she was sure that the plane which I was taking would burst into flames and crash. At first I laughed at her, but she wept and got herself into such a state that I had to promise to put off my departure until the next day. If it had been a question of an opening at the theater in Cairo I would never have delayed my trip; but, after all, it was only Farouk's private party. I listened to Maria and left the following day.

When I got to Cairo I found a group of annoyed officials waiting for me at the airport.

"It's a good thing," they said, "that the party didn't take place. Otherwise you could have caused a diplomatic break between France and Egypt."

"And why didn't it take place?" I asked.

"Because of the death of the King's aunt."

Later Maria calmly declared, "Of course she's dead. I diverted the evil spell onto her . . ."

As soon as the performances of *L'île Heureuse* were over, Maria came to be with me in Cairo.

We stole away for a few days to visit Luxor and the Valley of the Kings. Maria was fascinated by the Egyptian architecture and spent hours in discussion with the curators of Luxor and Carnac. She was so affected by it that when I suggested we stop at Athens on the way back, she refused, because she didn't want to tarnish her memory of the Egyptian temples by learning about the Greek ones.

We were expected in Rome to make *La Vendetta del Corsaro.* On July 13 we celebrated our eighth anniversary there.

Maria gave me an Alfa Romeo. To christen it we drove through Rome at dawn. The city, deserted, belonged to us. For

Maria, I designed a pair of earrings which I had made at Bulgari's. They were platinum with small round and baguette diamonds that tinkled each time she moved her head.

I'm describing these earrings, because I was to run across them again, later, in strange circumstances.

To say that Maria was popular in Italy would be an understatement. She was worshiped there. The unrestrained affection with which the Italians treated her went beyond the conventional homage given to film stars. This was something warmer, more profound. In Maria, who was Latin like them and exuberant like them, they recognized a kindred spirit. Street urchins didn't bother her by asking for her autograph, they blew kisses. One evening when we were dining at Santa Maria de Trastevere, some kids approached our table. One of them fell to his knees and, reaching for Maria's hand, said: "Give us another film, I beg of you, please, give us another film."

During our stay in Italy we had lunch with a gauntfeatured woman who was hiding behind an enormous pair of dark glasses. It was the Countess Ciano. None of the heroines of Shakespeare or Corneille had known a destiny as violent as hers. She was the daughter of a peasant who became the ruler of Italy and who made all Europe tremble. Wife of the Minister of Foreign Affairs, during the course of one month she saw her husband betray her father and her father condemn her husband to death. Then Mussolini himself was hanged a few days later. On her face I could make out the famous mask of *Il Duce*, and also the mask of tragedy. But both were for the moment effaced by the banality of an inconsequential conversation. She said, "I was in Paris last June. How beautiful it is! How I love your city . . ."

In June! Ten years before her father had launched a cowardly attack on us. They say that Edda Ciano had a lot of influence on him at the time. Perhaps the fate of whole peoples depends on strokes of chance as fragile as the destiny of any single man. If fate had wished Edda Ciano to know and love

Paris ten years earlier, maybe Italy would not have attacked us, and the war would have taken a different course.

Right after *La Vendetta del Corsaro* I made *Les loups chassent la nuit* in Venice. Maria followed me a few days later. I had said to my colleagues: "You are going to see Montez arrive with an escort of a hundred trunks." But she walked out of the airplane with one little valise, no evening gown, and not the least desire to take part in the Venice Film Festival. When I had to leave for Trieste to shoot some more scenes, she insisted on accompanying me. Fearing that she would be bored there, I wanted her to stay in Venice.

"It's not too far, I'll come back to be with you every evening."

"But I want to be with my husband in the daytime too."

The morning we were supposed to leave, Maria, who was hardly an early riser, woke at 4 A.M. and joyfully saluted the dawn. The same Maria who hated riding in a convertible with the top down insisted on riding all the way in the wind. Never had I seen her happier than on that morning. First, in the gondola which took us across the canals from the hotel to the garage, then in the rising sun on the route from Venice to Trieste.

Did she know or sense unconsciously that she only had thirty days left to live?

The time at Trieste slipped quickly away. Maria, to my great surprise, settled into a deck chair to watch the filming. When I wasn't working we went swimming a few miles from Trieste. But Maria, who swam so well, seemed to be afraid of the water. Her astrologer had always warned her to be wary of it.

When we got back to Cannes, where we were planning to spend a few days, the porter of the Carlton greeted us with a sad face: "What a misfortune, what a great misfortune . . . have you read the papers?"

"No."

"Louis Jouvet is dead."

This was a terrible shock for me. So many beautiful memories linked me to him; I had such gratitude and admiration. Maria shared my grief. We returned to Paris.

A few days later we were invited to the festival of Palermo. "Would you like to go there?" asked Maria. "Then we'll go." She added, in a tone of surprise, "Do you realize that I've been doing everything you want for some time now?"

I protested, but she added with a shadow of melancholy, "What's happening to me?"

She had stopped putting on so much as a dress or a piece of jewelry without consulting me first; although she would have preferred to live in Paris, she agreed to rent a new place in the country just to please me. She who was always late began to wait for me patiently. She who had always been impulsive became calm and reflective. The night before her death we had a few friends over for dinner. They were going on about Maria's beauty, Maria-Christine's brightness, and the charm of our way of life . . . All of a sudden I was afraid. I went up to our room and prayed: "My God, I know that I am fully happy, but I swear to you that I appreciate it . . . Please just make it last . . ."

The following morning, I left for the studio, where I was finishing the last takes of *Les loups chassent la nuit*. I was late and contented myself with giving Maria a quick kiss as I ran out the door. Aside from Adita, who was still sleeping, the house was empty. Maria's other sisters were on a trip. It was the domestics' day off. As for Maria-Christine, I had taken her to my brother's, where she was supposed to have lunch.

Around noon my brother called me at the studio.

"Maria fainted in her bath. Adita called me. I called the doctor. Come."

"Is it serious?"

"Up to this point we haven't been able to revive her."

I rushed to Suresnes. When I got to the house there was already a pack of bystanders milling around in front of the door. Inside, two doctors, plus firemen with their resuscitation equipment. I called a heart specialist. He came immediately. Wasted effort. There was no longer anything anyone could do. Maria had become unconscious in a bath which was too hot. Adita had not been watching her . . . The telephone hadn't rung . . .

From a simple fainting spell, from which she could have been revived if it had been noticed in time, Maria, alone, had slipped away . . .

I have often wondered if Maria hadn't sensed that the end was near. Never had we been more happy, never had we had so many wonderful plans, but Maria had known she would die while still young and happy.

Not only was she not afraid of death, she was familiar with it. She had an earnest curiosity about the world beyond, a need to know what existed after life. Her bedside books were: *The Mystery of Eleusis, The Sanskrit Anthology, Summary of the Secret Doctrine*, and the *Book of Things Known and Hidden*.

I was jealous of this curiosity to which I felt a stranger, I, who later on perused these same books, searching desperately for some key, some hope, used to stop Maria each time she broached the subject of the supernatural. Sometimes she said to me with surprise:

"Then you don't believe in anything but what you can see or touch?"

One day I asked her: "How is it that the time of our death isn't given in our horoscopes?"

She answered: "But death isn't an end, it's a continuation, an improvement . . ."

She spoke of God with a familiarity which was surprising for a Spanish girl brought up in a convent. One day she told me: "When I find myself in front of God, I will fall on my knees before Him and say, 'My God, there is surely something beyond You. Let's search for it together."

She also believed in ghosts: "Look, my ghost has come to visit me." She would show me her arm and I would see, or would think I saw, the marks of five fingers.

The night before her death, her ghost came looking for her. She received it more seriously than usual. I asked her to read the lines on my hand as she often did. She refused. Surprised, I insisted. She grudgingly agreed, gave it only a rapid glance, as if she already knew what was there, and said sadly, "There's a new line in your hand."

I tried to jest. "That seems like a good omen to me."

She didn't answer.

Later she complained about her heart. She couldn't feel it beating anymore. That happened to her sometimes, and I didn't worry about it.

Is it possible that fate is cruel enough not to make us understand these signs? Can one actually give his wife a last kiss without knowing that it's the last? I saw nothing, sensed nothing.

Nothing . . . Ah! If I had only realized how short my happiness would be, how carefully I would have fenced it in!

How many times since have I repeated to myself: "If I'd only insisted that she see the doctor . . . If I'd stopped her from dieting . . . If she only hadn't taken such hot, long baths . . . If Maria-Christine hadn't gone to lunch at my brother's . . ." There's no real answer. You have to believe in God or else go crazy.

Maria's death was like a personal bereavement for millions of people who didn't know her. These tears, letters, and little bouquets on her tomb were not for a movie actress, but for a tender and generous and radiant woman.

I left for New York with Maria-Christine. It was impossible for me to stay in that house. I also knew that my father, who adored Maria, would be needing us. For several weeks, Maria-Christine didn't ask for any news of her mother. One day she told me that she didn't love her anymore, and I suddenly understood that she believed Maria had abandoned her. I armed myself with all my courage and more or less told her the truth. Her reaction was both surprising and comforting. She sighed happily, "Then that's the reason Mama hasn't written." She added, "We've got to write the Good Lord right away."

She dictated this letter to me:

"Dear fine, good, nice God, would you mind returning Mama? But if she's really well and you want to keep her, send us to heaven too, because we miss her a lot. And make sure Papa doesn't die before I do, because otherwise I'll be all alone. And make it always nice weather while we're in New York and not raining like today. It's Maria-Christine Aumont who signs this note for Mama, and don't lose it, God, until Mama is alive again."

13

GRACE KELLY AND
THE THEORY OF RELATIVITY

~~~~~~~~~~~~~~~~~~~~~~~~~~~

The five years which elapsed between the death of Maria and
my meeting with Marisa seem to unwind in my memory in slow
motion, shrouded by fog, like a film by Marguerite Duras or
Alain Resnais. In time grief loses its hard outline. One even
knows moments of selfish euphoria like those survivors of ship-
wrecks. You're surprised to be alive. You open your eyes. You
breathe. You can't believe that the sun is still there. You remember that there is a little girl who is not responsible for your
unhappiness and who is now doubly in need of your attention.

At first you know only despair, then a kind of lull, then
emptiness, willed with sudden stabs of pain as memory plays
tricks on you.

I don't think I could have made it through this period if my
brother and brother-in-law, with their wives, children, and
baggage, hadn't gathered around me.

I had sold our house in Hollywood. Not only did I never
want to see it again, I didn't even want it to belong to me
anymore. At La Malmaison I rediscovered the marvelous oasis
of greenery where I had started my career as a shepherd in an
operetta twenty years earlier. Large trees like the ones in the

Vosges, a river which ran down from the ponds of Sain-Cucufa, a grotto where Bonaparte and Josephine had their secret rendez-vous . . .

We all crowded together in that house: Lucita and Jean, François and Djin. Djinn was François' wife, a lovely Hindu who had langorously coasted down from the snowy Himalayas. Her eyes lost in constant reverie, she seemed to belong to another planet rather than to another continent. With a regularity that is to their credit, six children were born: Jean-Pierre and Yvie Roy on one side, and Mara, Patty, Jean, and Venita Villiers on the other. Today they are all big and handsome. Do they know that they were my only reason for living at that period of my life?

Every morning they came to wake me up in the attic that I'd reserved for myself and which I continue today to use as a refuge for reading or writing. Each had a well-defined duty. One brought the coffee, the other the mail, another the paper, another pulled the curtains. One of them dialed telephone numbers for me. And one of them went around searching for the chewing gum I had hidden for them to find.

Life dragged on in spite of everything. Never have I made so many films and been in so many plays as during those five years. And the only thing I recall about most of them is their titles.

The first of these films, however, I remember quite well. Not with much pleasure. It was called *Lili* and I made it in Hollywood. In spite of the exceptional success of this production (its publicity slogan became: "How many times have *you* seen *Lili?*") it is my one bad memory of a film.

I have always had a strong need to be liked by my director, my fellow actors, the technicians, even the propmen and the electricians. No doubt, I am spoiled, since I've always accomplished this without the slightest effort and I've always returned it in full.

But this time the director, Chuck Walters, couldn't stand me. From the first day he showed signs of hostility. I tried to get an explanation for his attitude. He answered, "You've done everything since the beginning to undermine our film."

I was stupefied. There wasn't the slightest particle of truth or common sense in what he was saying. After a lull of a few days he began treating me like an enemy again. Finally, unable to stand it any longer, I went to complain to Dore Schary, the new head of MGM. There were still a few days of shooting left, and Schary decided to have my scenes completed by Eddie Knopf, the producer, who liked me as much as I liked him.

The next film I made was called *The Charge of the Lancers*, an historical epic on the Crimean War which, strangely enough, was billed as a western. Paulette Goddard was my co-star. Our roles consisted mostly of looking professional when we climbed onto a horse and shouted "Charge!" or "Giddyup!" With a shade of embarrassment Paulette inquired if I would mind working on our lines with Mme. Applestrudel, formerly encountered in connection with Lilli Palmer. I refused.

The next day, as we were rehearsing our equestrian rhetoric, the director said to Paulette, "What's the matter, you seem depressed."

She didn't answer. The truth was that my old nemesis Applestrudel had been working with her, forcing her to inject into her "Charge!" and "Giddyup!" as many pauses, thoughts, and emotions as would be necessary to play Lady Macbeth.

With or without pauses we gamboled about on horseback for several weeks and by the time the film came out there were, I'm afraid, very few spectators to ascertain the profundity or absence of our thoughts when we crossed the panoramic screen at a gallop, at the head of our armies. My only thought, in any case, was to keep my horse from getting out of control. I doubt that Mme. Applestrudel could have helped me at all in this endeavor.

A new epidemic was ravaging the world, more virulent in America than anywhere else. Television closed movie theaters, emptied concert halls, stadiums, and theaters, undermined the morals and education of the young, even altered the structure of family life. Because I had always considered myself a man of the theater (when I made my first film, I thought it would be my last), it never occurred to me that I would one day be struggling across that bizarre little screen of glass in France or in the United States.

My first appearance on television was in New York, in a role that Laurence Olivier had played on the stage. My co-star in *No Time for Comedy* was Sarah Churchill, daughter of the Prime Minister. Just as the program started the director whispered in my ear, "Don't forget that fifty million viewers are watching you." I found out that Laurence Olivier was watching me too, which gave me more stage fright than the fifty million spectators . . .

It was a little sad, leaving in the night with your box of make-up under your arm, after a single performance. On the other hand, how many times would you have to perform a play to reach fifty million spectators?

In other broadcasts I played Louis Braille, the inventor of the reading alphabet for the blind, Lafayette, and Shaw's *Arms and the Man*. I even appeared opposite a very affectionate dolphin by the name of Flipper.

Bill Friedkin, who was later to make a big splash with *The French Connection* and *The Exorcist*, started his career filming me singing "Where Have All the Flowers Gone?" in Chicago. That he chose me over Marlene Dietrich (who had made this her theme song) was flattering.

I also did *Crime and Punishment*. This classic was condensed—to say the least—into twenty-six minutes. I was Raskolnikov; and Raymond Burr, now famous for *Perry Mason* and *Ironside*, was Porphyre. Remember, this was a live show. You can imagine my surprise the night of the broadcast, when, just as I was about to stab the old usurer, I saw a man step before the camera, nudge me aside, and say: "You are about to witness the crime of a young student. Why is he committing this crime? Because he's nervous. And why is he nervous? Because he doesn't smoke Chesterfields."

Then I was pushed back in front of the camera, where I went on stabbing the usurer.

When I was offered the role of Audubon, the celebrated ornithologist, I asked who, aside from a few vultures and spar-rows, my co-star would be. They gave me the name of a young actress who had just shot a film bit but wasn't yet known: Grace Kelly.

Miss Kelly arrived, very pretty, very blonde, a tall girl with blue eyes that could turn to steel in a moment's notice. She began reading her lines. At the end of each of our scenes she had to say, "Look dear, a bobolink," or "Look dear, a starling," or "Look dear, a crested flycatcher."

It was monotonous but pleasant. Miss Kelly exhibited great resourcefulness in the different ways she enumerated her winged creatures, but I must confess I never would have thought, to listen to her, that two years later she would win an Oscar.

When we broke at noon, I invited her to lunch. She an-swered, "No, thank you, Mister Aumont."

For several days, in this country where everybody calls you Bill, Mack, or Tom on sight, "Miss Kelly" continued to hand me "Mister Aumont" and to behave with reserve. She irritated the hell out of me.

The room we rehearsed in was used for dances on Saturday night, and the walls had been decorated with slogans. Tired of putting up with her coldness for the fourth day in a row, I took Grace Kelly by the arm and pointed at one of these slogans. She adjusted her glasses and read: "Ladies, be kind to your cavaliers. After all, men are human beings too."

Grace burst out laughing. The ice was broken. We became the best of friends and saw a lot of each other until my de-parture for Paris.

Two years went by. We wrote letters from time to time. Then I was invited to the film festival at Cannes, where I was happy to find Grace, who was showing her film, *Country Girl.* In the interim she had become one of Hollywood's biggest stars. Each of us was glad to see the other again, me because I thought she was adorable, and she because I was the only French person she knew. We spent our days together and went to see all the films. Ignoring the fact that we were old friends, the newspapers described it as love-at-first-sight. The most innocent walk was quickly transformed into proof of a torrid love affair. An American reporter waylaid me as I was crossing the hall of the Carlton:

"Would you like to marry Grace Kelly?"

"Who wouldn't?" I answered, laughing.

The next day papers throughout the world published my answer, as if it were the most important statement of this century.

From that day on, the photographers never left us alone. We couldn't take a walk, eat lunch, or go for a ride without being shadowed by a crowd of newsmen. Hundreds of photos were taken, certain ones with our permission, but more often without our knowledge by the use of telephoto lenses.

Both in America and in Europe the magazines were full of our every move. "Will they marry? When? Where?"

Some articles depicted me as a marvelous fellow, a great actor, a war hero, a symbol of all French virtues that Grace Kelly should be happy to grab. Others treated me as an ambitious gigolo, a dubious adventurer, a minor-league Casanova who was trying to use this innocent child for publicity.

That same week Einstein died. Some papers accorded less space to this event than to Grace and me buying an ice cream cone. My friends grumbled: "They've talked more about you this week than about Einstein's death."

"That just proves again," I answered, "how right Einstein was about the theory of relativity."

One day when we were lunching at the Blue Star, Grace told me that she had been invited by the prince of Monaco to visit his palace and private zoo, but that she couldn't accept because she was to appear on stage at the Festival that night and had made an appointment at the hairdresser's. I tried to explain to her that the visit to the Prince was more important. I added that if she refused, she would risk jeopardizing the good relations between the United States and the principality of Monaco.

She finally decided to go. When she came back, three hours later, I asked her how it had turned out.

An impossible child, age six.

A sketch by Jean Cocteau. (S.P.A.D.E.M.)

At sixteen, as Pierrot.

Above: La Machine Internale. *On the left, Louis Jouvet; on the right, Pierre Renoir. (Photo Lipnitzki) Left:* Lac aux Dames. *The scene in the barn with Simone Simon.*

Above: With Louis Jouvet in Drôle de
Drame. Right: With Annabella in
Hôtel du Nord. (Photo SEDIF)

Left: With Philip Merivale and Katherine Cornell in Rose Burke, *my first appearance on the American stage (Ernest A. Bachrach) Below: With Tonio Selwart in* The Cross of Lorraine. *(Metro-Goldwyn-Mayer Inc.)*

Right: "Maria knew that we would get married on July 13 because it was written in the stars."

Below: Three years later, with Tina in our garden in Beverly Hills. (Courtesy of Universal Pictures)

Left: 1944: on the Italian front with Marlene Dietrich. Below: May 24, 1944. The liberation of Pontecorvo.

Above: Return to Hollywood. With Yvonne de Carlo in Scheherazade: *this sadistic sailor, believe it or not, is supposed to be Rimski-Korsakov. (Courtesy of Universal Pictures) Right: With Ginger Rogers in* Heartbeat. *(Courtesy of Crystal Pictures, Inc.)*

Hands in cement: immortality guaranteed.

Maria Montez as Antinea in Atlantis. (Photo United Artists Corporation)

The *magician in* Lili. *(Metro-Goldwyn-Mayer, Inc.)*

With Lilli Palmer on Broadway in My Name is Aquilon. *(Photo Vandamm)*

In Cannes with Grace Kelly. (Photo Michel Simon)

Left to right: Lilli Palmer, the author, Vivien Leigh, Laurence Olivier in Portofino. (Photo F. Lupo)

In Buenos Aires with Peron. "I will die without knowing the reasons for Peron's amazing affection for me."

Julius Caesar in the arena at Arles. Brutus and Mark Antony take a cigarette break while discussing the fate of Rome. (Photo André Lafebvre)

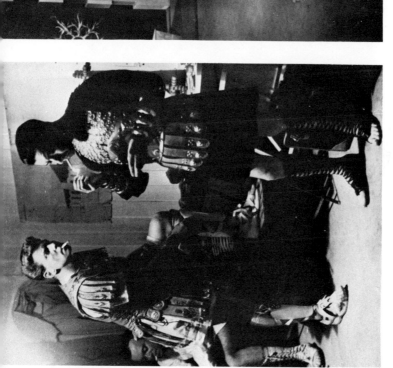

Amphitryon 38 with Françoise Christophe, as Alcmène and Jupiter. (Photo Pic.)

Marisa.

Our home at Malmaison. (Walt Disney Productions Limited)

With Jean-Claude and Marisa. (Photo Giornal, Milan)

With Vivien Leigh in Tovarich.
(Photo Friedman-Abeles)

*Maurice Chevalier congratulates us
after our nightclub act at the Persian
Room in New York.*

Above: With Burt Lancaster and Sidney Pollack during the filming of Castle Keep. *Left: With Jessica Tandy in* Camino Real *at Lincoln Center. (Photo Martha Swope) Opposite: Discussing* Day for Night *with François Truffaut.*

1974: on tour with Gigi.

As Dag Hammarskjold in Murderous Angels *in Paris and on Broadway.*

My favorite photo of Tina.

Jean-Claude at eighteen.

Patrick at sixteen.

1976: with Madeleine Renaud in Days in the Trees *on Broadway. (Photo Bruno Casa)*

She answered wistfully, "Prince Rainier is quite charming."

After the festival, Grace spent some time in Paris. I took her to Montmartre and Saint-Germain-des-Prés, just as she had taken me to Greenwhich Village, two years before. She was relaxed and free, a different Grace than anyone in Hollywood had seen before.

She came to La Malmaison to have lunch with Maria-Christine and my nephews and nieces. Jean Roy took photos of her playing with the children, listening to records, and knitting.

Unfortunately, these photos, which in our minds were destined for the family album, were spread all over *Paris-Match* and *Life*. The gentlemen at MGM Publicity were in an uproar. They had spent a fortune during the last two years trying to promote the image of a goddess who was haughty, sexy, and unapproachable at the same time, who always appeared in the most suggestive gowns and in the most flattering lights. Suddenly there she was, the "goddess," knitting in the country, with a pair of glasses balanced on the end of her nose and a handful of brats at her feet . . . MGM never forgave me for it.

Three months later I was in Hollywood shooting *Hilda Crane* when I received a telegram from Grace announcing her engagement with Rainier. I answered that I was delighted by the good news. I was sincere. I've always thought that Grace was born to be a princess.

A few days passed, then the papers published the news. That evening I was invited to a party. Everybody was talking excitedly about the engagement of their Grace to a prince. True, Pola Negri and Gloria Swanson had already married princes, but now, for the first time, it was a *reigning* prince. The women ran around asking, "Do you think it will be necessary to curtsy to her?" Some of them were practicing it already. Others insisted that Eleanor Roosevelt had not curtsied for the Queen of England.

Louella Parsons took me into a corner. Shaking a pudgy finger under my reluctant nose, she whined, "A little bird told me that you and Grace were supposed to get married once upon a time . . ."

I wondered if the little bird in question was one of the bob-olinks, starlings, or flycatchers that had appeared on TV with us. In any case, I answered, "Come now, Louella, darling, don't tell me *you* believe what you read in the papers!"

Hedda Hopper, more elegant but more treacherous than her rival, heard our exchange. "You must admit, Jean-Pierre, that it is more exciting to be Princess of Monaco, duchess of Valentinois, Marquise des Baux, Countess of Grimaldi, and to be called 'Most Serene Highness' than to be called 'Madame Aumont.' "

I entirely agreed.

At midnight I left the party. On the way home I had a slight accident with the car and fractured a rib. The next day Louella Parsons published the following on page one: "J.P.A. tried to kill himself!" The article began with: "A little bird told me that J.P.A. drove his car into a ravine because of heartbreak when . . ."

In 1954 a few friends and I were invited to present our recent films at the festival of Punta del Este in Uruguay. My brother-in-law, Jean Roy, had managed to come along.

We stopped at Montevideo. Expecting to see virgin forest, rivers filled with gold nuggets, and cannibals, we found ourselves in a city that looked a little less exotic than Brooklyn.

After two weeks at the local watering hole, Punta del Este, Jean and I decided to visit Buenos Aires, which was only an hour away by plane. The Uruguayans were indignant: "We're on bad terms with the Argentinians, you can't insult us like that."

"Look," I explained, "when we invite strangers to the Cannes Festival, they are free to visit Italy, Switzerland, or Germany, whatever our relations with those countries might be."

Then they found what they thought was a most effective argument for preventing our escapade. "Peron isn't in Buenos Aires right now, so you won't be able to see him."

Jean and I burst out laughing. We had not the slightest intention of trying to see him. We simply thought it was idiotic to be only an hour from B.A. and not visit it.

Our arrival in Buenos Aires was not without its problems. Jean was undressed from head to toe in a search for cameras hidden in his armpits. After a few further annoyances we were set free. Imagine my astonishment the next morning when we received a telephone call from the Minister of Information telling us that Peron was waiting for us.

At the scheduled hour, the Minister ushered us into the President's office in the Casa Roja.

We were, needless to say, biased against all dictators. But the apparent absence of security measures and the warm reception which Peron offered us charmed us immediately. He was stout and pockmarked but young, gay, and full of exuberant cordiality. He took us in his arms in the traditional *abrazzo*, had us sit down, offered us coffee, and chatted with us for an hour, half in French and half in Spanish. At the end of the conversation he said, "You are my guests for two weeks. I'm going to put my private plane at your disposal while you visit Argentina."

"Mister President," I stammered, "I have to return to Punta del Este (at this he frowned slightly) because my film *Koenigsmark* is being shown. That's the reason I was invited to the festival."

"Hop over there," he said with a twinkle. "I'll keep your brother-in-law here as a hostage, so you'd better come back. And bring all the friends you wish."

When I returned, Cecile Aubry, Alexandre Astruc, and Henri Vidal accompanied me. The president's glistening plane was waiting for us. Two pilots, two aides-de-camp, and a doctor escorted us. We took off for Bariloche on the borders of Patagonia. Unfortunately, violent storms prevented us from landing. We had to content ourselves with visiting the central part of Argentina with a long stopover at Mar del Plata, a Miami Beach of reinforced concrete where we spent our time visiting the day nurseries. God knows I like children, but I got a little sick of them by the twenty-fourth nursery.

The return to Buenos Aires was triumphal. All the ministers gave parties in our honor, everybody was happy—everybody except the ambassador of France, who couldn't understand the reason for this attention since relations between our two countries were strained. He had been waiting a year for an audience with Peron. He asked me suspiciously what I had done to obtain such favors. I couldn't answer him, and will die without knowing the reasons for Peron's amazing affection.

My companions returned to Paris and I took off for Santo Domingo. There, four of my brothers-in-law, strangers to me, were waiting at Barahona to drive me to meet Maria's mother. We had never seen each other before. I spent a week with them. They initiated me into hunting and deep-sea fishing. I couldn't succeed in imagining Maria's childhood in this tropical village.

I spent the next evening in Trujillo City. People had come there to inaugurate a street called Maria-Montez. Donkeys were walking around loose. Women in cotton shifts balanced provisions on their heads.

When I got back to France, I began rehearsing the part of Mark Antony in *Julius Caesar*, under the direction of Jean Renoir. It was a generous Renoir, full of contradictions and enthusiasm.

"Who did the adaptation?" we asked.

"Oh," he answered, wagging his head, "a little couple whose name I forget. They're very nice . . . They seem to understand English . . ."

Renoir wanted Henri Vidal for Caesar.

"It's Shakespeare's finest work. I know every line by heart," said Henri.

"Great," answered Renoir, "come to rehearsals tomorrow."

Henri arrived the following day, trembling with indignation.

"What's the matter?" asked Renoir.

"What's the matter? I just discovered that there are five acts!"

"So?"

"So? Julius Caesar is stabbed at the beginning of the third. That'll have to be changed."

Nothing was ready in Arles the day before the opening of

Julius Caesar. The extras—meaning the local grocer, the hair-dresser, the postman etc.—had never been rehearsed. None of the microphones worked. Renoir was happy, confident, and relaxed.

"Of course, I know that no one will understand a word of your text, but it doesn't make any difference. I like it that way."

Playing a tragedy in the open air in an arena constructed for a Roman circus while moving among twenty-four microphones isn't an easy task. A mishap under similar circumstances had occurred a year earlier. An illustrious tragedienne whom we shall refer to as Madame X had been requested by the sound engineers to direct her voice toward the microphones and not to speak when she found herself between two of them. Madame X was indignant: "How dare you teach me how to act!"

The evening of the performance, she walked across the immense arena without a thought for the sound system. No one was able to hear a word she was saying. A few seconds before the end of the show she caught her foot on one of the wires and fell flat on her face. As her mouth collided with one of the microphones, she was heard to scream "Shit!," her only audible word during the whole evening.

At nine o'clock the strong breeze of the mistral could be felt, the stars came out, people filled the immense arena.

Shakespeare, Renoir, the tragedy of power and ambition, the ghosts of Julius Caesar, Mark Antony, and Brutus, combined with the flapping standards to form a spectacle of unforgettable grandeur.

We were celebrating the second millennium of Arles.

"Eh! oui," sighed an old Arlesian. "Two thousand years already. Time flies . . ."

Each summer Lilli Palmer and Rex Harrison invited my daughter and me to Portofino. At the summit of a hill that could only be reached by a goat path, their villa overlooked the sparkling Mediterranean.

Lilli was as precise and controlled as Rex was dreamy, naive, and impressionable . . . I can never keep from laughing when I see my friend Rex billed as "sexy Rexy." I can believe that he is sexy. His numerous conquests have proved it. But after seeing his day-to-day life for five summers in a row, I think of Rex more as a little boy, often stammering, throwing tantrums, and hiding in corners so that he can do what has been forbidden.

One day we were at Portofino sitting on the terrace of a cafe when a journalist who recognized Rex came over to speak to him. After five minutes Rex hesitantly said, "You could . . . sit down . . . maybe?" Lilli, who didn't appreciate the company of the journalist, threw her husband an irritated look, to which Rex replied, like a child caught in the act: "I said maybe."

No, I'm afraid that no matter how hard I try to picture Rex as a playboy, or a Scott Fitzgerald hero at the prow of his yacht, all I can see is Professor Higgins himself, just as Shaw conceived him and as Rex so brilliantly portrayed him: a grand egotist, delightfully tyrannical, in love with himself as Napoleon was with Bonaparte, drunk with independence, then pausing abruptly in the midst of one of his escapades to think of the wife he has just abandoned, crying and ashamed of his own feelings: "Damn, damn, damn, I've grown accustomed to her face . . ."

14

MARISA

Albert Husson, whose *La Cuisine des Anges* (*My Three Angels*) was still a hit in Paris, had written a new comedy called *Les Pavés du Ciel*. It was an amusing, spicy play which Faye Emerson and I were later to do on Broadway under the title of *Heavenly Twins*. In Paris Micheline Presles and I acted in it at the Comédie Caumartin.

One evening Anna Pier-Angeli, whom I had known in Hollywood when we were both under contract at MGM, came to see me in the wings, accompanied by her twin sister, Marisa Pavan.

Timid, serious, silent, Marisa stood in a corner of my dressing room without saying a word. Something about her suggested a pure, profound, and secret charm. Like Giraudoux's Jupiter, I could have said to her: "This charm, this gravity which are as foreign to others as their clothing, are your flesh and your heart."

But I didn't say anything. Neither of us suspected that we would be married two years later. Nevertheless, I already sensed that we were bound to meet again, and that this haunting radiance of hers would not be easy to forget.

A few days later, the two sisters left for Hollywood. I accompanied them to the airport.

It was exactly twenty years since the premiere of *La Machine Infernale*. To celebrate this anniversary, French television decided to broadcast the play. I resumed the role of Oedipus that I had originated. Cocteau came to give us some last-minute advice. With precise fingers he remade our costumes, draping us in pieces of material, such as curtains or packing cloth. It didn't matter what he used; under his skilful hands, it became toga, cloak, buckler, or crown . . .

He took me into a corner and confided melodramatically: "Do you know what they've done to *La Machine Infernale,* to *our Machine?* Get this, my friend . . . A *classic.* What? It's just appeared in the paperback collection of Larousse Classics. Today children have to learn the Sphinx's monologue just as we had to learn 'To be or not to be . . .' *Homework,* my dear, that's what's become of our beautiful adventure. Children are going to yawn over my play and blunder through it because they're afraid of getting cuffed. Me, who gave my life for the young, now the young are going to hate me . . . or respect me, which is worse . . . eh?"

I enjoyed seeing him feign indignation. He considered this new honor a hoax. Laughing incredulously, he thumbed his nose at his early detractors—and at himself.

This wasn't a seventy-year-old man, the Jean Cocteau of the French Academy, who was musing aloud in front of me, but one of his own characters: Thomas the Impostor.

A few months later, René Julliard, the publisher, invited me to lunch. I thought at that time of some notes I had been taking and some portraits I had composed for my own pleasure. Gathering the dusty pages into a thick, illegible manuscript, I arrived with it under my arm and handed it to him. "Whenever you have the time," I said, "whether it be six months or six years from now, I'd appreciate your glancing at this."

The same evening Julliard called me. "I've looked over your

manuscript. I'll publish it." I was a little worried by the small amount of time given me to clean up this hodgepodge of writings—to cut, piece together, and give body to something which had no precision or unity.

In July the book appeared under the title *Souvenirs Provisoires*. It didn't break any sales records, but it earned me my stripes as a writer and won me the esteem of people I admired. Among the number of letters I received was one which caused me immense pride. It was a handwritten note from General DeGaulle which began: "My dear friend, Your book is like yourself; lively, earnest, human . . ."

That letter brought me such joy that I put it under glass and kept it on my desk. During hours of discouragement, doubt, and the blues (and God knows I had them), I often glanced at this talisman. It gave me back confidence in myself.

Alas! pride, and especially vanity, are always punished. When I returned from vacation that year, the sun had effaced the text of the letter. The writing had disappeared like a mirage. The only thing left was the printed heading: "General DeGaulle."

Plays, films, plays, films, what does it all matter if you can't share your successes and failures with someone you love?

Loneliness was a heavy burden. My friends, whose loving care had sustained me for five whole years, were now powerless to help me.

Darryl Zanuck offered me a role in *Hilda Crane*. I left for Hollywood once again.

At midnight, New Year's Eve of 1956, I arrived at Zanuck's home.

At five in the morning I started the new year with a solitary pilgrimage to my old house on Tower Road. Dawn began to break across the hot, starry night. I prayed to God to grant me anew a little of the happiness I had known in this house.

My prayers were answered; it was given me to meet Marisa for the second time.

The important events of our lives happen in their own time and cannot be controlled by our wills. When Marisa and I had met two years earlier, the time had not yet come for us to fall in love. But now . . .

I waited until the thirteenth of February, my lucky day, took Marisa's mother to a Polynesian restaurant, ordered some exotic beverages to give myself courage, and asked her for her daughter's hand, pointing out all the objections that she had a right to make. First there was the difference in our ages, and then my desire to live in France.

There was also the question of Maria-Christine. I went to get her in New York and brought her back to Hollywood. As soon as we got off the plane, Maria-Christine threw herself into Marisa's arms and asked me, "Can I stay with her?" The next day she pursued the matter further.

"Why don't you marry Marisa?"

"I'd love to," I answered.

"Hurry up, go ask her right away. Let's hope she won't say no!"

On March 27 we were married at Santa Barbara. We would have preferred Lake Tahoe but Benny Thau, an executive at MGM who was to be my best man, convinced us that Nevada wasn't a dignified state to get married in. I'll never understand what a dignified state is, nor know how many of them there are in America; but California must be one of them, since he seemed thrilled by our choice.

Pier Angeli was the maid of honor for her sister. Patricia (their younger sister) and Maria-Christine were the flower girls. That same evening Beno Graziani of *Paris-Match*, a lifelong friend, drove us to San Francisco and we took off for the Hawaiian Islands.

"I have not had time," said André Gide "to write about the happiest hours of my life. I've only had time to live them."

After Hawaii, we prolonged our honeymoon at Ischia in a villa shaped like a cathedral. The arches of our terrace framed the Oasis of Forio, where Anna Magnani was shooting a film.

Magnani had won an Oscar for *The Rose Tattoo*. Marisa, who had been nominated for her role as the daughter in the same film, had accepted the Oscar for Anna, who was unable to come. We had dragged this gold statuette along with us all through our honeymoon. Marisa was so frightened of losing it that we kept it with us in the planes, hotels, restaurants, even on the beach. We did everything but go surfboarding on the Pacific, cradling Oscar in our arms. At Ischia, we could finally deliver the precious object to its owner.

Both of us were used to la Magnani's excesses, her tragic depressions, and her devastating exuberance. Now, however, we encountered a detached and ethereal Magnani who kept blessing us. When we learned that she was playing the role of the mother superior of a convent, it all made sense.

We returned to Paris. Marisa was supposed to shoot a film there for Gerard Oury. It was about twin sisters who travel through France in 1944, guiding Allied aviators to the Spanish border. The twin sisters were supposed to be played by Marisa and Anna Pier-Angeli, but when the film was finally made, the casting was changed and their roles were given to André Bourvil and Louis de Funes, which is like giving Lillian and Dorothy Gish's roles to Abbott and Costello. The film was called *La Grande Vadrouille* (*The Big Spree*).

MGM offered me a role in a new version of *The Painted Veil* by Somerset Maugham. I left for Hollywood. Marisa and Maria-Christine came with me. We had hardly settled ourselves in the hotel when we received a telegram. I thought it was some message of welcome from one of our friends, but instead it was a notification of the death of Jean Roy.

Ever since Jean had taken off for Suez two weeks earlier, I had been fighting against an uneasy presentiment. That same morning we had coffee together. He had seemed too serious, almost sad, a rare mood when we were together. For the first time, I wasn't able to drive him to the airport, and I had a funny feeling about it. The death of another reporter for *Paris-Match*, Jean-Pierre Pedrazzanni, murdered in Budapest, had been a shock to us all and forced us to think more carefully about the dangers that Jean was exposed to.

I asked MGM to put off our film for three days and returned to Paris. During the long night on the plane, I relived those marvelous hours in the last ten years that I owed to Jean. Ten years of shared emotions, crazy laughter, tragedies, discoveries, voyages, and disputes too, which were so many proofs of our affection. Ten years during which we lived our tumultuous adventures mostly for the joy of recounting them to each other.

When he had left for Egypt two weeks earlier, sporting grenades and bravado, he had been in his element. As a student he had escaped from the Gestapo and reached Berlin in the midst of the war to gather information for the Resistance network to which he belonged. During the occupation, at the age of twenty, he had become a paratrooper. He had to go on living dangerously, intensely.

We now know how he spent the last three days of his life. He was the *enfant terrible* of the Allied troops. Taking possession of the most beautiful villa in Port Said and the jeep of an Egyptian general, he changed the number on the license plate to Balzac 00-24, the telephone number of *Paris-Match*.

He drove about in his jeep, breaking down the iron grills of the shut-up stores to distribute flour and milk to those who were dying of hunger. When the English soldiers threatened to fire on him, he guffawed: "Shoot, go ahead then!" His smile was his shield. He went alone into no-man's land, vulnerable, but sure of himself, gathering the wounded and feeding the children. It was these starving, naked children who instinctively found the nickname that in our hearts we all wanted to give him: "The angel in the red beret."

Never had I taken less interest in a film than in *The Painted Veil*, which MGM had rebaptized *The Seventh Veil*.

During the few weeks which it took to make this movie the executives at MGM fired first the producer, then the director. Our female star was affected by all these changes. We lost long days discussing lines she no longer wanted to say or chairs it displeased her to sit on.

Normally I would have taken these delays philosophically, but besides the fact that I couldn't stop thinking about Jean, I was anxious to return to Paris, where Giraudoux's *Amphitryon 38* was waiting for me at the Comédie des Champs-Elysées. Finally, the film was over.

In Paris, I plunged myself into Giraudoux's text with delight. *"Si le mot plaire ne vient pas seulement du mot plaisir, mais du mot biche en emoi, du mot amande en fleur, Alcmène, tu me plais."** This sentence, which Pierre Renoir had once recited, was now one of my lines, and I was saying it on the very stage where I had made my debut. Many years ago Jouvet, dressed in blue, had welcomed me in this theater, while Jean Anouilh was wandering about backstage. "Si le mot plaire . . ."

Sometimes, during the course of the third act, my spirit stole away to the wings to discover the ghost of my younger self in the shadows, that awed beginner I had been, still am, and hope always to remain.

The thirteenth of August, 1957, brought me the greatest happiness of my life: the birth of my first son. Of course, I'd already had a child. Eleven years earlier, Maria-Christine, now Tina, had been born, and I had experienced an immense joy from it. But a boy . . .

I felt as if he completed me, expanded me, perfected me. A son is a friend for life and an accomplice to each moment. Today he is nineteen. Never has he disappointed me. At every age and every moment, he has done nothing but amaze me. I feel as if his sudden changes of temperament and his thirst for independence are on a level with mine. He has always been the friend I've taken the liberty to give advice to, and who's taken the liberty not to follow it.

Jean-Claude is modest and secretive. He feigns impatience when I hug him or show him any tenderness. But when I return from a trip, I can see happiness in the corner of his eye.

"Ça va?"

---

* If the word *please* does not come only from the word *pleasure*, but from the words *startled doe*, from the words *almond blossom*, Alcmène, you please me.

"Ça va."

No effusions, just the glimmer of complicity . . .

Kings fire twenty-one-gun salutes at the birth of a son. There's a little of the king in every man.

The joyful chaos of living with my relatives and their boisterous friends at La Malmaison inspired me to write a comedy.

Two friends live in peace, or nearly, in a garret in the Latin Quarter of Paris . . . One of them, Maurice, is honest and sensitive. The other, Jean, known as Farfada, is volatile, indifferent, unconscious, cruel without knowing it and unhappy without realizing it. Because he doesn't run after women, they run after him. Even a powerful industrialist allows himself to be taken in by the charms of Farfada. For this character casts a spell over his victims until the day when . . .

Just like my other three plays, *Farfada* was accepted by the first producer to whom I gave it. Those were happy days when all you had to do to get a comedy produced was to write it.

I had at first intended to play Farfada myself, but I afterwards decided that it might be more elegant and more clever to have someone else play it. At any rate I felt too old for the part. I could already hear the sarcastic laughter of J. J. Gautier, our most influential critic: "Why hasn't Mr. Aumont let a younger actor interpret this character? *Farfada* would have gained from this in innocence, unconsciousness, ingenuity . . ."

Accordingly, we look for a Farfada. The name of Philippe Lemaire came up. Upon hearing it our bookkeeper fainted. Philippe was her idol. He was hired.

At the same time they started rehearsing *Farfada*, I was doing *Amphitryon 38* on tour. Each chance I had, I rushed to Paris to follow the progress of my own play. The night before it opened, Georges Herbert, who was both the producer of *Farfada* and the organizer of the *Amphitryon* tour, allowed me to miss a performance so that I could watch the dress rehearsal of my play. Everything went well. There were a lot of laughs and a lot of applause. Philippe Lemaire was dazzling, swift, relaxed . . . a bit too light, however, for my taste. After the show I took him into a corner and congratulated him on the zest of his performance. Then I reminded him that the character he was playing was cynical because of his unhappiness, the kind of boy who felt everybody could go to hell because he had once been deeply wounded. "I'm not asking you to play Hamlet," I added, laughing. "Just try to work against the comic elements a little, and remember that I wanted to depict one of those boys who came out of the war and the occupation; perhaps this play is less easygoing then it appears to be . . ."

What demon sometimes pushes us into pronouncing our own executions and becoming our worst enemies? The very next day, boarding the train for Brussels where I was going to perform *Amphitryon*, I was seized by panic. How could I have been stupid enough to interfere with the performance of my leading actor, a particularly sensitive young man, on the night before the opening? Since everything had gone splendidly, what had driven me to give him advice which contradicted that of his director? Was Philippe going to take me at my word and paint his character black?

At the risk of missing the train and the performance at Brussels, I rushed to a phone booth. I wanted to tell Philippe: "Forget everything I said. I'm an asshole. Play it like you did last night . . ." Alas, there was no answer.

That evening I played Jupiter while thinking only of Farfada. I, who rarely flub lines, ended a scene by saying (with the majesty you would expect from the God of gods): "Alcmène, lick me," instead of "Alcmène, leave me." My fellow actors burst into uncontrollable laughter, but I didn't feel like laughing. I called Georges Herbert. In a trembling voice I asked him how things had gone. He answered: "I don't get it. We rehearsed a light comedy for six weeks. Suddenly, this evening, in front of the critics, it became a somber drama. Phillipe was playing *Hamlet*. I don't know what came over him."

I knew. I went to have supper with my friends. They all asked me how the play had gone. "Very well," I said. And I got drunk. Two days later the all-important and fatal review by Jean-Jacques Gautier appeared: "Maybe M. Jean-Pierre Aumont did not intend to rehash the themes of *The Emperor of China*. He has, however, done exactly that. Sometimes we can't escape from a character which haunts us . . ." There followed a description of Farfada as cynical, bitter, and sad. The last lines of the review were doubly crucifying: "Philippe Lemaire's portrayal of Farfada accentuates the faults of the play and our discomfort. Ah! if only Jean-Pierre Aumont had played it himself."

Despite this poor review, there were 150 performances of *Farfada*. Philippe went back to his original interpretation and the comedy once again became joyous and light.

I couldn't be present at the last performance because that very night I was doing *Amphitryon* in Marrakech. Philippe Lemaire sent me this short note: "I've had two joys this year, knowing you and Marisa, and meeting Farfada. Now he's gone . . . I've lost my best friend . . ."

A tour should be short. At Marrakech, we just couldn't stand it any longer. Everything which had been fun at the beginning was becoming a bore. We could only repeat the same lines over and over again. I'm not speaking of the text of the play, for which we continued to exercise an effort, but of our own lines in real life, now drained of all juice. Contemplating our group, Alcmène blurted out: "I'm sick to death of you all!" This summed up eloquently the general sentiment.

The last performance of *Amphitryon* took place there at Marrakech. Unlike all the other cities of France, Switzerland, Belgium, and Tunisia where we had played, the Moroccans were not amused.

At the end of the final scene, Jupiter advances toward the public: "Gods and vermin, let us disappear toward our zeniths and our caves. All of you, spectators, must withdraw without saying a word, and forget the spectacle you have just witnessed."

A superfluous recommendation.

15

CAMEOS

I've always had more faith in pure chance than in elaborate schemes. If I hadn't caught sight of Irwin Shaw crossing Avenue Montaigne, I wouldn't have dared ask him to let me adapt a play from his novel *Lucy Crown*. I chased after him and blurted out my request. Although he was rather surprised, he accepted. I began working.

The Theatre de Paris seemed to be the ideal place to stage this drama. I paid a visit to its director, Elvire Popesco.

"So tell me about it."

"Well," I said, "you see, it's about a woman, still very beautiful . . ."

"That's enough," cried Elvire. "I understand everything. It's me, twenty years ago."

Without letting me reply, she called Edwige Feuillere.

"Dah-ling, I'm sending over a su-blime play! [she hadn't read it, of course], with the role of your life. Stop by and sign your contract tomorrow."

Without waiting for an answer, she hung up.

It was just a matter of luck that Popesco was looking for a play and that Feuillere was free. For the part of the husband, we agreed on Bernard Blier.

The principal role of the young teacher remained to be cast. Pierre Dux, who was directing the play, wanted to give the part to one of his students, François D.; but I preferred Jacques Riberolles, who had been my stand-in for two or three films at the beginning of his career.

Because we couldn't come to any agreement, I went looking for Jean-Louis Trintignant, who everybody thought would be right for the role. Finally I found him in the back of an army barracks where he was wearily fulfilling his military service. Since his sole duty at the time, folding gauze bandages, hardly seemed essential to our national defense, I asked his colonel to let him do the play. The colonel refused. In his eyes, Jean-Louis was an indispensable recruit.

We held auditions. The actors who filed in front of us didn't have anything in common with the young leads of my day. They were terrified of expressing the slightest emotion. Making a declaration of love seemed the height of absurdity to them. This generation had come out of cellars. Hunted and poorly nourished, scarred by the occupation, it had burrowed itself into a bitter taste for misfortune, revolt, and nonconformity. Among the hundred actors whom we auditioned, we found only carbon copies of Montgomery Clift or sullen Marlon Brandos who had not yet acquired the irony of a smile. In vain we searched for the luster, health, and enthusiasm which had typified youthful leads before the war. In 1938 we were all blonde, but in 1958 they were all dark, physically and spiritually.

Finally Dux decided to rehearse his candidate, François D., and my candidate, Jacques Riberolles, alternately. In order not to lose time he asked each of them to watch the rehearsals of the other. They agreed to it, although both of them considered the game a cruel one. "Don't you remember the days when you were starting out?" Riberolles flung at me in a surly voice.

Oh yes, I remembered them. And the ones that followed too. It's our profession which is cruel. Hesitating between two novices, we ask each of them to watch the other rehearse, not out of sadism, but so that each can keep up with the day-to-day direction. Of course, a beginner has to be at his best every minute. If established actors are not in top form at a rehearsal, no one worries about it. Everyone knows what they are capable of. But if a novice actor is not in good form, we become worried, because we are completely ignorant of his potential. Perhaps this is unjust, but it's inevitable. Yes, our profession is cruel. Cruel and indelicate. We're not selling vegetables or cement, but the most sensitive and secret parts of ourselves.

Of course, a writer, a composer, a painter, also strips himself bare; but he does it without witnesses. An actor exists only in front of his audience. He's a little like a man who can make love only in front of voyeurs.

After a week of competition between the two rivals, we found ourselves deliberating in Edwige's dressing room. As the author, I was given the first word. Forcing myself to be as fair as possible, I said, "François has made progress, but Jacques is physically more believable as Edwige's lover." Since the majority of those present agreed, Riberolles was hired. My God, what patience and diplomacy had been required of me, who had none!

As I left the theater, I saw Riberolles standing in the great dark hall, looking very alone. "You got it," I said. "Oh, shit!" he blurted out, and began to cry. I had tears in my eyes, too. Both of us knew that his whole career, his whole life, could depend on the success of this play. I drove Edwige home. In front of us, on the sidewalk, I saw François D., who had just been informed of his failure by Dux. I imagined him going back to his place, telling his wife that he had been given the sack . . . his foundered hopes, his doubt, his search for another job, the bitterness which might now be filling his heart. Alas, everything is unjust. All competitions, all tests, all selections. And during the war, when one guy was killed and the other lived, was that just?

I would have liked to stop and talk to François, to invite him to have a drink, to tell him about my own failures and disappointments. Even though the experience of others rarely helps, he possibly would have felt less miserable. The cars in back of us began honking. Like a coward, I let him walk on alone.

In the autumn of 1958 I went to Madrid with Marisa; she was going to film *Solomon and the Queen of Sheba* with Gina Lollobrigida and Tyrone Power. Tyrone, warm, affectionate, modest, and generous as always, was married to a young woman named Debby. They were happily expecting a child, and Tyrone, who already had two daughters by Linda Christian, prayed for it to be a son.

After dining together one evening we separated very late at night. The next morning I took the plane to Paris. On the papers at Orly airport blazed these headlines: TYRONE POWER IS DEAD! Thinking that it was a matter of some awful mistake, I called Marisa, who confirmed the sad news to me. He had been rehearsing a dueling scene with George Sanders when he collapsed. By the time he arrived at the hospital he was dead. Knowing how depressed Marisa would be, I flew back to Madrid.

The two or three days between the death of Tyrone and his burial were absurdly grotesque. There was a rivalry between the cosmetician at the morgue and Tyrone's personal make-up man. These two artists were debating who would add the last touch of pink to the cheeks of the unfortunate cadaver. "I'm the one who always makes up Mr. Power," said one. "I know what he likes."

The other would answer, "Corpses present different problems than live people. I've never had the least complaint about my work."

The producers had other worries. After offering their condolences the insurance companies made it clear that the film must proceed without any delay. Panic-stricken telegrams were sent to the agents of Gary Cooper, Robert Taylor, William Holden, and Charlton Heston. No one was free. Besides, every time a new name came up, Lollobrigida's agent shook his head: "I feel for you gentlemen, but Gina had a contract to shoot a film with Tyrone Power."

"But he's dead," bellowed the producers.

"It's not in the contract," retorted the agent.

Finally Yul Brynner was agreed upon. The agent kept asking: "Who is he, this Yul Brunner?"

Brunner or Brynner, Yul didn't waste any time making himself known. As soon as he got to Madrid, he sized up the situation. If Gina arrived twenty minutes late, he managed to arrive twenty minutes after her. If she was escorted by five or six people, he had himself preceded by a whole battalion: valets, bodyguards, secretaries, chauffeurs. Slowly, he would ascend Solomon's throne. Then he would snap his fingers. One of his slaves would offer him a cigarette, another a match, and a third would hold out an ashtray.

Yul was no fool. He had decided to out-star the star. But as soon as he was away from King Solomon's throne and back with his friends, he would make fun of himself. For Yul's heart belonged to an activity which he considered far more important than the make-believe of technicolor. Without ever mentioning it, he had been working for UNICEF for several years. Many of those who had escaped the slow death camps during the war now found themselves in other camps where death was even slower. Yul visited these refugees, collected funds to help them, struggled with governments, committees, prison guards, and laws to release them from this hell.

I take my hat off to the man.

The filming of *Solomon and the Queen of Sheba* dragged on for months. Afterwards Samuel Bronson, the producer, asked Marisa to stay in Madrid for *John Paul Jones*. We dug into our encyclopedia to discover that this Jones fellow was an eighteenth-century sailor who had made the tour of the royal courts of Europe to collect subsidies. His greatest claim to fame was the words "Full speed ahead!", a phrase that became as immortal as "Kilroy was here" or "Vive la différence."

Robert Stack, who had not yet acquired the badge of Eliot Ness, but who already seemed untouchable, was chosen to interpret this historical figure. Marisa played his wife, who waited patiently at home while her husband kept making historical statements. There were also several "cameos" in the picture.

Someone should celebrate as he deserves the man who invented this term. A producer wouldn't dare offer a role that's too short to a known actor. But a cameo . . . Any star would be flattered to be offered one. There's a strange magic in the word.

Bette Davis crossed the Atlantic to play Katherine of Russia, and Charles Coburn to create his version of Benjamin Franklin. I was offered the role of Louis XVI.

We started to shoot, under the direction of John Farrow, a tall and polite gentleman who was the husband of Maureen O'Sullivan, Tarzan's original mate. They had an incredible number of children. One of them became Mia Farrow.

Robert Stack was just returning from his honeymoon, telling everybody, "I had a ball." That was a new expression to me, which I found, rightly or wrongly, extremely funny. One day, when he was telling me again that during his honeymoon, in Hawaii, he had had a ball, I said, "I hope your wife had the other one."

He was kind enough to forgive me.

I was especially happy because this was the first time that anyone had ever offered me a character role. I would finally be able to shed the image of "young leading man" with which I had encumbered the screens for so long. More wrinkled every year, but a young leading man all the same.

But that belonged to the past. Now I could finally prove my talent to the thirsty masses without owing anything to my appearance. In order to make my character believable, I bought all the books I could find on the royal family. I went through all the museums, got copies of all the prints, drawings, or paintings which showed Louis XVI. I visited Versailles, Varennes, the Conciergerie. I kneeled piously over the spot where the king had been guillotined. I made my devotions at the church where his remains were buried. Then I ordered a false nose, as Bourbonian as possible, and a false belly.

Rigged out in this manner, I arrived on the set for the first day of shooting. No one recognized me, which was gratifying. The assistants walked in front of me shouting, "Where is Mr. Aumont? Have you seen Mr. Aumont?" without suspecting that this obese extra with the hooked nose could be me. Finally I revealed my identity. One of the executives nearly keeled over with horror. After he had regained his self-control he said: "Mr. Aumont, if I cast you, it was so that you'd appear on the screen as you are. Not with an additional twenty years and thirty pounds."

"But I've been made up to look exactly like Louis XVI. He's a well known figure. He can't be represented differently."

"I want sex and elegance."

"I'm sorry, but Louis XVI was not elegant. He was common. As for sex, he had a few problems when it came to that . . ."

"Stop babbling absurdities! He was extremely seductive. Remember the parc au Cerf? I know my history of France. And Pompadour, huh? And Du Barry?"

The horrible truth became apparent. He was confusing Louis XVI with Louis XV.

Finally we worked out a compromise. I cut off half my nose and half of my stomach and played a kind of "Louis XV and a Half."

Everybody was happy.

16

DeGaulle, Sinatra, and Melina Mercouri

In 1960, Benoit-Leon Deutsch, owner and manager of the Théâtre de la Madeleine, asked me to act in Sacha Guitry's *Mon Père avait Raison*. Though doing it appealed to me, I'd already signed for a film in Rome and a play in New York. I could only do *Mon Père avait Raison* if Deutsch authorized me to rehearse no more than two weeks and give no more than fifty performances. At word of this he began tearing his hair and gnashing his teeth. I went to talk things out with him at his home.

By a stroke of luck his two-year-old toddler took a spontaneous liking to me. We began romping on the carpet; he climbed on my back; I helped him do somersaults. Deutsch was so touched by our immediate affection for one another that he gave me everything I wanted.

Then, as soon as my fifty performances were over, I took off for New York. I got there on a Sunday and hopped onto a stage. Robert Dhéry, the star of *La Plume de Ma Tante*, had asked me to appear at a gala benefit he was organizing for the survivors of Fréjus, a small town in the south of France where a dam had broken and hundreds of people had been killed. Rex Harrison, Claudette Colbert, Sir Laurence Olivier, and I did nothing put pass unannounced across the stage, carrying a prop, sweeping the floor, or saying a line or two. The audience had a good time picking us out. What an odd sensation it was to play Saturday night in Paris and Sunday night in New York.

In the midst of all this, DeGaulle arrived. He had changed considerably since that time not so long ago when he had come to Italy and the Vosges to inspect our troops. In those days he had been forced to prove himself. He had had to fight against his allies as well as his enemies to be recognized as the leader, the representative, and the symbol of France. Churchill had found the Cross of Lorraine heavy to carry. Roosevelt had called DeGaulle a prima donna, had set up Darlan against him, and then Giraud . . .

But today it was the President of the Republic who was coming on an official visit to New York. And he was given a reception befitting a hero. It was Lafayette or Lindbergh all over again, Lincoln or Vercingetorix. He was touched by so many honors and so much enthusiasm. The turnaround in his fortunes, which renders certain men more intolerant, had made DeGaulle more human. That haughtiness which had chilled us before had given way to a relaxed manner. Even during his public addresses his voice was softened. His style had become more familiar without losing its grandeur. He no longer needed to prove that he stood for France; he was France.

We gathered at the consulate to welcome him. After he had chatted with Jacques Maritain, Charles Boyer, and myself, he met Robert Dhéry who, stated the consul general, "was lucky enough to have collected three hundred thousand dollars for the Fréjus victims in a single gala."

DeGaulle patted Dhéry's shoulder absentmindedly: "That's too much, my friend. Much too much . . ."

Obviously, he was thinking of other things . . .

Inspired by the presence of DeGaulle in the United States, my second son decided to be born. At the time, I was in Hollywood, in Loretta Young's sylph-like arms, filming a TV show. Miss Young was making a small fortune (not for herself, mind you, but for her charities) by penalizing her colleagues each time a foul word escaped their mouths. Even the most innocent "damn" obliged one to fork out a dollar. One of the actresses on the set had forgotten her lines and yelled out, without thinking, "shit." With a charming smile Loretta wafted over to the culprit.

"Ethel, my darling, it breaks my heart, but I have to ask you for three dollars. Would you mind very much?"

"Not at all, my dear," answered the other in a honeyed voice. "But how much would it cost me to tell you to go fuck yourself?"

Three dollars richer, Loretta threw herself back into my impatient arms. Our frolics were interrupted by a call from the gynecologist. Tearing myself from the embrace of my partner, I ran to the hospital without taking the time to remove my make-up. I collided at breakneck speed with a hospital cart and sent a half-conscious young woman sprawling onto the floor. It was Marisa, who had just delivered. After hoisting her back onto the cart and kissing her, I ran to a window where you could see the newborn infants. A nurse showed me mine, who, to my great embarrassment, I must admit, was the spitting image of all the others.

I sprinted back to the studio and continued my love scene with Loretta. When we finished working at seven o'clock, I went back to the hospital with Dalio. I showed him my son. Dalio started making monkey faces and strange noises. I pleaded with my son to look at us just once. Nothing helped. Neither Dalio's contortions nor my tender exhortations could draw the slightest smile from him. At that moment I knew he would be a difficult child. But newborns are what they are; and the sooner we learn to recognize their nature, the easier it is to figure out how to handle them.

Marisa and I decided to call our son Patrick. Our American friends couldn't get over that. They put forth great objections, contending that the child of an Italian girl and a Frenchman couldn't in all decency have so typically Irish a first name. We hadn't thought of Ireland; we were simply attracted by the sound of the word Patrick. Patrick it stayed. Or sometimes, when he was particularly well-behaved (rarely, to tell the truth), Patrickino.

The papers only commented upon the birth of Patrickino with a few indifferent lines. Those all-powerful empresses of the gossip columns, Louella Parsons and Hedda Hopper, called us to say that they were absolutely shocked that neither Marisa nor myself had deigned to inform them the same night that our child was conceived. To punish us, they relegated the announcement of his birth to the fifth page.

Not that it mattered. This third child brought total happiness for me. I felt young, strong, and blessed by the gods.

In February 1960 the rehearsals for *Second String* began. The show had been taken from a play by Colette, *La Seconde*, which she adapted from her novel, and which had run in Paris some years earlier. The principal character was to be played by a great American actress, Shirley Booth. I was both delighted and surprised to have been chosen to be her partner. The least we could say is that, having a slight French accent and looking at the time much younger than my real age or than the age my part required, I didn't appear to be the obvious choice to play Shirley Booth's husband. If there ever was a bit of off-beat casting, that was it!

I promised the producer that I'd age myself as much as I could. I glued on a mustache and put some white on my temples.

The other actors in the play formed an even more heterogeneous family. My mistress was an American intellectual from Boston and my son was a cowboy from the Midwest.

My cowboy son was studying at the Actor's Studio. This was much to his credit, though it presented no end of problems for us. Aside from scratching himself constantly, leaving doubts in the audience's mind as to the habits of hygiene with which his mother and I had raised him, he mumbled so much you couldn't understand a word he said. Twenty minutes before curtain he lay on the floor and closed his eyes. The only problem was that he chose the space right in front of the door where we were supposed to enter the stage. Just before each entrance, we had to leap over his inert body.

In his efforts to explain this exotic behavior to me, he

pointed out a line at the end of the third act in which he mentioned that he'd been sleeping. It was for this line that he prepared himself two and a half hours in advance. It didn't really matter that there were other scenes, other actors, and other lines in his role besides "I took a nap." No, it was on that one line that he had decided to construct his character.

With condescending patience he explained to me, "You must try to understand; by the Method we get into our roles outside of the text, we play the situation and not the words, we establish a rapport with every character."

"So?" said I. "Isn't that what all actors in all countries have been doing since theater began?"

My cowboy son couldn't get over this revelation.

The problems of my aristocratic mistress from Boston were of a different order. She couldn't say a line without the advice of her psychiatrist. If our director asked her to smile, she became livid. Before smiling she had to know the family history of her character. Why should she smile? What had her grandmother done to justify this strange behavior?

Leonard Sillman, our producer, was an enlightened dictator whose moods fluctuated rapidly between the conquering exultation of Napoleon at Austerlitz and the hopeless dejection of Napoleon at Waterloo. Because of his size, furors, and megalomania, we nicknamed him "Napopo."

We opened in Detroit. The night before, Napopo asked me to courteously receive a journalist who wanted to interview me about the play. She arrived at my suite with notebook in hand and glasses slipping off her nose. Without saying hello, she asked: "Where is Croquette?"

I hadn't the least idea where Croquette was, nor even who she was. Faced by my startled silence, she consented to enlighten me.

"Maybe I'm not pronouncing her name well. Where is Coquette?"

Coquette? Coquette? I was becoming more and more lost.

"I'm talking," she said finally, with impatience, "about this play that you are going to do . . . It's written by somebody, isn't it?"

It was then that I realized she was talking about Colette.

"When will she be in Detroit?"

Discreetly I explained that Colette had been dead for five years. I sensed that the young woman would never forgive me for it.

Every evening Napopo entered my dressing room without knocking and began shouting and chewing me out for not spraying enough white on my temples.

Were we doing badly at the boxoffice? It was because my temples weren't white enough.

Was it snowing? Had China developed an atomic bomb? Had Shirley Booth caught cold? Again, my temples were at the root of it all.

God knows I was doing all I could! Aside from my mustache, which muffled all my lines and made me sound as if I had a harelip, I had tried powder, chalk, flour, and white lead on my hair. The whiter I became, it seems, the younger I looked. I couldn't understand, in any case, how a few grams of powder on my head would improve this feeble work of art.

But Napopo would not give up. He insisted that if my hair were whiter the play would run for five years.

Second String didn't run for five years but only several unbearably long months. The dreary rain which had cloistered me in New York during these performances was alleviated by a sunny sojourn in Hawaii to film *The Devil at 4 O'clock*. The island of Oahu displayed its indolent charms with a dreamy indifference. Spreading palms, bamboos, waterfalls, orchids, and giant bananas welcomed the arrival of our film company and its two most illustrious members: Spencer Tracy and Frank Sinatra.

It takes more than film stars to ruffle the serenity of the Hawaiians. They have been persuaded that God created their island before any other land. To thank him they sing softly, accompanying themselves with guitars. When problems appear they chase them away by murmuring, "No hui hui."

"No hui hui" means: "Don't make such a big deal out of it. Just leave me in peace."

Our troupe didn't share this peaceful philosophy. The director, Mervyn LeRoy, screamed at the cameraman, who screamed at the soundman, who screamed at the assistant director, who screamed at the extras . . .

Spencer Tracy, a genial man who was not well at the time, couldn't work past the morning. The problem was that Sinatra would only work in the afternoon. In the morning he hired a private plane and hopped from island to island trying to convince the startled inhabitants to vote for Kennedy in the next presidential election. Around two o'clock he returned, exhausted, at the precise moment when Tracy was retiring for the day to his rooms. How, in these conditions, the scenes between Tracy and Sinatra were shot is a mystery to me.

Sinatra knew that I couldn't vote because I wasn't a citizen, so he wasn't going to waste any time with me. On occasion, however, he looked at me amicably and murmured "Hi." I would answer, "Hi," but these exchanges occurred only on the days when he felt particularly talkative.

Fortunately for me, there was Dalio. In an immense straw hat he looked like a cotton-picking slave before the intervention of Lincoln. Anyone who has seen Dalio performing in Paris at Castel's or playing one of his inimitable butlers or maitre-d's in a Hollywood film is already witness to a highly colorful spectacle. What is there to say about Dalio among the Polynesians? Unable to acquire the good graces of Sinatra, who had other things to worry about, Dalio had taken Tracy under his wing. Every time Tracy stammered or missed a line, Dalio sputtered, "Oh, it's *my* fault, Spence, it's really my fault." Even when the mistake occurred in scenes where Dalio didn't appear.

One day, to my great surprise, I discovered our whole company in a state of absolute calm. There was no question of any shouting or fighting. On the contrary, everybody spoke in soothing tones and sat down to rest or fan themselves intermittently. I asked Dalio what had happened.

"You haven't heard that Gable is dead?" he said.

"I know that. Is it as a sign of mourning that our friends . . ."

"Not at all. But when they learned that Gable had had a heart attack they all panicked and called their doctors. Their doctors told them, 'Take it easy, don't push yourself, relax, smile.' They're so afraid of croaking that they've been changed into lambs overnight."

During the months that remained, it looked as if someone had been feeding our company tranquilizers. The Hawaiians, with mistaken pride, were convinced that we had adopted their philosophy: "No hui hui."

"I don't want to see him," shouted Jules Dassin. "I like Jean-Pierre too much. I don't want to have to tell him that he's absolutely wrong for the part."

This was the situation which presented itself when Arthur Lesser, producer, and Albert Husson, adapter of an Italian comedy, *Il Benessere*, offered me the chance to play opposite Melina Mercouri in Paris.

I had read this story of a bungled love affair, and had liked it a lot. I was tempted to try my hand at the role of the husband, a faded and cynical roué who repents suddenly, but too late. But what could I do? Dassin was the director of the show and neither the author nor the producer could impose an actor on him.

What I did was take the bull by the horns and go see Dassin at the studio where he was filming *Phaedra*. In his eyes, I realized, I was still the clean-cut young man whom he had directed in Hollywood more than twenty years before, in *Assignment in Britanny*. I cornered Julie (that's what his friends call him) on the set and tried to intimidate him by shouting in his face: "So you think I'm too young and too nice? Look at me closely. I'm old and nasty!"

It was a stupid thing to do but I was satisfied. That same evening Arthur Lesser called me. "I don't know what you did to Dassin but he swears by you now. He even refuses to do the play unless you're in it." Fine.

The next step was to find a French title. The literal translation of *Il Benessere*, a voluptuous word in Italian, was a little tame in French: "Bien-être" ("Well-being"). I proposed "Je reviens, Giacomino" ("I'm Coming Back, Giacomino") which seemed to me to sum up the content of the play pretty well.

"A title doesn't have to sum up the content of the play," said Husson. "For instance, when I was young, I called one of my comedies *Her Tits on the Table*. Well, I assure you it wasn't primarily about a table."

In face of such logic we opted for *Flora*.

Flora was Melina Mercouri, who arrived at the rehearsals like a tigress escaped from the Parthenon.

She began working, stopped, cried, lay down on the ground, stood up again, and screamed to Dassin (who was her husband): "I can't do it, Julie. I'll never get there. You're asking impossible things of me." Dassin calmed her down, then swore at her, then embraced her, then scoffed tenderly at her. She started to rehearse, stopped again, and took me as a witness: "Why don't you say it, Jean-Pierre, since you're thinking it. Go ahead, tell Julie he's an asshole."

"I don't think he is."

"My God, you're such a coward!"

On opening night, while I was waiting in the wings for my cue, the stage manager hurried up to me. After having exchanged the customary "Merde," he seized me by the arm and said with emotion, "Oh, Jean-Pierre, I really feel sorry for you."

"And why do you, my friend?"

"Because you have such a horrible part."

It was on that comforting note that I walked onstage.

At the end of the show, the first friend to appear at my dressing room said straight out: "I don't like it." The next was Micheline Presle: "You're good but I don't like the play." Then it was Carné's turn: "Oh, was that awful!" Just as I was about to collapse I heard an actress I knew screeching in the corridor: "*Maa*rvelous! Absolutely *maa*rvelous!" I felt a glimmer of hope. She entered: "Dassin is a *maa*rvelous director. He's no more made for the theater than I am for being Pope, but he is *maa*rvelous! Mercouri is *maa*rvelous. You can't understand a word of what she's saying, but she's *maa*rvelous. You, my dear, you are *maa*rvelous, but it's not that much fun to be in a flop, is it?" She walked out, thrilled at having accomplished her mission.

I've always been shocked by the offhand manner of some people who enter a dressing room on opening night and say they don't like a show. What would they think of a guest who came to their house, took a look around, and said, "How can you live in such a place?" If we are acting in a play, it's because we believe in it, right or wrong. Such a reaction is an insult to our taste.

The day after an opening night is like a hangover. When I arrived at the theater Melina welcomed me with blood in her eye:

"Have you figured out what's happening?"

"What's happening, my darling?"

"If you don't understand by now, you're a jerk."

She thought that there was a plot against us. The word is too strong, but it did seem that no one was willing to forgive her for the exceptional success of *Never on Sunday*, the large billboards which had been put up on the Champs-Elysées to advertise our show, the excess of interviews and articles on the production, and the incongruous Greek music which accompanied our comedy.

The following morning our publicity agent telephoned me at dawn. Gasping for breath, he managed to say, "Somebody read me J. J. Gautier's* article. It's not so bad." Then he hung up.

I hurried to the theater. Melina had regained hope. "Gautier isn't so bad." The stage manager entered my dressing room at a gallop: "Gautier isn't so bad." Soon the whole theater was echoing with it. Color returned to cheeks, postures straightened up, voices mounted a tone, dejection gave way to euphoria, a wind of victory passed over the battlefield.

"But what did he say about the production?"

"He liked it."

* Jean-Jacques Gautier was the Clive Barnes of Paris.

"He liked it," "He liked it." They whispered it to themselves from dressing room to dressing room, and each wondered, "What did he say about me?" But no one dared to ask for the precise details.

Dear Jean-Jacques Gautier, do you realize the terror that you inspire? The ruin that you sow?

For thousands of directors, producers, scene designers, stagehands, and electricians your pen is the sword of Damocles.

Were you conscious of your responsibility when you scribbled out your review on a café table? And don't answer by saying, "What I write affects only me and a few readers who have confidence in me." Alas, these are no longer the days when the theater in Paris, like the circus in Rome, was the daily bread of the people. Once upon a time theater was the very center of cultural life; but now it is the diversion of an elite. And that elite no longer even wants the luxury of choice, but follows blindly the dictates of its soothsayers.

Alas, my friend, alas; three times alas, or more . . . (this is the first line of a five-act tragedy in verse which I began at about age eleven. I didn't go any farther, because I couldn't find a second line worthy of the first.) Alas, most of the critics were contemptuous of *Flora*. "The theater is not a successful vehicle for film stars," wrote M. Paul Morelle. And Poirot-Delpech, critic for *Le Monde:* "The stage doesn't forgive; it's not as complacent as the camera."

May I remark to M. Poirot-Delpech that Melina Mercouri played Aeschylus and Sophocles long before appearing in front of any camera? What point is there in criticizing her passionate excesses, her fire? A volcano is not a rolling meadow, not does a tornado have the same delicacy as a summer breeze . . .

But let's forget about a demoralizing and partial press. Instead of complaining about the number of people who will read these reviews, I try to take comfort thinking of the much greater number, in Greenland or Tasmania, who will never read them.

"We celebrated the 100th performance of my play the night of the eightieth performance which of course was only the sixtieth," Bernstein once said. The sixtieth performance of *Flora* was also its last.

At least we finished in style, in front of a full house in which lurked Marcel Jouhandeau, the greatest living disciple of Gide, draped in a 1900 cape, and his wife Caryathis, eyes kohled like an Assyrian warror. They came to see me during intermission. While I chatted with them, a very serious gentleman in tails entered my dressing room. He announced that "you know who" was in the audience; that He had the intention of honoring us with a visit at the end of the performance; and that it would therefore be necessary for us to welcome Him backstage.

Moved and flattered that General DeGaulle had taken the trouble to come, all of us lined up at attention as soon as the curtain had fallen. The serious gentleman—surely he was the chief of protocol—appeared again and verified our bearing with a trained eye before stepping aside to let the great man through.

To our amazement, it wasn't General DeGaulle who made his entrance, but, gracious and olympian, Maurice Chevalier.

I took the Jouhandeaus to supper with me, and during the meal they began to tear each other to pieces. She reproached him for not being interested in her literary works.

He (in a weary and distracted tone): "What works, my dear? And what literature?"

Here also, it seemed to be a question of a recurrent routine, but this one was less tender than the one executed by Melina and Dassin. The Jouhandeaus sifted through their ancient gripes, incapable as they were of adding new ones to them. For the hundredth time, without a doubt, Jouhandeau looked at Caryathis and said: "I think the greatest proof of love one can give his wife is to kill her."

17

A Foolish Decision

⟨∽∽∽∽∽∽∽∽∽∽∽⟩

The quarrels between my wife and me were neither as frenetic as those of the Dassins nor as cunning as those of the Jouhandeaus. But in the end, I must confess that quarrels there were. It all began one lovely day in summer, under a placid sky, because of a broken window.

Without asking any questions, Marisa blurted out: "It must have been Tina."

In fact it hadn't been Tina who was at fault but the servants, who admitted it.

Unfortunately, from then on, Tina became an excellent pretext for problems and arguments.

Caught between two tigresses, my life was not easy. Certainly there were still pleasant times and long calms, but my wife and my daughter no longer had confidence in each other.

If I supported Tina during a fight, Marisa reproached me. If I said Marisa was right, then Tina would give me the mournful look of an abandoned child.

Up until then Tina had adored Marisa. She'd called her "mama" and considered her as such. Marisa had performed the duties of motherhood with infinite love. Between the two of them there had been a tenderness and complicity of which I was often the willing target.

But Tina was becoming difficult. Fourteen is a dangerous age for girls and an exhausting one for their parents . . .

Marisa and I were soon sabotaged by misunderstandings. She became jealous, not only of my friends, but of the book I was reading, the cigarette I was smoking. When we were together, she spent her time upbraiding me for the hours we were apart.

All couples, especially after six years of marriage, have their bouts. Usually she will content herself with slamming the door in his face and he will go out for a defiant 24-hour pack of cigarettes. But Marisa is stubborn. She's Italian, and, worse, she's Sardinian. She isn't the kind of woman who will stand for compromises and half-measures. Since it is impossible for her to arm herself with patience and philosophy, her approach to life is all or nothing. As for myself, although I seem to be easygoing, I'm apt to make rapid and definitive decisions, and these are all the more final because I make them at the last minute.

Instead of wisely separating for a short time to think it over, we decided to get a divorce. The first lawyer that Marisa consulted told her that she had been lucky to marry me and that she'd be better off getting rid of her mother . . . By the greatest of coincidences he happened to be a friend of mine. When she came back to the house, she was honest enough to tell me the story. Fate seemed to be watching over lovers. It looked as if the happy years of our marriage were going to continue. Perhaps an obstinate belief that problems will work themselves out and that in the end everybody will love everybody is one of my faults.

Unfortunately, it didn't happen that way. Another lawyer was found who would expedite the situation right up to the finishing strokes. But Marisa's lawyer and mine were dumfounded when they discovered that there was no motive for our decision. There wasn't the least infidelity, no insults, not the slightest desertion. Nothing. We had to invent something.

Each of us was thus obliged to telephone two friends and ask them to write two letters, one certifying that Marisa had insulted me in public and the other that I had hit her in front of witnesses. Thinking that we'd lost our minds, our friends refused; but after much explanation the deed was accomplished.

A curious sort of peace descended in our household. After all, deciding to get a divorce is already agreeing on one thing.

The preliminary divorce proceedings were to take place at Versailles, a few weeks later. In court, the judge seemed hostile to me. However, when my lawyer revealed that my wife had refused to sleep with me for two months, the judge leaned forward and patted me on the shoulder with sudden tenderness. "You poor guy!" Maybe he was in the same position.

Obstinate children that we were, we kept to our decisions. The divorce followed its course. As we left the courthouse, lawyers and clerks shook hands with each other and congratulated themselves on their success.

Marisa and I went for coffee at a nearby bistro. In all frankness, we felt much closer to each other at that moment than we had on the day of our marriage.

I left the next day for Lisbon to film *Vacances au Portugal.*

The seven hills of Lisbon sloped gently into the Tagus River. Pigeons on the Place du Rocio brought to mind the Piazza San Marco in Venice. Barefooted street urchins chased the trams which nipped in and out of alleys so narrow that they sometimes grazed the terracotta walls.

We crossed the Tagus to arrive at Setubal, a fishing port where we established our headquarters. Here I renewed some old acquaintances, Daniel Gelin, Michel Auclair, Françoise Arnoul, and discovered a blonde newcomer, looking like a lost Ophelia, secretive and austere, a dreaming, golden stalk of wheat: Catherine Deneuve.

When the newspapers later asked about our divorce and remarriage (remarriage there was—in fact, the children never knew a thing about our separation), it was easy for me to treat it lightly. I've always preferred to inspire envy rather than pity. In 1962, however, in a Portugal which seemed like the end of the world, I felt very alone and very sad.

What a mess I'd made of my life . . . what a cruel and foolish act our decision to divorce had been. I looked at my acquaintances. Most of them were married. Most of them had known trying times with their wives, but they were still together. Love had become tenderness, or at least complicity.

I envied them.

Waves of regret assailed me, waves of tenderness and remorse. Tenderness for someone to whom I should have tried to be more protective, more understanding. Remorse, since there were faults on both sides, as always. And especially regret: so many chances stupidly squandered, so many hours of happiness that I'd taken for granted . . .

If I passed a child on the street, the tears came to my eyes. The sight of a couple in each other's arms was unbearable.

While I was working everything was okay, but when night fell I felt alone, unloved and empty. Associations were strange: One night I started to cry, not in front of a photo or an old letter, but on finding Marisa's voter's registration card in a small bundle of papers. Even though I had suffered from my wife's recent coldness, I still knew that one smile from her, one tender expression to crack the mask that her face had become, would be enough to make me pardon all, to promise anything, to throw myself into her arms . . .

Perhaps, I thought, this is what love is: the need, the desire to be with her every time I saw something beautiful: a beach, a church, a cloud, a child's smile . . .

Sometimes, alone at the prow of the boat as we crossed the Tagus, I caught myself murmuring: "Come, the sun is warm. We'll take a ride on one of these funny old ferry boats crammed with sheep. Look at that Christ behind us with the outstretched arms. Doesn't he remind you of the one on the Corcovado where we climbed up together? Come. There's a woman in black balancing a basket of cork-tree bark on her head. Let's go to Castel San Giorgio. There's a beautiful view from the top. I'll hold you by the shoulders and you'll call me 'my baby' just like you used to do when we were in love . . . Come, I still need you . . ."

Whenever I wasn't filming it was difficult to keep myself

from jumping into the first airplane to Paris. What for? I would have arrived like an intruder to find Marisa cloistered, guarded, and under the spell of her mother. I called her instead. A voice answered, so impersonal that I thought it was the operator. "The lawyer this," "the movers that"—. When I asked her if she was happy with our decision, she answered: "I haven't had the time to think about it," and hung up.

I wrote her and didn't send the letters. Maybe one day, by chance, she would find them. She'd discover a husband much more in love with her than she could ever imagine. I addressed a poem by Aragon to her:

> Mon bel amour, mon cher amour, ma déchirure,
> Je te porte dans moi comme un oiseau blessé . . .
> Il n'y a pas d'amour heureux . . .*

October 1962. Marisa was preparing to go to Rome with my sons and I to New York to rehearse *Tovarich*. The house was filled with suitcases, trunks, and bags. I'd just stumbled against a low, metallic one. It reminded me of a coffin.

With much secrecy, Jean-Claude had just brought me a little piece of paper on which he had written: "If I could only stay here forever." Poor little five-year-old, he didn't know anything, but he understood everything . . . and he was suffering from it, too.

Marisa was reading under a bad light in a bed that was too narrow. When I bent to embrace her, her expression seemed more hesitant than obstinate. As I stood up I noticed the Delft tiles imbedded in the fireplace. I'd lived in that house for ten years and never noticed those tiles before.

At Orly airport we said our goodbyes as if we were going to see each other the following day. I was stricken, sad, defeated, but I was hiding it. Was it also a sort of reserve that made Marisa seem hardened, or was she expressing that proud indifference of women who aren't in love anymore?

> * My beautiful love, my darling love, my rending,
> I carry you in my heart like a wounded bird . . .
> There is no happy love . . .

Jean-Claude had started acting cold to me. He seemed to hold me responsible for this separation. At the last moment, however, he kissed me sweetly. Patrick seemed sad, too, but who can read the mind of a two-year-old? They moved away toward the airplane together, Patrick wiggling his little legs and Jean-Claude walking with that swinging gait in which I recognize myself. A vague gesture of farewell from the boarding ramp . . .

I returned to La Malmaison. Empty.

I heard the voices of my kids playing in the garden: "Papa! Papa! . . ." I saw Marisa again, at that not so long ago time when we were in love: "Come, my baby, come quick, I'm so cold . . ." I was twenty years older than she. She called me her baby. It didn't seem strange at all.

That deserted house, that silent garden without children. Marisa fleeing to Rome in search of a new life while I stayed alone with my memories. What a mess . . .

PART THREE

18

Vivien Leigh

While I was playing *Flora*, an American director, Delbert Mann, had offered me a role with Vivien Leigh on Broadway in a musical adapted from Jacques Deval's *Tovarich*. Much as I would have liked to play opposite Vivien, I hesitated. I had never sung or danced in my life and I felt it was too late to begin.

I called Vivien in London. She had never sung before either. "So what?" she said. "Sounds like it will be fun."

I signed the contract.

In December I flew to New York. Accompanied by our producers, Abel Farbman and Sylvia Harris, Vivien was waiting at the airport.

How beautiful she was . . . as regal, as young, and as radiant as she had appeared to me twenty-five years earlier when I had seen her for the first time.

It was in 1936 or '37. I was having dinner in a restaurant in Soho with Tony Bushell, an English actor with whom I had just made a film. Standing opposite us and escorted by a man who was clearly older than herself was the most ravishing creature that can be imagined: immense eyes that passed from melancholy to the most ironic vivacity, a little insolent nose, and an oval face lengthened by a frail neck. "Un cou blanc, delicat, qui, de la neige, effacerait l'éclat."

She wasn't paying any attention to us, and still less to her companion. Pursuing some interior dream, she sometimes glanced briefly toward another table. At that table sat a blonde woman and a younger man whose dark, romantic looks were marked by something intense and secret. I said to Tony: "That young woman and that man sitting at the other table are madly in love with each other."

He burst out laughing. "That's a Frenchman for you. They think only of love! It so happens that I know both of them very well. Her name is Vivien Leigh. The man she is with is her husband. The young man at the other table is Laurence Olivier and he is with his wife. As far as I know, Larry and Vivien have never even met. Ah! these Frenchmen!" And he laughed again.

Whether they had met or not didn't really matter. Their love shone across the restaurant. It was to last more than twenty years.

Later, *Gone with the Wind* would make Vivien the idol of her generation. Larry Olivier had been alternating performances of Shakespeare in London with Hollywood films (including *Wuthering Heights* and *Rebecca*) and was considered the most prestigious of the English actors. They shared so much glory, youth, beauty, love: it seemed as if Shakespeare had written *Romeo and Juliet* for them. They decided to play it on Broadway. The failure of the show was a cruel blow.

The following year, Katharine Cornell and Basil Rathbone, who had neither the right age nor the right appearance for their roles, played Romeo and Juliet. It was a hit. Such are the fearful mysteries of the theater.

In 1943, Claude Dauphin and I found ourselves in England. Larry and Vivien invited us to Slough, a hamlet with a certain damp charm situated near London. Vivian had abandoned Hollywood, and all the glory of stardom which she no longer cared about, to share with her compatriots the ordeal of the Battle of Britain. Larry was on leave from the Navy. He was directing *Henry V* and playing the principal role in it. At midnight we left them. London was blazing under the bombardments. All my life I will remember the frail silhouette of Vivian as she accompanied us under the porch roof, looking serious and serene, nestled in her husband's arms, and illuminated by the reddish flashes which signaled that a "V-1" had just destroyed another district in London.

As time went by, my friendship with the Oliviers grew, and so did my admiration. Whenever I could I went to see them, whether they were playing together or separately. There were a series of memorable evenings between 1950 and 1960: *Antony and Cleopatra, Caesar and Cleopatra, Hamlet, A Street Car Named Desire, Candida, Oedipus, School for Scandal.* At the beginning, Vivien had to fight against her exceptional, aristocratic beauty. It took the London critics a long time to accept her as a real actress: she looked too refined, too elegant, too insolently seductive. Nevertheless, they had to admit that she sometimes equaled the man she loved. She played with him like a mouse with a cat, notably in Shaw's *Cleopatra.* But at the same time that her talent and fame began to be recognized, her health began to wane. The tuberculosis that she thought she had cured reappeared, and her emotional stability was affected by it. She could no longer stand to be apart from Larry. While she was making a film in Ceylon, she had to interrupt the shooting to return to London, because of nervous collapse. The birth of a child, which she had so intensely desired, was refused her. Destiny was avenging itself.

In 1957 the Oliviers came to the Sarah Bernhardt Theatre to play *Titus Andronicus* and to receive the Legion of Honor, which Vivien was to wear proudly on all her dresses till she died. Taking advantage of their day off, Vivien, Larry, Marisa, and I left for Touraine. At every stop Vivien would go into a shop and ask in perfect French: "How's Mme. Dupont? And little Pierre, how's he doing in his studies?"

Even though I knew she had taken this same trip several years before, I was astounded. I didn't know that wherever she went she always inquired, with a passionate concern and curiosity, about the health and problems of everyone, whether it was the mayor or the postman. She had an incredible memory and always remembered last names, first names, and family affairs. That year, she made her attentive and benevolent inquiries throughout the province of Touraine, like a sovereign visiting her vassals.

Chenonceaux was inaugurating its *Son et Lumière* show. All four of us went to see it. There were no other spectators. Silent, we sat watching the splendors which emerged from the darkness. Larry had his arm around Vivien; they were at times illuminated by a red reflection which reminded me of those hellish flames in London thirteen years before.

During those years Vivien had reigned at Notley Abbey, a feudal castle where the phantom of Henry VIII wandered. But in 1962, after she had been divorced and Notley Abbey sold, Vivien had taken shelter in Sussex at Tickerage. This manor of old rose bricks, nestled between fields and marshes in a melancholy and romantic countryside, suited her. It was there that I went to find her and work on *Tovarich.*

Stretched out on a chaise lounge, manuscript in hand, with her mood constantly changing, there was something of the Empress Josephine about her, of whom Napoleon had said: "She was spoiled, whimsical, excessive . . . but you forgave her everything, because she was generous and loyal. And above all she was alive. All that was necessary was for her to appear, or even for someone to speak of her, to make everything sparkle."

In December we met in New York again and began rehearsing *Tovarich.* Vivien was radiant. For both of us it was a debut in a new world, highly colored, turbulent, and so different from the intimate stages to which we were accustomed.

We rehearsed in every cranny of New York. As soon as dawn broke I rushed to Greenwich Village to don breastplate and mask. Then I did two hours of genuflecting, feinting, and parrying in an attempt to learn the art of fencing.

Just as rheumatism started to run me down I would drag myself to Brooklyn, where the musical director would undertake

the perilous task of teaching me to sing. His name was Stanley
Lebowsky. Oh, Yves Montand! Oh, Chevalier! Oh, Sintra! you
lucky guys are your own masters; you stop when you feel like it,
you modify the tempo, you breathe, you shorten or sustain a
note at your fancy. It wasn't like that for us. We had to tie our
vocal chords to the tone, rhythm, and style which Stanley imposed. In a musical comedy the musical director is second only
to God.

I begged him to let me sing two octaves lower. I of course
didn't have the slightest idea of what an octave was (nor a sharp
nor a flat), but I believed, in any case, that two octaves lower
than "whatever it was" would be easier. I was wrong. In this
kind of show it is preferable to sing high.

"What if I'm off key?"

"Who'll notice it?"

With my larynx in the same state as my knees, I next
crawled to Broadway, where we rehearsed the dances in a kind
of garage. Herb Ross, our choreographer, seconded by his wife,
Nora Kaye, a former ballerina, showed me the steps. If I didn't
get them on the first try, he would raise his eyes heavenward
and count once again: "Seven, eight, nine . . ."—I don't know
why, but he always began with seven—and all with the mar-
tyred smile of a professor in the Sorbonne who has been asked
to teach the alphabet to a retarded person.

Winded and bowlegged, I would grab a taxi to go to rehearse the comedy scenes. Another difficulty awaited me there.
I had to speak English with a Russian accent. I resorted to a specialist who overwhelmed me with so many suggestions that I
would no doubt have seemed Russian had I followed them, but
no one would have understood a word of what I was saying.

I spent my evenings with Vivien, during which we fed each
other lines. At midnight, reeling with fatigue, I would try to
leave her. But midnight was the precise hour when Vivien (who
had, with the exception of fencing, followed the same routine as
I) began to bloom. My going to sleep was out of the question.
At a more normal time nothing could have enchanted me more.
She had eyes that—like Colette's favorite cat—changed from

grey to mauve, and a little impudent nose: a face that you could only weary of admiring if you had spent sixteen hours singing, dancing, leaping, parrying, panting, learning lines, and rehearsing. But my exhaustion only made her laugh, since Vivien, who was capable of every generosity, couldn't imagine anyone being tired in her presence. Alas, men are not made of bronze, iron, or steel like those fragile creatures!

On Christmas Eve I felt particularly lonely. I had received no news from my wife and children, who were living in Rome. Maybe Marisa was thinking of me and suffering from our separation too. Maybe she'd met some young, handsome Italian . . .

At midnight, at the precise instant when the churches were celebrating the birth of Christ, Vivien announced with an enchanting smile that she wouldn't take part in our show. Not without reason she felt that my role was superior to hers. A full rehearsal had taken place for the first time the night before. With dismay I had noticed that my lines had gotten more laughs than Vivien's.

On top of that, Vivien hated my songs, she hated the songs of Taina Elg (who had a secondary role), she hated the twenty-five minutes (she'd counted them) when she was offstage. She hated our director, Delbert Mann.

But it got even worse. There was a scene in the second act in which the grand duchess Tatiana (Vivien) confessed that she had been raped by one of the jailers before escaping from the Bolsheviks. Vivien was repelled by this passage. She kept trying to have it deleted. We kept trying to convince her that this confession was indispensable to the plot. She finally gave in.

I thought that her behavior was a matter of caprice, but I was mistaken. Something profound and pathetic which perhaps stemmed from a faraway, personal drama was troubling her. I was wrong at the time not to attach any importance to these symptoms. Whatever the reasons might have been, they were to prove tragic.

We left for Philadelphia. Up until that time, we had rehearsed with a piano. But in Philadelphia we discovered with terror that there were dozens of violins, flutes, trumpets, guitars, trombones, a harp, and some cellos, but not a single piano. What had happened to the melody? In that ocean of music, I felt like a man who didn't know how to swim. It seemed as if the only function of this orchestra was to hide the melody and render the songs that the composer had written unrecognizable.

Vivien thought of the musicians as so many enemies. "Thirty against two," she said. "It just isn't fair."

Thank God there were a few laughs to lighten the blackness of our fears. One day, Stanley Lebowsky, our orchestra conductor, shouted at a worthy cellist: "Madame, you have between your legs something which could give pleasure to thousands. Why do you content yourself with just scratching it?"

The first performance finally took place in front of a packed house. When Vivien entered wearing the little white collar and black dress of a chambermaid, looking so slender and yet so royal, and began dancing the Charleston, there was delirium. She did it with that grace and ironic elegance which belonged only to her; but had she danced one hundred times less well, she would have been just as big a hit. It was not her choreographic talents which created such enthusiasm, but the fact that this figure of legend, the wife and acting partner for twenty years of the greatest English actor, this Scarlett O'Hara, Cleopatra, Juliet, and Portia, was, at the zenith of her career, kicking her heels in a Charleston.

Bernard Giquel eloquently summed up this evening in *Paris-Match*. Under the title BROADWAY BETS 500,000 DOLLARS ON VIVIEN LEIGH AND JEAN-PIERRE AUMONT, he wrote: "On the stage of the Erlanger Theater in Philadelphia it's like Cape Canaveral at the blast-off of a new missile. Twenty electricians and stage-hands, helmeted with earphones, wearing mikes under their Adam's apples, are proceeding with the final adjustments. In a few hours the countdown will take place. Broadway is betting on *Tovarich* to break the show business barrier.

"Fifteen minutes before curtain Jean-Pierre waits alone with his stage fright and the telegrams from his family scattered throughout Europe . . . Western Union, Rome: 'Am near you this evening with all my love, Marisa.' Marisa is Marisa Pavan, his wife, from whom he is separated. It is one in the morning in Rome and his two sons ought to be asleep . . . Western Union, Rome: 'Two million kisses from your two angels who love you so much. Jean-Claude, Patrick.' And what's Tina, my daughter, doing at this very moment? . . . Western Union, Paris: 'I'm right beside you. Love, Your Tina.'

"In the pit, twenty-eight musicians tune up their instruments. Six, five, four . . . zero, blast-off. When the handsome hero of *Lac aux Dames* and the divine Scarlett O'Hara first appear, there is a long round of applause.

"At the back of the theater, like aficionados leaning against the fence of a bull-ring, stand the producers, on the lookout for the reactions of the beast, the public. Sitting in the last row, Delbert Mann and his script-girl are tightening a few loose bolts on the machine. For the next three weeks in Philadelphia, and three weeks after that in Boston, the show will be mercilessly cut, rewritten, polished, and repolished. On March 9 in New York, the stagehand who knocks three times [no, Bernard, in America they don't knock three times like they do in France] will be able to say at the same time: 'Well, the cards are dealt. There's nothing else we can do!' "

In my dressing room—at last it was *over!*—there was a crowd as big as in the old days. All we needed was Ginette Spanier, international empress of fashion, with her immutable "You clever boy, you did it again." No, tonight, it was not "again."

It was certainly the first time in my life that I had ever been unself-conscious enough to sing seven songs alone or in duet. I wasn't too happy with myself. I had tried to actually sing instead of contenting myself with talking my songs à la Rex Harrison . . . My fears were confirmed when the orchestra conductor came to congratulate me. He began with "You were marvelous" and finished with "Let's rehearse all day tomorrow."

At midnight I had supper with Bernard Giquel. I was happy that he was there, evoking the scent of Paris, suppers at Lipp and drinks at Castel . . . Despite the fact that the show had been a success, I had the blues. Cherished ghosts were haunting me, living and dead, everyone who had formerly comforted me with tenderness in those hours of doubt for all actors between the lowering of the curtain and the morning papers. During that time we're like lost children, full of mistrust toward compliments, stung to the quick by the slightest reservation. At least Marisa hadn't forgotten me. If ever I had prayed for a telegram with my whole heart, it was hers.

Before going back to my room, I stopped to see Vivien. Noel Coward was keeping her company. She handed me the first edition of the morning paper. The critics praised us, but they thought the play was out of style.

"Merde!" I muttered.

"One couldn't sum up the situation any better," concluded Noel Coward.

Thereupon he began haranguing Vivien in that staccato voice of his that he shook under the noses of all his friends. He told her that she had been crazy to accept this role, that she didn't know how to sing, that the plot was stupid, the direction grotesque, the production shoddy, and that he was *forbidding* her to do it on Broadway. I was stunned, not by his criticisms, but at the thought of the number of hours it would take me to repair the damage he was doing. It wouldn't be easy. I would have to convince her that she sang better than Tebaldi and danced with more style than Margot Fonteyn.

The next day our producer decided to replace our director. He hired Peter Glenville. I knew Peter well. He had planned on producing *Un Beau Dimanche*, a play of mine, in London. I was happy to work with him.

I was a little less happy when he felt it necessary to change everything. To begin with, he cut several of the musical numbers which Vivien and I were fond of. Then he booted out two of the actors who had secondary roles and replaced them with other people. We were upset about being separated from friends with whom we had rehearsed, trembled, performed, and rejoiced. I• was unjust and cruel. I tried to have a say in the matter, but in vain. It seemed that such changes during the course of performances before reaching New York were common fare.

We left Philadelphia for Boston in an atmosphere of doubt.

Ah! who could ever describe the epic of Boston, last stage of massive overhaul before New York. What writer has enough lyricism, dramatic furor, and comic delirium to depict these nocturnal conspiracies in smoke-filled rooms? Who could immortalize the true tale of nervous breakdowns, tellings-off, embraces, fear, hope, love, hate, and cold coffee? We would argue about the shreds of a scene, the director pretending that a certain line got a laugh at Saturday matinee, the actor asserting that the same line laid an egg on Saturday evening.

We soon got to the point where we no longer knew what should be cut and what should be kept. At five in the morning we would suddenly decide to put the first scene of the first act at the end of the second. "Who knows? It might be more effective?"

The irony of the whole thing was that the old version which we continued to play was breaking all records at the box-office. We were outdoing Mary Martin in *South Pacific* and Rex Harrison in *My Fair Lady!* Despite the freezing weather and the tepid reactions of the critics, we continued to play to packed houses. So why, in God's name, were we changing everything? This mania for testing plays in Boston and Philadelphia before New York has often done more harm than good. The desire to try any change as long as it is something new, the tendency to listen to the advice of visitors from New York, make us lose our perspective. A different show would arrive on Broadway. Would it be a better one?

Vivien began regretting every line that Peter Glenville had taken out in order to please her. Everything new that was offered her, she refused. When I defended certain scenes she answered in angelic tones: "You like this play. I detest it. Why don't you do it with Taina Elg?" Taina Elg had become Vivien's understudy as a compensation for losing her role.

All day we rehearsed different scenes than the ones we performed in the evening, fighting to maintain the same importance that our roles had had in the first version. Little by little, each night, we replaced the old text by the new, inserting new numbers and testing out freshly minted songs.

As we left the theater after one of these rehearsals, Vivien pointed at the line in front of the boxoffice and said to me with a sigh, "Poor people! They're buying tickets to see one play, without suspecting that they're going to see another."

As for myself, I not only had to learn a new text in a strange language, including new songs and dance steps, but I had to stay with Vivien every evening in an attempt to convince her to hold on until New York, which for her was becoming an ever more terrifying prospect. No wonder people who saw me leaving her suite, exhausted, at dawn, assumed that we were having an affair. Certainly we were both in love: she still and forever with Laurence Olivier, and I with Marisa.

One night Peter Glenville told me that while I sang "I go to bed," which was the first of my seven songs, he was going to have Vivien dust our garret with a flamboyant feather duster. I was furious. Who the hell would hear even a word of my song if Vivien was fluttering around me with that grace which was one of her surest enchantments?

In order to console me, our composer wrote me a new song called "I'm Delighted to Make a Friend."

"Be at room 92 tomorrow morning at eight o'clock," said the stage manager. "There'll be a pianist waiting to help you practice."

At the appointed hour I ring at room 92. There is no answer. I knock. Finally an old gentleman appears at the door, furious at being awakened. I tell him that I've come to work on my new song. He looks at me as if I were crazy. It's no more fun for me than for him to rehearse this early in the morning, I tell him, but those are the instructions. He refuses to let me in. I state my name. This hardly excites him. He states his, which I don't understand. I keep insisting, "Are you a pianist, or aren't you?"

"Yes, I'm a pianist."

"Then would you please play, 'I'm Delighted to Make a Friend'?"

"No, I will not play 'I'm Delighted to Make a Friend.' "

"You don't like that tune?"

"I don't even want to look at it."

He tries to slam the door in my face. I pour out all the insults I know in English. He answers me in the same manner with a strong Teutonic accent. For a moment we almost come to blows. Finally he succeeds in slamming the door.

I go down for breakfast, buy a paper, and see a three-column photo of my Teutonic pianist on the first page. He has just given a concert in Boston last night.

His name is Rudolf Serkin.

But what the hell was he doing in room 92?

19

THE LAST PERFORMANCE

After endless months of problems, changes, panic, nights without sleep, doubts about the results, one would have expected Vivien, who was fragile and in precarious health, to be on the brink of collapse. Not a bit. I was the one who was falling to pieces. More and more radiant each evening, she tap-danced merrily over my corpse.

We were supposed to preview *Tovarich* in New York on Thursday, Friday, and Saturday and open officially the following Monday with a gala premiere.

When I landed in New York I discovered that I had completely lost my voice. I was going to have to sing seven songs without the least idea of how to fake them. I rushed to a specialist who told me: "It's nothing serious. Just don't talk for about ten days."

I went to a second laryngologist, Dr. Kanev. He understood right away that my vocal cords were not at all damaged, but that I was physically and emotionally near collapse. If I skipped the Friday and Saturday performances, he said, I would be fit as a fiddle by Monday.

Friday evening was a nightmare for me. It was the first

time in my life that I had missed a show. I paced about my hotel room like a beast in a cage, immune to sedatives.

Saturday afternoon I couldn't stand it any longer and decided to slip into the theater and hide in the shadows. When the producer saw me, he became panic-stricken and tried by force to prevent me from entering. I escaped his clutches and rushed into the house, just as the lights had quite fortunately plunged it into darkness.

During the intermission I went to congratulate my understudy, a Russian with an equally superb beard and voice, Michael Kermoyan. When I tried to embrace Vivien she flew into a fury.

"How dare you make an appearance when you're dying!"

"I'm not dying. I've just lost my voice. I can't sing, but that doesn't prevent me from coming to the theater."

"Only a Frenchman could have the nerve . . . All amateurs . . ."

Sunday was a dark night.

Monday. The hour for me to go to the theater arrived. Crammed with pills, syrups, shots, drops, sprays, gargles, fears, and hopes, I was getting ready to leave my room when the telephone rang. It was Air France notifying me that Marisa was arriving with my two sons on flight 707 and that she wanted me to find her an apartment and a nursemaid immediately. I was overcome with joy at the prospect of seeing my wife and sons again, but this wasn't exactly the ideal moment to find a nursemaid and an apartment! I'd hardly had the time to recover from this when the telephone rang again. It was my brother, calling from Paris. He wished me good luck, adding:

"When you entrusted your daughter to me, you asked me to look after her virginity. That's getting more difficult every day. I'm sending her back to you."

"Fine. Send her over in a few weeks."

"A few weeks? What are you talking about, dear fellow? [I know, by experience, that when my brother refers to me as 'dear fellow' he's about to announce a catastrophe.] Tina will be in New York this very evening. I put her on a plane this morning."

"What flight?" I asked with a gasp.

"Air France 707."

So, by an unbelievable stroke of fate, every member of my little family was going to arrive on the same plane, at the precise moment when I would be making my entrance on stage. I called one of my best friends, Dr. Parente, and begged him to go to Idlewild instead of coming to see *Tovarich*. I wanted him to welcome my precious planeload, put them in two taxis, and keep them out of the theater until the end of the performance. It occurred to me that a doctor might also be useful to administer sedatives to my two fine ladies after their plane trip. They hadn't spoken one word to each other for months. Would Marisa ever believe it was pure chance that out of 365 days in the year and ten flights each day, they would both end up on the same plane? As a finishing touch, the stewardess had recognized both and, thinking that they would be pleased, had seated them right next to each other. The Atlantic Ocean and my two sons became the thunderstruck witnesses to a seven-hour silence.

With doubts and foreboding I hurried to the theater. Vivien received me coldly. I put on my make-up with trembling fingers and got dressed somehow or other. The din of a full house, curious, excited, and ready to applaud or devour surged through the curtain.

The lights lowered. The din became a murmur. The musicians took their places. Vivien joined me, becoming more and more glacial. She seemed in full possession of herself and faced this New York premiere with the same confidence with which she would have approached a thousandth performance in Dayton. Just as we were about to enter I pulled her close, saying, "Listen to me carefully. I don't know what I've done to offend you, but whatever it is, don't you think this is the right time to patch things up? We've been waiting a whole year for this very moment. We've worked so hard for it. Kiss me."

She kissed me. The orchestra went into the overture. The gods were with us. *Tovarich* was a hit.

It was a night for reconciliations. After a few moments' hesitation, Marisa and I were reunited in each other's arms. She had even smoothed things over with Tina. All of us agreed that when summer came, I would rent a farmhouse in upstate New York where we could all spend our vacation together. I would shuttle between the country and New York City to play every evening there.

In the meantime, *Tovarich* continued to roll merrily along. In spite of Vivien's contradictions and moodiness, I watched her each evening with delight. All she had to do was enter, move, come and go with that royal ease, or let her fingers flutter with that airy gracefulness of hers in order to conquer every heart. It really didn't matter whether she was in character or playing the situation. Her very presence created a special magic.

The audience fell prey to her snares, became fascinated, overwhelmed. This was more than talent, grace, or elegance. It was a kind of spell. One evening when my father heard me complaining about something that Vivien had done on stage that I disapproved of, this usually collected man leaped up and shouted at me, "How dare you? How dare you criticize Vivien?" For him, as for the rest of the public, Vivien could do no wrong.

Although I was as sensitive to her charms as anyone else, I couldn't help regretting that she never varied her interpretation. At the very first rehearsal she had decided once and for all how she was going to say a phrase, in what rhythm and with what gesture. The earth could have collapsed before she changed her resolution.

Strange actress . . . on the screen she was sublime in *Gone with the Wind*, staggering in *A Streetcar Named Desire* or *Ship of Fools;* but she was less exceptional on the stage. Lively and saucy when she was saying her own lines, she sometimes seemed lost when it became someone else's turn to express himself. She had to speak or walk for her magic to function. As soon as she finished a line or a passage she appeared to lose interest in the situation and would contemplate her partner with an impatience which soon became annoyance. That another actor could have something to say seemed like a crime of lese majesty.

Peculiar personal taboos made her detest certain stage business. When Tatiana and Mikhail (the two characters that we played) would leave their garret, Vivien couldn't stand having to pack our bags.

When she was constrained by the demands of the plot to be disguised in a maid's uniform, she accepted the flattering costume with its black sheath, short white apron, lace collar, and little bow for her hair. But she rebelled at the idea of having to touch a broom or move a chair. Words like "dust" or "clutter" didn't come easily to her lips. She didn't understand that the very fact of her really being a "lady" was what made her characterization of a chambermaid all the more interesting.

"Let's face it," said Dalio, "Vivien is a goddess, but she doesn't have our gypsy blood."

When we had passed the three hundredth performance, I began modifying my interpretation little by little. I would slow down or speed up my delivery to surprise her, as a way of combating the routine into which we were slowly but surely sliding. But Vivien refused to follow me.

Every evening after the show we sat in her dressing room, permanently decorated with a photo of Olivier, and discussed our different conceptions over a bottle of champagne.

In an attempt to convince her that I was right, I told her about my first years as an actor. In *La Machine Infernale* I had little by little modified Jouvet's direction (which was certainly more serious than modifying the tone of one line). Far from criticizing me for this, Jouvet had congratulated me.

Vivien remained stubborn and condemned Jouvet, too. "Ah! these Frenchmen . . . all the same, Jouvet, Chanel, De Gaulle, or you, all amateurs . . ." (I couldn't help noticing that she was actually wearing a Chanel suit, which looked divine on her, and was not at all a product of amateurism.)

As chance would have it, I happened upon an article written by Laurence Olivier for *Life Magazine*. In it he affirmed that the only way for an actor to conserve some spontaneity was to vary his interpretation every evening and find some new element in the show which would lend it a lifelike, fresh, unpremeditated quality and make the lines spring forth as if they had just been invented.

I placed Larry's article delicately on Vivien's make-up

table. She didn't breathe a word to me about it, but from that day on she stopped calling me an amateur.

When summer came, I rented an estate bordered by a river and a row of birch trees near the edge of a forest in Mamaroneck.

Marisa, Jean-Claude, Patrick, and Tina were there with me. Tina had fallen in love with Philippe Le Tellier, a correspondent for *Paris-Match* whom I liked from the very first. One evening they announced their engagement to me. Tina was only seventeen and a half at the time. I tried to persuade her to wait a few more months before marrying, but she insisted. I gave in.

Vivien had recovered her health and her good humor and came to see us almost every day. It is there, more than anywhere else, that I still see her in my heart! Buoyant, gay, and relaxed.

She would often bring us some Chinese dish that she had concocted herself and we would picnic together on the grass.

One day she showed me a letter that she had received from a London journalist asking her to write a eulogy for Noel Coward. I jumped up. "Is Noel dead?"

"Don't be silly, Noel will never die."

"I don't understand."

"It's to complete his obituary file, that's all. I'm really flattered that I was asked to write an article on Noel. That won't make him die. Larry wrote one on Churchill fifteen years ago. It's perfectly normal."

"And what will happen," I asked, stupefied, "if between today and Noel's death, which I hope will be far away, your sentiments change?"

"I'll telephone the paper and tell them to change my copy."

"It's monstrous."

"I'd be very happy, said Vivien, musing, "if my friends wrote now what will be published after I die . . ."

Autumn spread through Mamaroneck forest, and our hearts. In September we switched theaters. The sparkling and joyous Vivien who danced like an elf on stage or among my birch trees, the Vivien who seemed so lively—the summer Vivien—soon gave way to an anguished, exhausted Vivien.

Her understudy had to play her part, not Taina Elg any more but Joan Copeland, the sister of Arthur Miller. In any case, Vivien was never very fond of the young women who stood in for her, whoever they might be. She began missing more and more performances.

By the four hundredth, her role, with its seven songs, taxing Charleston, and many costume changes, had exhausted her. And then those sleepless nights. It was decided that the show would close for a week in November and that Vivien would go to London during this time to receive the treatment she was supposed to get at least once a year. Johnny Parente, my friend, had this to say: "Vivien is going to become unbearable to justify in her own eyes the need for getting cured." I shrugged my shoulders, hoping that he was wrong.

Meanwhile, Tina had returned to Paris, escorted by Philippe Le Tellier. Learning that I was going to be free for a week at the beginning of November, she decided to get married at that time so that I could be at the ceremony. I sent her a telegram: "Will be there. Very happy for Philippe and you." Just as quickly, I received an answer. (This doesn't happen every day in Tina's case): "Papa, you've become senile. It's not Philippe I'm marrying, it's Christian."

I had not the slightest idea which Christian she was talking about.

We were supposed to finish this first series of performances on a Saturday night. On Friday, Vivien, whose nervousness had become increasingly serious, decided to invite us all to her place after the show. I projected a little 16-millimeter film which I had taken of *Tovarich* and of our happy vacations in Mamaroneck. There were some close-ups of her that she didn't appreciate and she became abusive.

The truth, I think, is that there were also a lot of shots of my sons in the Mamaroneck episodes. Normally, she would have enjoyed seeing them, for she liked Jean-Claude and Patrick a lot; but in the state she was in, the sight of my two boys reopened an old wound. She had desperately wanted to have children with Laurence Olivier and had been refused this happiness. Then Larry had a son and a daughter from his new wife, Joan Plowright. Who can understand what takes place in the heart of a woman who is suffering and who has lost control of her nerves? Despite all our efforts the evening ended in disaster. Vivien kept drinking and continued to fling insults at us. She talked, smoked, danced, took pills, drank more, hurled herself against the walls like a poor, maddened bird.

The next day we were playing a matinee. I walked into Vivien's dressing room to find her in tears, a photo of two children in her hands. She held it out to me, murmuring, "My grandsons." The dresser, the stage manager, and I looked at her with astonishment. We had never heard anything about her having any grandsons. She had put a tape-recorder on her table. She was listening to the waltz from *Gone with the Wind* . . .

The performance began. Vivien was pale and trembling. From the very first scene I had the feeling that she should not be performing. She sang her first song three times as quickly as she usually did. Stanley Lebowsky desperately tried to follow her. The musicians stood up, trying to understand what was happening on stage. Then came the moment for our first duet. I was supposed to appear cocky while singing: "You love me, you love me. If there's one thing you can't resist, it's me . . ." Throughout the number she was supposed to look at me in rapture. But that day she turned her back to me, opened her pocketbook, and began to read her personal mail. I was torn between a desire to strangle her and a feeling of infinite pity. All during my song, I kept telling myself, "Just one more performance after this, just one more. She'll go to London, they'll take care of her; when she gets back she'll be herself again: tender, and warm, and generous . . ."

Intermission found us in our dressing rooms like boxers between rounds of a match.

The second act began without either of us speaking one word to the other. Then came the jealousy scene in which she was supposed to admit having been raped by her jailer. At that moment, her old repulsion for these lines (that she'd expressed since the first rehearsals) rose up from the depths of her subconscious. She began to claw me, slap me in the face, and kick me in the balls. Since it was a quarrel scene I tried to make the audience believe that this boxing exhibition had been planned. It was a bit excessive for a domestic quarrel, but at least the little old ladies who filled the theater on Saturday afternoon might not find the outburst entirely out of keeping.

Unfortunately, Vivien stopped suddenly and, wrapping herself in total silence, looked at me, then through me at the entire world, with hatred. I began to improvise in an attempt to lead her back on the right track: "Speak to me, Tatiana . . . Tell me what's in your heart . . . Don't look at me like that . . . What happened?"

The explosive silence continued.

I went on: "I understand what happened in that prison. I forgive you for it. But what did you do next? . . . Speak . . . Answer me . . ."

Then Vivien came to the edge of the stage. She looked out at the whole auditorium and spoke carefully, enunciating each syllable: "An actress has to think before answering," and she walked off.

The manager dropped the curtain, called desperately for two other actors, and had them do a number that they had already performed in the first act.

The show ended with a waltz danced by the whole company. Vivien appeared again, so beautiful in the court costume that Tatiana exchanges for her apron. I tried to lead her in the waltz. She wouldn't budge. There we stood, immobile in the center of the stage. The curtain fell as rapidly as possible. Vivien received her usual ovation. The little old ladies seemed to appreciate the unprecedented abuses they had just witnessed.

Three hours later, when I returned to my dressing room for the evening performance, I discovered that all the photos of my wife and children which I had attached to the wall had been torn off and ripped to pieces . . . There were two doctors in Vivien's dressing room trying as best they could to give her a shot of morphine. The stage manager had told her that she was in no state to perform, but she had come back to the theater just the same.

She asked me to let Michael Kermoyan play my part.

"O.K.," I answered, "if you let Joan Copeland play yours."

The mere mention of Joan sent Vivien stalking back to her dressing room to get ready for the show.

The curtain rose. Tatiana was not in the first scene. I performed in a state of near-panic, wondering whether Vivien or Joan would appear in the next few seconds. It was Joan. During the whole show we couldn't concentrate on anything but Vivien's screams. She was struggling like a wounded animal against the stagehands, who were trying to keep her from making her entrance. Obviously the morphine was not having any effect on her.

Many years before, Sarah Bernhardt had collapsed in her dressing room while putting on her make-up for the dress rehearsal of *Un Sujet de Roman*. When she came to, her first words were: "When do I go on?" But she never went on again. Bedridden in her home, she kept her script by her pillow and reread it each evening, saying her lines at the exact moment the actress who had replaced her was saying them on the stage.

That is what Vivien did. All during the evening, imprisoned in her dressing room, she went through the costume changes and said every line with her dresser and her two doctors as her only audience.

Sarah Bernhardt was old. She had fulfilled her destiny. But Vivien still had so much to offer . . .

Vivien Leigh died three years later, apparently of tuberculosis. But I know that, like so many others who are too beautiful, too gifted, too fortunate, she died of disenchantment. She died of despair for a love that was gone . . . for children that she couldn't have. She died of sadness.

20

THE KENNEDYS

The day after that tragic evening, while Vivien, finally subdued by morphine, was taken unconscious in an airplane to London, I flew to Paris. At Orly Airport, Tina was waiting for me with Christian. I had discovered that my daughter's new fiancé was Christian Marquand, the tempestuous movie star whom I had known for years.

By way of formal request for Tina's hand, he had sent me a telegram: "Hate this kind of ceremonies, but if it makes everybody happy, o.k. for beginning November. Bring me three tee-shirts."

No, it didn't make everybody happy. My family was apprehensive about the kind of life Christian had always led, dividing his nights between his cronies and his many amorous conquests. But with that optimism which has always been my Tunic of Nessus, I replied that Christian was twice the age of Tina and had already sown his wild oats. That bourgeois side of myself that I detest, but cannot deny, preferred to see Tina become Christian's wife rather than one of his mistresses.

So I arrived in Paris, armed with three tee-shirts. Although the drama with Vivien had left me a bit shaken, the presence of

Christian at Orly struck me as both comic and preposterous. My companion on so many nocturnal expeditions was clinging to my daughter's arm with a dignified and deferential expression.

That night I wandered in the streets of Paris. I wanted to embrace the trees. The trees! Suddenly I realized that they were what I missed most of all. Churches, too. Saint-Etienne-du-Mont, Saint-Germain-l'Auxerrois . . . I was awed by their proportions, their age, their scars. For hours I strolled aimlessly. In my delight, I became a tourist all over again. The boutiques, the passers-by, the posters . . . everything seemed friendly to me . . . everything seemed my accomplice.

Paris was like Marisa. I was too used to them. I had to be away for a while to realize how much I needed them.

Tina's wedding was supposed to take place at Banon in Provence. She flew to Nice, and Christian, Roger Vadim, and I started out for the Côte d'Azur in a car. This trip with his best friend and future father-in-law was Christian's way of saying goodbye to his wild youth.

We made a small detour, of course, to Saint-Tropez, to get the blessing of Brigitte Bardot, recently divorced from Vadim. Then we headed for Banon. I tried to persuade Christian to buy two wedding rings, but he looked at me in horror. Clearly, this kind of purchase wasn't part of his personal mythology.

Banon is one of those ancient villages in Provence, austere and welcoming at the same time. We arrived hours late.

All our friends were there. A small plane dropped orchids on the procession. The schoolchildren clambered over the mayor's platform. The girls who worked in the post office left their windows to ask for autographs.

At the moment of the fateful "I do," to tease Tina, Christian feigned hesitation. Vadim and I pretended to push him into it: "Come on now, just one bad moment and it'll all be over. Courage . . ."

The reception took place in the courtyard of an inn. During dessert I got up to make a toast. Striving to appear both dignified and succinct, I declared, "Since I am forbidden, for reasons which escape me, to marry my daughter, I am happy, Christian, that you are the one to do it."

Nobody was listening; everybody applauded.

Around five o'clock we decided to leave the newlyweds alone with each other. Christian seemed surprised that neither I nor any of his friends were staying for the wedding night. Even Tina seemed to find it curious that I was abandoning her so soon.

I had a real need to be alone. The marriage of my daughter, preceded by Vivien's nervous collapse two days before, had left wounds. They needed some time to heal.

The next day I flew back to New York to take up my role in *Tovarich* again. As soon as I arrived, I was advised that Vivien had been treated with electric shock, had stood the ordeal well, but would not be able to perform for several weeks.

In the meantime we had changed theaters. I would be acting with Joan Copeland at the Winter Garden.

As time went on it became clear that Vivien would not be returning soon, so our producer began looking for a big star capable of replacing her. After having tried to obtain Marlene Dietrich in vain, he cast Eva Gabor. I knew the Gabor sisters well, since I had already filmed *Lili* with Zsa Zsa. Eva proved to be charming, both on and off stage. Though she didn't have Vivien's royal bearing, she compensated for this by her good humor and her communicative warmth. The play wavered a little. Instead of the story of a grand duchess who is transformed into a maid, it became the story of a lovely young thing who disguises herself as a grand duchess.

The day Eva started in the part, I had stage fright. I knew from experience that in these cases it's the veteran of the production who makes the flubs, and not the newcomer. Furthermore Eva expressed herself in a spontaneous and chirping hungaro-twitter which I didn't always understand. In short, for her debut that Saturday, I decided to take two pills as soon as I woke up so that I'd feel in better shape for what was to come. A little while later, I realized that I had made a mistake. Instead of swallowing two stimulants, I'd downed two sleeping pills. Frantically, I called my faithful Dr. Parente, who told me: "Bah! Don't worry. Sleep all day and tonight you'll feel fine." I hung up and went back to bed. At two o'clock the stage manager called me: "What's happened to you? Have you forgotten that we're doing a matinee?"

I plunged into a taxi. Parente came to my dressing room and gave me a stimulant. Between each scene, I drank coffee. Eva warbled. Everything went well.

One day during the New York run of *Tovarich*, I received a telephone call from Porfirio Rubirosa inviting me to a party at the home of a certain Mrs. Smith. "Put on your dinner jacket and meet us after the show." Because I had a matinee the next day and hated putting on dinner jackets, I declined the invitation.

"You'll be sorry," said my friend.

His tone intrigued me. I went to the party.

Park Avenue. Midnight. At the entrance to the building I can see a dozen strapping fellows who look as if they are waiting for something. I don't pay them any attention. The mistress of the house meets me at the door and leads me into the living room. In the center is a man talking with his back to me. Mrs. Smith interrupts him: "Jack, this is Jean-Pierre. Jean-Pierre, this is Jack." And I find myself face to face with the President of the United States.

Mrs. Smith was one of his sisters. The two men with whom the President was talking were his two brothers, Bob and Ted. It was the fifteenth of November, a Friday, a week before he was to be assassinated.

The President invited me to sit and chat with him and Bob. Bob was then Attorney General. Some interior fire consumed him, some concentrated mission. One moment he would seem austere, and then a dreamy expression would pass over him. A surprising mixture of vigor and timidity.

As for the President, he had all the gifts. He was warm, friendly, and witty. I was fascinated by Bob, but I was under the spell of the President.

Nine years afterwards I got to know the other Kennedys.

One summer, while I was playing *South Pacific* at Hyannis Port, I was awakened early by a telephone call.

"This is Ethel Kennedy. Hi, Jean-Pierre? [We'd never met.] Ted wants to know if you'd like to come sailing with us."

Ted holds out a large and powerful hand to me: "Come on, Jean-Pierre, I'll show you my new boat."

How kind they all are, in the purest sense of the word, how hospitable, open, spontaneous. Bob Kennedy's eleven children have a moving resemblance to him. I can't keep from remarking on this to Ethel, who answers with a radiant smile, "Yes, it's great, isn't it?"

Her place and those of her brothers and sisters-in-law are grouped on a peninsula among other properties. They are comfortable without being ostentatious. The house where John and Jackie used to live is not even on the waterfront. The garden is small. One has the feeling that the President bought it only to be near his parents.

How this clan touches me, with all its children running barefoot from one house to another . . .

Ted Kennedy has returned last night from the Democratic Convention in Miami. I watch him, strong, sure of himself, as he maneuvers his boat and gives orders to the crew, composed of his children, nephews, and nieces. When we talk about politics he is less direct. He doesn't have the President's glowing grace. Nor has he that secret, burning, and ascetic trait which distinguished his brother Bob. His charm is more down-to-earth.

Ted Kennedy has brought Pierre Salinger with him from Miami. Both of them recount inside anecdotes about the convention. The choice of the Vice Presidential nominee reminds me of the way an actor is cast for a part. "Oh, no, not X," cries one person, "I can't stand him." "Oh, no, not Y," roars another, "he stutters." "Oh, no, not Z, his wife is such a bitch," etc. Finally, everyone settles on some person who wins the support of the weary delegates simply for lack of any glaring flaws.

Our sailboat skims merrily along. Because of the wind we are obliged to shout. I ask Salinger if he thinks that Chaban-Delmas has any chance of becoming the next French President.

"Definitely not, he's just been involved in a scandal," Salinger shouts back. "Scandals in politics, you just don't recover from them."

Ted Kennedy tends to the trimming of the sails.

The weather is gray, so is the ocean. The children begin struggling with the rigging while the adults relax, bloody marys in hand. I feel a part of this family which I admire.

Certainly I'm not the only one who admires them. Alas, fortune, power, and beauty also engenders resentment. Pierre Salinger, arriving at night the preceding week, had become lost. He asked a man sitting on his doorstep not more than one hundred yards from the Kennedy property, "Excuse me, sir, would you tell me where Mrs. Robert Kennedy's house is?"

"Kennedy? Never heard of them," said the man.

Jackie didn't come sailing with us. She stayed to keep her ex-mother-in-law company. I watch the two of them: The old, indomitable matron, like some ship's figurehead corroded by salt. The deaths of three sons have not vanquished her. Shriveled but erect, she continues to watch over her dynasty with a defiant smile.

And Jackie, so fragile, so vulnerable under her mask of confidence and strength, which is the natural armor of all the Kennedys.

When one of the children seizes a stick and points it at her, playfully imitating the noise of a tommy-gun, she begins to tremble. Her expression becomes haggard, pathetic . . . No, whatever the pageantry of her life, the islands, the yachts and diamonds, I don't believe that Jackie will ever succeed in escaping a certain day in Dallas . . .

John-John, who is remembered playing on all fours in the President's office, and who stirred the world at the age of three, erect and proud at the funeral of his father, as he gave the military salute on the steps of the White House, no longer wishes to be known as John-John. This boy who, since he was born, hasn't been able to take a step without being photographed, pursued, applauded, jostled, closely surveyed by the Secret Service, could not have escaped his childhood without some trauma. Now, proud and secretive, he hides his bruises and goes out to rejoin the other boys with the apparent toughness of a young rooster.

21

SHARPS AND FLATS

Ever since the close of *Tovarich* my agents hadn't stopped talking about my doing a nightclub act.

My first reaction was to fly into a fit. "Are you completely crazy? It's a totally different profession and I don't know anything about it. In *Tovarich* I had co-stars, I was playing a character. In a nightclub, you're out there alone . . ."

My agents protested that it was a lot easier to sing in a place of intimate dimensions than in huge theaters. They also promised me a portable microphone which would allow me to whisper, and the luxury of choosing my songs.

"But when it comes down to it, I'll be the victim of those drunks who holler insults, and I won't know how to respond."

"First of all, there won't be any drunks in the kind of establishments we're sending you to . . ."

"Can you imagine my face if somebody shouts something like 'down with De Gaulle'?"

"Just answer, 'He says the nicest things about *you!*' "

I ended up letting them convince me, but I demanded two or three months to prepare myself and after that a year's tour in small, remote towns, before attacking New York or Chicago.

Then Easter vacation arrived. I went to spend it in Capri with Marisa and my two sons. When I came back to New York, tanned and relaxed, my agents nonchalantly told me, "You open in three weeks in Chicago."

I roared: "I told you that I wanted to spend a year in small towns!"

"Chicago isn't that big."

We began working. There were twenty songs: ten were French hits by Becaud, Aznavour, and Trenet. The others were American tunes for which my musical director, Stan Freeman, was writing special material for me.

The time of my debut was getting nearer, and I was getting nervous. Finally I went back to my agents. "I will not open in Chicago without trying out somewhere else first."

Enter a man who owns a nightclub in Dayton. My agents introduced me to him. This fellow, whom I shall call Bill, complimented me on my tan for hours. He had never seen such an even, healthy-looking tan in his whole life. I was hired to sing in his club for the week preceding my debut in Chicago. I had only two weeks to rehearse.

The day before I left for Dayton, I begged my agents to let me sing in any dive, that same evening, without being paid, and under a false name, so that I could polish my routine.

They finally hunted up a club in farthest Brooklyn where several octogenarians were gathering to celebrate the birthday of one of their cronies. I was supposed to be a guest. At the end of the bash I would get up and begin to sing, as if someone had begged me to. Everything went as planned, except that these nice elderly people recognized me. I explained that one of my great-aunts had been a member of their association and that therefore, in her memory, I felt I should join them. Around ten o'clock, when they seemed to be at the point of falling asleep, I pushed Stan Freeman, my musical director (I ought to say, my director of conscience) toward the piano.

My first song was a mongrel version of "Never on Sunday." Stan had whipped me up some verses which proved to be risqué enough to wake up my audience. I took it from there. Never in my life have I been as bad; but, the more I sang off key, the more these old folks demonstrated their enthusiasm. I heard a woman cry, "He's simply scrumptious! I could eat him up!"

The evening ended in embraces and promises to return.

Dayton. Mr. Bill was waiting for me at the airport. He looked at me with undisguised disappointment and, before he had even said hello, asked, "Where's your tan?"

"What tan?"

"When I hired you, three weeks ago, in your agent's office, you had a tan."

"Obviously. I'd just arrived from Capri."

"Where is it?"

He talked about my tan as if it were a musical instrument I'd forgotten, something indispensable to my singing tour.

I explained that a tan fades away in three weeks, and I had been too busy working on my songs to think about the color of my cheeks. Things were starting out badly.

Afternoon rehearsal in his club. I listen to the orchestra and content myself with quietly humming my songs in order to save my vocal cords for the evening. Obnoxious Bill thinks I am giving my maximum. He takes Stan into a corner and says to him: "This is a catastrophe. I've never heard a singer than can be heard less . . ."

Stan shrugs his shoulders. "What can I say? In Brooklyn they wanted to eat him up . . ."

That evening the place was half-empty. Contrary to what one might believe, there is an enormous difference between half-empty and half-full. And this place was definitely half-empty. Obnoxious Bill didn't even notice that I was singing louder than I had in rehearsal. He was too busy counting the number of unoccupied tables. Somehow or other everything came off. To say that I was a great hit would be going too far, but I was cordially received.

The following afternoon Stan and I decided to make some changes in the program in view of our opening in Chicago. After all, this week in Dayton had no other purpose than to polish up our act. We cut several songs and added others. Obnoxious Bill stuck his nose into the hall when we were rehearsing, and, after verifying that my tan had not returned, called my agents: "There's no way I can pay Mr. Aumont's fee. First of all, he has no talent. All you have to do is read the papers tomorrow morning to see that! Secondly, he is as pale as a dead fish, which means he had to put on make-up to look decent under my spots, which are the best in Ohio. Last of all, he's using my hall for rehearsals to improve his nightclub act, which is evident proof that he's not up to the mark."

My agent answered that the tan was not part of our deal, that Arthur Rubinstein rehearsed five hours every day, and that no one had ever reproached him for not being up to the mark. As for the newspapers, we would just have to wait.

Well, to my great surprise and the confusion of obnoxious Bill, the papers were enthusiastic. One review opened with: "Thank you, Mr. Aumont, and come back to see us as often as possible." The other with: "There isn't any doubt that America has henceforth gained a song stylist in the grand tradition."

Obnoxious Bill was forced to honor our contract.

The following Monday, Chicago. The Camelia Room of the Hotel Drake, which is the most difficult, elegant, and sophisticated nightclub in America. Twenty-five musicians in the orchestra. No excuses this time. Here comes the moment of truth.

I slip into my dinner jacket, say my prayers, go down to the club, and grab hold of Stan. "Play the melody," I cry to him, "*just* the melody, and pound it out!"

Poor Stan! It's not amusing for a musician of his class to be condemned to play the melody with both hands! He throws me his wounded spaniel look and goes back to the pit, sighing. The orchestra goes into "Elle roule, roule, roule . . ." which serves as my introduction. I wait in the corridor, behind the door. Two waiters are supposed to open it at the end of the introduction to reveal me entering under a spotlight.

I try to calm my fears. "Who do you think you are? Whether you sing on key or off, it's not the end of the world.

Think of the war and of your friends who lost their lives in it. Really, whether you're good or bad isn't of cosmic significance."

I can hear the master of ceremonies announcing: "The Camelia Room is proud to present . . ."

There it is . . . I knock on wood, take out my wallet and kiss the photos of my children, breathe deeply . . . The doors open. With all my teeth exposed I bounce forward. At this precise moment, an old man who is passing through the corridor takes hold of my arm: "Pardon me, sir, Where is the men's room?"

Midnight. It's a hit. One of those hits based on imponderable factors that only arrive once in a lifetime.

The next morning's papers are full of me, as if Vietnam, unemployment, and crime have lost all importance. "Magnificent . . . terrific . . . sex appeal personified." If my name and photograph hadn't been there to accompany these comments I could never have believed that they were about me.

I learned a lot during these three weeks at the Camelia Room. I learned to look each person in the audience in the eye, to make a friend or an accomplice of everyone. This was the most difficult part for me. When you've been used to looking only at your partner and ignoring the audience for years on stage, it's not easy to do the opposite. I learned to flirt with the women without inviting the resentment of their escorts. I learned to improvise, to tell jokes. It's a lot easier in a strange language. All you need is a slight French accent and they'll forgive you everything. All your faults get chalked up to ignorance of the language. Platitudes, spiced by a French accent and French gestures will pass for a kind of rakish charm. I learned to change the order of my songs, according to the mood of the evening. I learned to shake hands, to hobnob with the crowd. I learned, in a word, to become a huckster.

My next engagement was in Cleveland. This was not as bad as Dayton, but not nearly as good as Chicago. It seemed I was more popular in Illinois than in Ohio.

The local paper came out with an article that pleased me immensely, though it was not particularly flattering: "It's a great pleasure to listen to Mr. Aumont . . . although you can't really figure out why!" And it ended with: "He doesn't have a lot to offer, but he knows how to offer it better than anyone else."

The next evening, after my third song, a fat lady climbed onto her chair, blew me a kiss, and cried: "Baby, what you haven't got, you don't need!"

I blew her a kiss back.

Other cities followed . . . Sometimes everything went splendidly. Sometimes it was awful. A hit in Denver. A flop in Windsor. A hit in New Orleans. A flop in Caracas . . .

In the cities where they liked me, I felt like the prince of showbiz. Neither Chevalier nor Sinatra could hold a candle to me. After all, it was me, me alone, whom they were applauding. I didn't have to share the limelight with my fellow actors, the director, or the author, as you have to do in the theater.

In the cities where they didn't like me, I was on the edge of suicide. After all, it was me, me alone, who was the failure. I couldn't throw the blame on my fellow actors, the director, or the author . . . as one does in the theater.

I couldn't even have a drink with other members of the company to console myself. There was no company, except for my faithful Stan, who was getting sick of beating out the melody. He began allowing himself a few flourishes, which I listened to with a haggard eye.

Finally, after these peregrinations, I came back to Chicago, where Marisa was waiting for me. The manager of the Hotel Drake had said to her, "I'm hiring Jean-Pierre again. But for this second engagement I want you, too." She had begun working without too much effort. Italians receive the gift of song from heaven at an age when the rest of us are learning how to walk. With great pleasure I found myself once again in the Camelia Room and with even greater pleasure I found Marisa at my side.

In a warm and easy voice she sang two songs in Italian, two in English, and some duets with me: "I Remember It Well," "Let's Do It," "I Wish You Love" As an ending to our act, I had written a sketch in which Marisa was "Lili." I was both the magician that I had played in the film and the puppeteer that Mel Ferrer had played.

At the end of the sketch we would leave the stage while the orchestra struck up, "Hi, Lili," in muted tones and with lights slowly lowering: "A song of love is a sad song, Hi, Lili, Hi, Lili, Hi lo . . ."

It was romantic, a bit sad, in mezzotints . . .

After Chicago, the Persian Room in New York booked us. The supreme tribute!

"Watch out," cried our friends in chorus, "you can't possibly end with 'Hi, Lili.' It's too depressing. No one has ever—EVER—ended an act on that kind of note. You need something brilliant, spectacular. You can't flout all the rules of show business."

New York. The following day. The house is superb, full to bursting. In the first row are Maurice Chevalier and our two sons. During the whole show, Patrick, who is five, sleeps like a log.

As I pass in front of his table during one of my songs I pinch him gently to wake him up. He takes a pair of dark glasses out of his pocket and resumes his forty winks.

Maurice Chevalier came to our dressing room. He congratulated us: "You showed a truly human . . . humanity." Then he added: "The Persian Room! You're at the top! The only way you can go now is down."

The next day the papers sang our praises. "Marisa Pavan is adorable. She has a captivating voice, especially for ballads. She and Jean-Pierre finished with an evocation of 'Lili.' This was a dramatic and moving sequence which won the audience's bravos."

We were right to be stubborn.

For two years we made all the television shows. Then the Bermudas, Detroit, Miami, Los Angeles, Boston, etc., and Mexico City. Everywhere it went beautifully. Except for Mexico City, which was a veritable torture.

We were supposed to appear in the most elegant club in town. To our amazement, it turned out to be the oldest and dirtiest place imaginable. In order to get on stage in our dinner jacket and evening gown we had to hop over garbage cans and slide over banana peels. The rats found us enticing. Our orchestra was a hodgepodge of gauchos rattling ancient guitars which probably had been used as zip guns by Juarez. The piano wasn't tuned. The drummer was dead drunk. The violinist didn't know how to read music. The audience talked at the top of their lungs. First they greeted each other with loud *abrazos*. Then they shouted their comments on the show from one table to the other.

"Where'd she get her dress?"

"Dior."

"She really should have worn a Courrèges."

"And him, how old is he?"

"I thought he'd died a long time ago."

The contrast between our precious Persian and Camelia Rooms and this exotic dive was a bit rude. By the second evening we had cut all the ballads and other romantic numbers and had kept only the songs with punch which we could bawl louder than they could talk. Nevertheless, the papers liked us: "Despite the irresistible need of the audience to discuss the virtues of the singers in a loud voice, the Aumonts received an enthusiastic welcome." It was true. The bravos at the end of the show made almost as much noise as the comments during it.

My experiences with bel canto didn't stop there. For some mysterious reason—though I protest—Americans continue to think of me as a singer. Ah, the miracle of a French accent!

Thus, I performed four other musical comedies: *South Pacific, Carnival, Jacques Brel Is Alive and Well and Living in Paris*, and *Gigi*.

Gigi and *Carnival*, which I sang with Marisa, weren't too much of a problem. The other shows were another story.

South Pacific is a classic. Its score is more like an opera than a musical comedy. The principal number, "Some Enchanted Evening," was recorded by its creator, Ezio Pinza, and has sold millions of copies.

I begged the orchestra conductor to lead into the song before I started singing so that I could pick up the melody.

"Don't worry," I told him, "I'll catch up to you."

But he wouldn't listen. He insisted that I begin and he would follow. Finally I resorted to starting off this great and gallant aria by talking it, trying to look nonchalant. Then I would slide into a cooing baritone as soon as I felt sure of myself.

My friend Louis Jourdan and his wife Quique saw my debut in Los Angeles in an immense, open-air theater. When the orchestra began the introduction to "Some Enchanted Evening," Quique discovered that her husband had disappeared. Finally, she found him hiding under his seat.

"I just can't watch," he said to her, sighing. "I know Jean-Pierre's limits. He'll never be able to sing that song. People are going to throw tomatoes at him."

"They're out of season," answered Quique, imperturbably.

I made it to the end of my song. No one threw tomatoes at me. Louis Jourdan couldn't get over it. Neither could I.

Jacques Brel promised other horrors. Even in *South Pacific* I had been playing a character. Before attempting my high "g" I had the chance to save myself with a dialogue. I could try to woo the audience, to please them, to sell my wares, as it were, so that the limits of my voice would be overlooked. But in *Jacques Brel* there was not the least text.

There were five of us who took turns singing songs which were not in any way linked to each other. The songs had been adapted by Mort Schuman and each of them had become a poem in English, new, yet faithful to the original French text.

The four other singers, two boys and two girls, were young, good looking, marvelous dancers, and angelic singers. The star of the show, unfortunately, was me—less young and less good looking, with very little notion of dancing and singing.

In order to save myself, I tried to put into practice something Nureyev had once told me. He claims that "presence" is not only a gift from heaven; it's a question of effort, will, and concentration. "I can attract the attention of an audience even if

I am standing still at the back of the stage, simply because I want to attract it."

Eva Gabor and I continued to perform *Tovarich* over the years at different places.

One day, when we found ourselves in Washington, Mrs. Johnson invited us to the White House for tea.

After about five minutes Eva asked, "But vhere is the President?"

"I don't think he'll be able to come," answered Ladybird. "He's up to his neck in work . . ."

"But I came here to see him," said Eva with perfect logic.

"Right now he's at a Cabinet meeting . . ."

Two cups of tea later, Eva again demanded the President in that Hungarian accent you can cut with a knife. We began to get a little embarrassed.

Ladybird called her husband, who answered that he was busy.

"Vietnam . . . you know," explained Ladybird, politely.

It was obvious that Eva had forgotten about Vietnam.

"He'll come as soon as he can," said Ladybird, soothingly.

"But ve're playink this evenink. Ve can't vait . . ." replied Eva with a completely European impatience.

Finally the President arrived. We rose. Eva walked toward him and exclaimed: "Darlink, you are exactly like me."

General consternation. No one knew where to hide. Then Johnson asked that ravishing eccentric what she was talking about.

"You're so much better lookink in person than on television" (an embarrassed smile from the President). "Darlink, promise me somethink. Promise me never again to appear on television."

The President beat a hasty retreat, no doubt estimating that it was easier to deal with the Vietnamese than with the Hungarians.

It was during the performance of *Carnival* that Marisa and I suddenly realized that we had totally forgotten to get married

again. Our divorce had become official during our second honeymoon, and the court had informed us of it, but we hadn't attached the least importance to that scrap of paper.

Thus, for several years, we had been living in sin! We
decided to remedy it immediately.

Our wedding took place on the shores of the Pacific, at San
Clemente, where the judge, a Baptist minister, asked us if we
wished to become part of his flock. We answered that it had
always been our most fervent desire. He took up his Bible,
asked us for a donation, and began to read the first verse,
"Wine, thou shalt not drink." My fervor cooled.

A number of our friends regarded our remarrying as something extraordinary. In my eyes it was totally natural. Since
marriages are not eternal, why should divorces be so? I think,
on the contrary, that marrying the same woman twice shows
consistency in one's ideas. In any case, it's proof of how much
you love her . . . Couples who only get married once don't
inspire confidence in me. I can't believe they're very passionate . . .

22

Snow in The Spring

When Sidney Pollack offered me a part in *Castle Keep* I accepted with pleasure.

The action of the script took place in 1944, during the last offensive of the Germans. Burt Lancaster was to play an American colonel and I was to play the owner of a chateau in the Ardennes. For the role of the lieutenant, the head of the studio wanted some one who looked exactly like Robert Redford.

"Why not Robert Redford?" suggested Sidney Pollack.

"You're crazy," answered the head of the studio. "He's absolutely wrong for the part."

The same implacable logic influenced the choice of the location. The executives decided that Yugoslavia was much more typical of the Ardennes than the Ardennes itself.

Since we needed the banks of the Meuse, only the Danube would do.

Thus, we found ourselves on the banks of a Danube which had forgotten about being blue since the days of Strauss. It is, instead, a rather foul-looking brown. A medieval chateau made out of plywood meant to simulate stone was constructed on the shore. It was supposed to be destroyed during the course of a fire. All of this, plus the rental of a Yugoslavian army, the transport of our 100-person company from Hollywood to Novi Sad, a backward village of Inner Serbia, cost a pretty penny. We were to stay on location for six weeks. Six months later we were still there.

The majority of the scenes in the film had to be shot during snowfall. Since it was the end of February, snow was getting scare. Then it stopped falling altogether, and we accordingly stopped working. March passed slowly, without our exposing a single frame of film. Then, without any warning, and to the great surprise of everyone concerned, April followed March, and May, April. The shrewd Yugoslavs tried to convince the Americans, who were making plans to leave for less clement skies—Mount Blanc, for example—that the snow was due any minute. It was simply a matter of being patient—spring in their country was the ideal season for representing winter. Soon spring burgeoned, young buds appeared, then flowers. A three-year-old child would have understood that we weren't going to see a snowflake until the following winter.

The studio made a heroic decision. Snow was brought over from Hollywood. One fine morning, under a radiant sun, three helicopters appeared and began dropping tons of white stuff on the astonished Balkans. The air was full of plaster, powdered marble, and flour, while fire hoses showered us with soapy water. We ordered two thousand soldiers from the Yugoslavian army. The flour descended gracefully. The sun shone doggedly, transforming it into biscuits.

By then Burt Lancaster, weary of waiting, had flown off for New York. Most of the other actors were equally scattered, in Rome, London, or Athens.

I had gone to Paris. It was the agitated Paris of May '68. I soon received an urgent telegram telling me to abandon the barricades of Boulevard Saint-Germain and come as quickly as possible to receive my portion of snow.

I was playing the lord of the chateau, who was obliged to lodge American troops in his home. Burt Lancaster played the one-eyed colonel who was smitten by my wife, acted—if I may dare to exaggerate—by Astrid Heeren.

My part required an excellent equestrian. I was placed in

the expert hands of a professional rider who spoke only a dialect of Serbo-Croatian. I didn't understand a word of his instructions, which would have been useful in figuring out how to make my horse change from a trot to a gallop. As this was a matter of a delicate maneuver, another teacher of horsemanship was imported from Hollywood. The results of our collaboration were not convincing, so a third specialist was hired, a Frenchman named François Nadel, who made me confident enough to gallop several successful yards.

On a certain Friday the burning of the castle, which was the chief attraction of the film, was supposed to take place. Unfortunately, the night before, my manor burned down accidentally. I was awakened by shouts and the smell of smoke. By the time I got there nothing remained but a hole.

I was used to ruins. All during the war, from Bizerte to Pontecorvo, I had seen many cities and villages bombarded. But of every house, every church, every burned building, something always remained: a section of a wall, a staircase, a part of the floor, some bricks. Here there was nothing. Emptiness. Constructed out of wood, the chateau had been totally consumed.

So we stopped filming again. It would be necessary to build a new chateau in order to burn it down again. And millions of dollars continued to flow down the drain.

Up to that point my relations with Burt Lancaster had been courteous but distant. Of course, as co-producer of the film, he had a right to be preoccupied. In an attempt to forget his worries, he exercised abundantly. After my fall from a horse and the premature burning of our manor, we became closer. Since he had nothing to do but wait for the construction of a second chateau, Burt rented a yacht at Dubrovnik and invited me as his guest.

Situated on the Dalmation coast, Dubrovnik is one of the most beautiful places I know. Almost an island, it is reminiscent of Capri. It is a Venice without canals, a jumble of Renaissance palaces, Roman churches, and alleys sporting pieces of laundry which look like standards fluttering in the wind. A jewel detached from time.

Around mid-June, with a fresh supply of snow from Holly-wood, we started frolicking in front of our new Versailles. I began to find my days monotonous. It was at this point that Marisa, Jean-Claude, and Patrick came from New York to spend some time with me.

What joy to see my two sons descending from the airplane! Jean-Claude, age eleven, with his determined step, forward jaw, dignified, stern—a junior Mussolini in conquest of Yugoslavia. And Patrick, age eight, quicker, more wide awake, tossing his glances around, also getting ready to conquer, but with a subtler tactic.

Traveling halfway around the world in twelve hours doesn't seem to bother them. At an early age they are as used to planes as I was to the bus. Jean-Claude finds it perfectly natural to fly New York-Belgrade-New York just to give his father a hug. Patrick finds it amusing. But neither of them is surprised or stirred to be in a new country, with a strange language and writing that he can't decipher. At the hotel my sons don't seem to experience the slightest culture shock. Patrick immediately strikes up a friendship with the bartender, just as always.

I take Jean-Claude on a tour of the ramparts. He is, of course, happy to be there, but he can't help worrying about his studies. How different we are! He is as conscientious, serious, and orderly as I, at the same age, was lazy, superficial, and mischievous. And yet, physically, of the two, he resembles me the most. The younger looks like his mother but has my nature. He doesn't give a damn about his work. Everything amuses him and attracts him except effort. Just like me, he has a taste for lib-erty and a desire to meet a great many people, while Jean-Claude already seeks solitude. Halfway through our excursion he leaves me. "I feel like going back alone." I watch him walk away, lost in his thoughts.

My other son has been anxious to experience women for some time. This began when he was seven. Whenever he had the chance, he would peer at his mother or his nursemaid through keyholes as they took their showers. Then he would run triumphantly to me:

"Papa, I saw Mama's breasts. You want me to tell you what they're like?"

I would try to calm his excitement. "No, thanks, I already know them."

Now he draws pictures of naked women all through the day. When we took him to a museum, he touched the buttocks of the statues with such an intensity that I was afraid the guards would throw him out. He doesn't talk about anything but the "splits" of these women, a word which he asks me to translate into French. I don't know how to answer him. What word can I use that is not too vulgar or too technical? I try to get the conversation onto another track, but he comes back to it. "Papa, yesterday evening, I saw Mademoiselle's split." I pretend to attach no importance to this. "So what? Is that more interesting than her knees or her hands?" His answer is a knowing smile.

His brother looks at him with amusement. From the summit of his eleven years he seems to be saying, "Me, too, I went through that stage, but I'm well over it . . ."

Their complicity is total. When they talk together, they do it in English, in a Western twang that they pick up from television. They roughhouse like sailors at the drop of a hat. Cries, bruises, scratches, screams. We separate them as well as we can. Two minutes later they're together again, more friendly than they were before the squabble.

Their intelligence amazes me. Already I can hardly answer their questions . . . Lasers, rockets, electromagnetic waves, all the modern technology which they hear about and which they want me to explain to them. Whether it's a matter of Mademoiselle's "split," or of satellites flying toward the moon, how difficult it is to answer children of eight and eleven years!

When I finally got back to Paris, I received a strange offer from some television producers. They wanted me to be the master of ceremonies and interviewer for a special one-hour show on Arthur Rubinstein.

I have a deep admiration for Arthur Rubinstein and I'm more than proud to be his friend, but to be honest, I don't know a thing about music. I can barely distinguish a sonata from a

polka. My answer to the producers was that, c
the Parisian musicologists, they could find some
fied than me for this task.

"You don't understand," I was told. "Your
make him speak—he doesn't need you for that, by
get him to shut up so that his guests will have a char.

How do you shut up an octogenarian who is not on
but dazzling, full of verve and humor, who can tell a s
ter than anyone else, and who takes delight in doing so?

Arthur Rubinstein's wife, Néla, called me: "Do it fo
beg you. Arthur's guests won't be able to get a word in ed
if someone isn't there to hold him back. and we'll be in tr
with all our friends. Any ordinary television intervie
wouldn't dare interrupt Arthur. But you can do it. He likes
a lot. He'll forgive you . . ."

It's impossible to resist Néla's Slavic charm. I accept. A di
ficult enterprise. In addition to the eight guests, all of them im
portant people, whom I must introduce and if possible draw out,
I also have to insure the showing of a dozen film fragments:
some Debussy by the Lowenguth quartet, a filmed conversation
with Pagnol, some extracts of Chopin and Beethoven played by
Rubinstein in Jerusalem.

I go over to Arthur's to try to plan the broadcast. He overwhelms me with anecdotes, becoming more and more comical,
but he obstinately refuses to tell me what he would like to talk
about or what he wants me to ask him.

"Arthur, don't you think that at the beginning of the broadcast . . ."

"Do you know, Jean-Pierre, what Einstein heard a violinist
(whose name I will have the charity *not* to mention) say? Einstein was playing the cello in a quartet as a way of relaxing.
When he started his part a second too late, the violinist got
angry, jumped up and shook a threatening index finger at him,
shouting, 'Don't you know how to count?' "

I try to lead him back to the subject. "For your conversation with the dean of the Sorbonne, which is supposed to last
around six minutes, have you . . ."

"And poor Chopin . . . Can you imagine, dearrrrr friend,

ıis being invited to the home of a lady who cunningly tries to ιat him at the piano as soon as the meal is over: 'Excuse me, Madame,' says Chopin, 'but I feel too weak to play. I've had so little to eat.' "

I try again: "After the dean you're supposed to talk with Malraux. Four minutes and a half. Do you think that . . ."

"My dearrrrrr friend, if you knew the number of young pianists who play better than me. . . . [He rolls those terrible eyes of his.] Oh! How I *hate* them!"

Sunday. Three o'clock. Five minutes before broadcast. Arthur still hasn't arrived at the studio. The guests, musicians, critics are there. They begin dumping their apprehension on me. They're all afraid that they won't be on the air long enough. Rubinstein appears at the last second and the broadcast begins.

I let him go on, contenting myself with punctuating certain anecdotes. He is happy as he speaks, he is funny, he is moving. The assistant director points nervously at his watch. After ten minutes the timing is totally destroyed. I try to make Arthur understand that he should cut short his anecdotes. But what does my cold sweat matter to him? What does it matter to him that the assistant director's gesticulations are becoming more and more hysterical? Did you ever see Sarah Bernhardt stop in the middle of a tirade? Could Nijinski remain suspended in the air in the middle of a leap?

The more time passes, the more effusive Arthur becomes. By showering his guests with compliments, he keeps them off screen. At the precise moment when the director signals "Ten seconds left," just as I am beginning a sentence to end the broadcast, Arthur, more royally relaxed than ever, utters these words: "My dearr friend, ever since the release of my film, *L'amour de la Vie*, do you know whom they've compared me to? Jerry Lewis."

The last word of the last anecdote has fallen right on the last second. Unlike Albert Einstein, Arthur Rubinstein knows how to count.

As soon as the broadcast is over, he drags us to his home on the Avenue du Bois de Boulogne. On the walls are his portraits

by Kisling and Picasso. On the piano, which is a gift of the municipality of Jerusalem, are photos of Toscanni, Golda Meir, and Queen Elizabeth of Belgium. On a piece of furniture is a gilded bronze cast of Arthur's hands—aerial, powerful, like a plow frame sculpted by Rodin. Néla has placed flowers around. Her presence, diaphanous, graceful, and glowing, brings to this house, which could be a museum, a soft warmth, the perfume of a perfect tenderness.

An admirer congratulates Arthur on his last concert. He seizes her hand.

"You see, dearrr friend, I'll never forgive myself for not having developed the talent God gave me. I play badly." (He pauses, sighing.) "But in spite of that, it works . . ."

Aghast, the woman cries, "God loves you . . ."

Arthur, musingly: "He seems to love me . . . He seems to . . ."

A year later, Marisa and I would be in New York applauding John Rubinstein, one of Arthur's and Néla's four children.

That baby, whom I had held in my arms when we were Hollywood neighbors, and whose mother recently told me, "He's vaguely interested in the theater," is today the star of *Pippin*. At the end of the show, we go to his dressing room. I ask him for news of his father.

"He's in New York, but, unfortunately, he's seriously ill. His shingles are making him suffer horribly. He's very weak, too. At the age of eighty-six, it's pretty serious . . ."

I call Néla for news. "Arthur's a little better, thank God." I ask her if I can say two words to him, if that won't tire him too much.

"But he's not here," answers Néla. "Tonight he's giving a concert in Los Angeles, tomorrow in Boston, the day after tomorrow in Milwaukee . . ."

Sensing my surprise, she adds, "What do you expect? The day he stops playing, he'll die." Then she adds: "If he played any worse, I'd have a reason to force him to stop. But he plays better and better . . ."

Eighty-six years old!

Thank God genius has nothing to do with perfection. One day when I asked Néla why they didn't record Arthur's concerts live, she cried, "Are you crazy? With all those wrong notes he hits?"

23

WITH OR WITHOUT CARTWHEELS

It goes without saying—so let's say it right away—that my mother-in-law is a saint. It's also a well known fact that ALL mothers-in-law, all over the world, come from a different planet. They are a race apart which has nothing to do with other human beings, at least not with sons-in-law.

Cocteau used to say of them that they have an aching attachment to their daughters, as for some organ cut out of them. At first, they don't mind their daughters marrying, since they are intelligent enough to realize that this ceremony is the necessary groundwork for divorce. So they put up with the gentleman in question, but they think of him as "The Man Who Came to Dinner" and who is wearing out his welcome. They open his mail—by mistake. They listen in on his telephone conversations—to be helpful. His house, which they originally described to their friends as slightly less imposing than Versailles, soon becomes an uncomfortable hovel.

Coming—inevitably—from a middle-class background, where respectable people put on white gloves to receive the delivery boy, they take a dim view of bare feet, of rolling in the grass, and of eating French fries with the fingers.

They begin the battle by telling their daughters: "I just found out your husband is old enough to be your father."

The poor victim starts to toy with the idea of bumping off the lady in question. He talks it over with his lawyer, who cannot guarantee that he'll get away with it, since most judges are scared to death of their own mothers-in-law.

I didn't resort to these extremes. Instead, I wrote a play.

In the first act, Madame Ponce, my heroine, hires a detective to follow her son-in-law. In the second, the son-in-law wriggles out of the situation by convincing the detective to marry her. Then Madame Ponce becomes the victim of an equally obnoxious mother-in-law.

When I read the play to my friends they howled with laughter. As for my own mother-in-law, she thought my comedy was interesting but wondered how I could have invented such an unbelievable character.

I gave the play to a few actresses. They didn't bother to read it. Not that it mattered. I'd performed an exorcism by writing it.

On the off-chance, I slipped the manuscript into the bottom of my suitcase when I left for New York. I put it on my agent's desk, more to get rid of it than for him to read it, since he didn't understand a word of French. One day the telephone rang. Somebody named Erich Segal had read the play. He thought it was hilarious and wanted my permission to adapt it for the American stage.

This was only a year before Erich Segal was to become the most celebrated writer in the United States. *Love Story* has sold nearly as many copies throughout the world as the Bible and Agatha Christie combined. But when he came to see me, Erich was only a modest professor of Greek at Yale. I found myself face to face with a brown-eyed dynamo, a mixture of Woody Allen and Rudolf Valentino. He talked about my play with such enthusiasm and in such perfect French that I immediately gave my consent, provided that we worked on it together.

The following day he came over, grabbed a pencil, and began scribbling away. Suddenly he jumped up, tore off his clothes, and bolted out the door in his shorts.

An hour later he returned, got dressed again, and went back to work. His behavior struck me as slightly unusual, but I didn't have the nerve to ask for an explanation. After all, I'm a foreigner . . .

The next day, after about an hour of work, the same ritual occurred. He got undressed and rushed outside. The fact that it was the middle of winter didn't help me come to any conclusions. I hurried out to my balcony in time to see Erich cross the street, go into Central Park, and begin running around the reservoir.

These track sessions didn't relax him at all. He came back more nervous than before and began chewing away at his pencil, spitting out translations of dialogue which made him explode with laughter.

Out of politeness, I joined in.

The English version completed, we began looking for a producer. We found Frank Loesser, who besides being a composer spent his spare time producing shows. Unfortunately, Frank couldn't stand Erich. My collaborator's constant nervousness, manifested in his leaps and yelps, set Frank's teeth on edge. When I refused to let Erich go, Frank declined to produce the play.

We sent it to another producer, the renowned and feared Hal Prince. Having gotten into the habit of writing me every day, Erich sent these words: "Hip, hip, hooray. Hal Prince has read our play six times. He's crazy about it. Of course, he has no intention of producing it, but after all, if somebody doesn't like a play, he doesn't read it six times in a row. I'm a professor and I've only read *Hamlet* twice. Hal Prince has read your play *six times already* . . ." Eric concluded from this that *Madame Ponce* was three times better than *Hamlet*.

I didn't share his enthusiasm. I would have preferred someone who had read the play only once—or even not at all—but who would go ahead and produce it.

Finally, it happened. After several tentative proposals, a certain Emmett Rogers came through with a solid contract. He declared to anyone who would listen that *Madame Ponce* was a masterpiece, and that we shouldn't change a comma. This healthy frame of mind lasted exactly twenty-four hours. Then he began changing everything, starting with the title. We lost two weeks trying to come up with others: from *A Devoted Lady* to *Naughty Girls*, from *Remember Me to Your Mother* to *Send Her Off to Tahiti*. Finally Emmett Rogers had a brilliant idea: *Madame Ponce* became *Madame Mousse*.

Now that we had a producer and a title, we still had to find the star. Emmett had his second brilliant idea: Molly Picon.

Molly Picon was the muse and star of the Yiddish theater. She was a plump, lively little woman who'd been the darling of the Jewish community for the last fifty years. The thought of having to translate my play into Yiddish was a little distressing, especially since neither Erich nor myself knew a word of it, but they assured me that Molly had been quite a hit in *Milk and Honey*, an English-speaking musical. She had read *Madame Mousse* and was excited by the prospect of a change of pace.

For the role of the detective we got Pierre Olaf, who was still in New York after *La Plume de Ma Tante*. For the second mother-in-law we signed Estelle Winwood. The role of the son-in-law remained to be cast. Emmett, on bended knee, begged me to play it. I accepted without too much persuasion, since I'd written the part for myself.

Word Baker was asked to direct it, a shy man, whose previous success, *The Fantasticks*, had been running then for ten years. It didn't take much to fool ourselves into believing that *Madame Mousse* would run for eleven.

Before rehearsals began, Emmett took us to Sardi's so that we could meet the press and some potential backers. All of a sudden Emmett had another brainstorm. He wanted me to hide the fact that *Madame Mousse* had once been *Madame Ponce*, a French play. "No French play's ever been a hit on Broadway," he told me. "We just can't take the risk."

"O.K., I'll say my name's Bill Smith and that I was born in Brooklyn just like everybody else." He was too worried to appreciate my sense of humor.

In an attempt to make Emmett happy I told the reporters who were present that my play had nothing to do with those comedies which are a hit in France but lose all their flavor in crossing the Atlantic. No. Nein. Nyet. Non. This was an original work, concocted in the good old U.S.A. (deafening applause). If it turned out that I'd written it in French, it was because of my fear of mistreating the language of Shakespeare for which I felt a stirring respect; but the subject of my play wasn't at all French. It was International, Universal, Eternal. (More applause, but less deafening.) Emmett was in heaven. Molly Picon, who had a tendency to put her foot in her mouth, and who, after all, had only accepted this dangerous escapade to get away from her usual repertoire, spoke up: "You're not taking Jean-Pierre seriously, are you? His play is typically Parisian, thank God." Emmett passed out.

Then Molly took me into a corner and asked me to change a line. "Just one, darling, just one. The rest is pure gold. To touch it would be a crime."

"But of course, darling, which line?"

"Well, you know where Paul talks about his mother-in-law and he calls her an 'old bitch'? Wouldn't it be nicer if he called her a 'little pixie' instead?"

"Darling. It's obvious that you *are* a little pixie. It's known all over the world. But it's really not a question of public opinion. Paul is speaking. Paul hates his mother-in-law. And with that sense of excess that characterizes him he calls this 'little pixie' and 'old bitch.' He's the one who's going to seem ridiculous."

"Of course, darling, of course. But I consider it essential that he call me his little pixie."

Naively believing that it would be the sole concession I'd be asked to make, I surrendered.

The next day we began rehearsing. We also started having sessions with our producer, who, little by little, was ordering us to change everything.

With massive cuttings in some spots and rewrites in others we went on rehearsing. We were supposed to play four weeks on the road before New York. The first performance would be in Westport.

The day before the opening, Molly Picon took me aside. Sporting an angelic smile she raised her skirts and showed me her legs; very shapely, I had to agree.

"Darling, I want to turn two or three cartwheels."

Me (haggard): "Where?"

"Wherever you like. You're the author. It's up to you to find the right scenes for my cartwheels."

"In God's name, Molly, why?"

"Darling. You remember of course that I played *Milk and Honey* five hundred times? Wouldn't you like me to do *your* play that many times?"

"Of course I would."

"So? My cartwheels were what made *Milk and Honey* such a big hit . . ."

This time I stuck to my guns. We opened in Westport without cartwheels.

Westport. The theater, made completely out of wood, is reminiscent of Elizabethan prints. I love it. It's like playing in a barn. The cars pull up on the grass close by. Members of the audience walk past the dressing rooms and greet the actors affectionately before taking their seats.

The house is packed. It will be that way all week. Molly Picon is a big draw on the summer circuit.

She walks on stage. Fantastic ovation. I'm happy. We're off to a good start. Unfortunately, as the play goes on, it becomes apparent that my scenes are more effective than Molly's. The audience has a good time with the son-in-law and takes his side against Madame Mousse.

At the curtain call, frenetic applause for Pierre Olaf, then for Estelle Winwood, then for me. When Molly comes out for a bow, the applause is merely polite. For the second time in my life, I'd had more success than the star of the show. For the second time, I was going to pay dearly for it.

After an uncomfortable supper I closeted myself with Emmett, trying to figure out what had happened. The explanation was simple. To see a doting Jewish mother suddenly become a shrewish and possessive witch whose sole desire was to see her daughter divorced, was an insult, a crime, and a heresy. It was almost as if Roger Vadim had chosen Golda Meir to do the nude scenes in *And God Created Woman*.

At dawn the reviews came out. Everything went well at first: "The confrontation between the two mothers-in-law is one of the funniest scenes we've seen. The public didn't stop laughing." Then it continued a little less well, confirming Emmett's verdict: "Molly Picon's fans were surprised and disappointed to see their idol in the same situation as a fish out of water. To tear their Molly up from her native Brooklyn and transplant her to Paris, depriving her of her Yiddish accent, was quite a shock."

When things aren't going so well, it always helps to find a scapegoat. Emmett found two: the director and Erich Segal. He decided to get rid of both, nd asked me not to tell Erich what was happening until we had found someone else. I refused. To continue to work with Erich, while knowing that they were looking for a replacement . . . I just couldn't do it. So I went to find him and tell him the truth. The same person whose outbursts had driven us crazy took the news of his dismissal with philosophical calm. Did he have an intuition that his guardian angel was watching over him and that a year later he would be selling millions of copies of *Love Story?*

John Berry appeared on the scene as the new director, a robust and hairy giant who boomed with laughter at each new catastrophe. With a few slaps on the back, some anecdotes and whiskey, he convinced us that the answer to our problems was a third mother-in-law. The second mother-in-law would also end up marrying and take her turn at being the victim. It was a little farcical, but it would do.

I tried to write the new scenes in English myself. It wasn't easy to turn my shrew into a saint, my "old bitch" into a "little pixie." Estelle Windwood, mother-in-law #2, didn't help. "You can change Molly's role all you want as long as you don't change a syllable of mine." She was getting a little old and didn't want to learn another line—not even a cut. Since most of her scenes were with Molly, I had to transform the dialogue of one without touching the dialogue of the other.

"Where are the snows of yesteryear?" the poet asks—and where was the play I'd written with ferocious delight two years before?

On the one hand we were breaking all records at the boxoffice; and on the other, everyone was on the brink of a nervous breakdown. When I asked Estelle Winwood, "How are you, darling?" she responded, "What the hell do you care?" Pierre Olaf wasn't speaking to me anymore because he thought I was responsible for letting Word Baker go. Molly was sure that the only problem was the lack of cartwheels.

One evening—we were then in our second week—Molly told me: "Tomorrow's my fiftieth." I congratulated her, and made a note to send her some flowers. "It wouldn't bother you that I make an announcement, would it, darling?"

"Of course not, darling."

The following evening, as usual, we take our bows at the end of the show. And, as usual, the applause is meager for Molly. Suddenly she steps forward to the edge of the stage and declares: "Today is my anniversary. I've been on the stage for fifty years." A long ovation. She continues: "It's also fifty years that Yunkle and I are married." Thunderous applause.

Encouraged by this unexpected reception—unexpected by everybody except her—she begins telling Yiddish jokes. These last about half an hour, with all of us impatiently standing behind her. Laughs, cries, applause, raves. The audience has finally found their Molly again.

From that day on, Molly finished the play as quickly as possible, as if it were some insignificant hors-d'oeuvre, and only began giving herself to her dear public after my comedy was over.

It was no longer a question of asking, "Would it bother you, darling." She'd found a way to recapture the success to which she was accustomed, and she wasn't going to give it up.

As a matter of fact, it *did* bother me, darling; but I couldn't blame Molly for it. She'd tried to shed an old image and failed.

Yiddish jokes or not, Molly refused to do my play on Broadway. At the end of our third week of tryouts, after the last curtain call, the last Yiddish joke, and the last ovation, I gathered everyone in my dressing room and told them: "I have the firm intention of doing this play in New York. With or without a producer, with or without Molly. If certain of you want out, I understand. But if you care to stay with me for the battle of Broadway, that will make me very happy. I'm not saying *adieu*, I'm saying *au revoir* . . ."

Of course, that meant absolutely nothing. How would I have found a Broadway theater, without a producer and without Molly? But I've always been a ham. It was a good exit.

Long weeks followed. Emmett, by tearful pleading, had hunted up a co-producer, a man of experience, Max Gordon. We started at the beginning again. Max Gordon convinced me to let Yunkle, Molly Picon's husband, do a new version of my play. "After all, she adores her husband. She's not going to refuse anything that he's written."

When Yunkle, a most endearing man, had finished working on the play, we all got together at his home. Monopolozing one corner of the mantel with a kindly solemnity, he began the task of reciting his opus. He began with: "*Madame Mousse*, a play in two acts by Jean-Pierre Aumont." He stopped for a moment, regarded me with moist eyes, and said, "You see, dear boy, it is still your play."

Alas! He continued to read. Madame Mousse entered with a cartwheel, as had been expected. Then she became a ghost. A spry, teasing, bustling, jocular ghost who whispered to her daughter: "Couldn't you be a little nicer to your husband?" The exact opposite of my character. No, dear Yunkle, it wasn't my play anymore.

After the reading of the first act, which I listened to with angelic patience, Max Gordon stood up.

"I've got it! This isn't a play about a mother-in-law. It's about a *detective*. I don't give a damn whether it's written by Aumont, Yunkle, Shakespeare, or the janitor, as long as it's about a detective."

Emmett burst into tears.

Molly fainted.

Madame Mousse disappeared.

But I haven't lost all hope of seeing her back on the stage some day.

With or without cartwheels.

24

APPLES OF MY EYE

In 1970 I wrote four novellas under the title *La Pomme de Son Oeil*.

The first copy brought me true joy. Set in fresh paper, with neat margins and harmoniously cropped chapters, it seemed like a new book, so much clearer and more precise than the manuscript I had pecked out on my typewriter, itself quite different from the one I had written by hand, six months earlier.

I rushed to my editor's office and, without even inquiring how he was (but he must be used to that), asked him in which papers he intended to publish advertisements celebrating my new work. Obviously, there was more pressing business at hand. I was shut up in a room with two hundred copies of *La Pomme de Son Oeil* destined for journalists, critics, editors-in-chief, newswriters, and gossip columnists, three-quarters of whom I had never heard of.

"Try to say something personal," suggested the charming secretary.

It was then that I learned that writing a book is really nothing compared to the resources of imagination and diplomacy required by public relations.

I began scribbling: "To Mr. B. whose work is a constant inspiration to me." (Had Mr. B. ever produced the least work? Bah! thought I, who doesn't think he's worked in one domain or another?)

"To Mr. and Mrs. Z., an admirable couple, whose rare and shining example my immoral protagonists would do well to follow." (Off target again! This admirable couple had just gotten divorced.)

It was with a shock of pleasure that I saw my little book appear for the first time in the window of a bookstore in Saint-Tropez. Inside the shop, the book was well displayed, though a bit eclipsed by a collection of Freud's works. I was unable to prevent myself from feeling a slight jealousy toward Freud. Surreptitiously, I moved his volume to one side—just to give mine a little more air and make it a bit more noticeable.

A man in a bathing suit entered, an extremely distinguished man with imposing biceps and a wholesome curiosity for literary matters in his eyes. With a manly gait he steered toward my book and seized hold of it. Maybe he would be the first person in the world to buy it! I wanted to press that intelligent, eclectic, enlightened being to my heart. With much attention he read my biographical notice (flattering, I must admit) and the blurb printed on the left-hand flap of the cover: "Four short stories, very different in tone, each of an irresistible verve and liveliness." (If blurbs are to be believed—and why wouldn't I believe this one, since I'd written it?)

A few seconds passed. This member of the intellectual elite took his time. Then, suddenly, while the breeze casually rocked the yachts in the harbor, suddenly, while thousands of illiterates blankly drifted across the beaches, and while other customers contented themselves with facile magazines, suddenly, I say, this vulgar, shifty individual, this pot-bellied, tasteless, tactless tourist, who had no desire for entertainment or instruction—this idiot—put my book down and left without buying it!

At that moment I understood the meaning of murder.

*La Pomme de Son Oeil—The Apple of His Eye—*was both the title of the book and of the first novella. In this story I examined the relationship between a stern father, who is a French ambassador, and his daughter, who is completely off her rocker. At the age of fiteen Beatrice becomes uncontrollable. She passes through many phases: a mystic, a hippie, a member of the Salvation Army, a communist. She changes not only her personality but her appearance, her voice, and her name.

The story was produced for television. Michel Polnareff composed the music. He was a thin, angular fellow with an aquiline nose, wavy hair, and a touch of genius. He played us his score. From time to time he would stop and declare: "Sublime."

I had to sing several songs. In one of them I was supposed to express my concern after learning that my daughter had a lover.

"During this song," said Polnareff, "I want you to gyrate your hips, moaning, 'Yeah, yeah, yeah,' like Elvis. It'll be earth-shaking."

"Listen, Michel, on the one hand, I've passed the age for such contortions . . ."

"You go, 'Yeah, yeah, yeah.' "

"On the other hand, I'm playing a French ambassador . . ."

"Yeah, yeah, yeah . . ."

"Then you haven't read my story? Just as the daughter is uncontrollable, the father is supposed to be stiff, strict, dignified, old-fashioned . . ."

"I don't give a damn . . . Yeah, yeah, yeah . . ."

The day of the broadcast I sang the song, but to the great disappointment of Polnareff, I didn't gyrate anything.

The second novella was an homage to Colette, whose style I tried to imitate by retracing, to the last days of her life, the ascent and downfall of a Belle Epoque sinner. It is the story of a woman who has known all the glamours and successes from the age of fifteen to the age of eighty, and who finds herself toothless, childless, and without lovers, awaiting the end. She pictures death in the form of an old friend, la Belle Otero, who says to her: "Come now, honey, getting the Balkan prince into bed was a lot more difficult than dying's going to be . . ." Her only funeral dirge is the mewing of a triumphant cat whom she detested.

The third novella is the story of a boy who pays with his life for his penchant for adventure, his overriding need to prove that he is capable of any exploit, no matter how noble or how sordid.

The story had been inspired by a down-at-the-heels lad I had known in New York, who, not being able to stand his anonymity, had ended up hijacking a plane, well before it became fashionable.

The last novella, *Yerbas*, was the story of an island, and of the strange fauna which inhabited it each year during the two months of summer: beautiful, bikini-clad girls, tanned athletes, shady businessmen, homosexuals, painters, actors, gigolos, drug addicts. One of the principal characters in my story was called Damis. He was a kind of grand lord, a solid, stocky man, always loaded with rings and gold chains, and perennially followed by an entourage, flaunting his joyously dissolute morality. Elmyr de Hory, who lived at Ibiza and whom Clifford Irving, before tackling Howard Hughes, had described in his book *Fake* as a genial forger, thought he recognized himself in my character. From the bottom of my heart I assured him that there wasn't the slightest connection between Damis and him, and that all authors use several models to make up one character. As Musset said: "You take a nose from one, a jaw from the other . . . and from the next . . . guess . . ." The whole ends up having very little to do with anyone in particular.

Elmyr pretended to believe me and, to prove that he didn't bear me any grudge, asked me to participate in the television special that François Reichenbach was doing on him for the BBC. As soon as the camera was on him, Elmyr shouted out with the lyric egocentricity of a small child, "Ladies and gentlemen, I'm the greatest forger of all time!"

Did he know what he was doing? was he conscious of the danger he was inviting? Did he realize what he risked by boasting of his own scandals?

This Great Impostor, this Houdini of the art world, can't

keep himself from throwing out challenges. It is in his blood. Sure, he could disavow the book by Irving, and so many newspaper articles; but how could he ever repudiate what he himself had said on television?

"I am the greatest forger of all time . . ." Ah! This moment of rapture is worth all the risks!

How had Elmyr escaped all the police investigations right up to the present time?

His defense is simple: "I paint for my pleasure, after the manner of Picasso or Matisse. Others sign these canvases, I have nothing to do with it. Others sell them . . . it's none of my business. All the experts declare that my works are real Picassos, real Matisses. It's rather flattering. The museums get puffed up about their new acquisitions. Good for them. Everybody's happy, everybody gets rich . . . except me. I'm not a criminal, I'm a victim."

Elmyr gets ready to paint for us. He begins making arabesques with his brush. He asks me not to smoke.

"I need my voice," says he, as if he were going on stage to sing *Tosca*.

With an aerial hand he does a Matisse drawing in seventy-two seconds.

"And now, a Picasso. This will take a little longer, because it's a pen and ink."

He draws without ever losing contact with the camera. In the course of it, he amuses himself: "Do you know what my dentist had the nerve to accuse me of? He said I had sold him a false Dufy . . . I said, 'My dear fellow, you sold me false teeth . . . We're even.' "

Two minutes later he has finished a glorious Picasso from the Toreador series, one of the most beautiful I have ever seen.

"Now we're going to burn it," he says, suddenly prudent.

The flames lick at Matisse's nude and Picasso's picador. It's painful to watch; copies or not, these are authentic masterpieces burning up before our eyes.

Besides, these are not really copies. Contrary to what he claims, Elmyr is not a forger. He is inspired by a canvas that he likes and he composes another from it, one that's almost more authentic than the original.

I know people who own a Velazquez and who have said to me—with a certain hope—that the painting may really be an Elmyr.

Strange and tragic destiny of an artist who was never able to sell a single one of his original works, but who has succeeded in filling museums the moment he allowed himself to be inspired by someone else.

Maybe Reichenbach was right when he said to Elmyr:

"You're a benefactor to mankind. You've given us works that the greatest masters have not had time to paint."

(This sequence, shot in Elmyr's workshop, will appear later in Orson Welles' astonishing and diabolically edited film, *"F" Is for "Fake."*)

25

AL PACINO AND
SUPPERS AT SARDI'S

Once more I came back to America, this time to play an Austrian Prince in *Incident at Vichy* by Arthur Miller. Of all the characters that I have portrayed, this is the one which moved me the most.

The play was directed by Harold Clurman, in the presence of the author. Joe Wiseman was the doctor and Roy Scheider the German major. We received a warm reception.

A while later, I was asked to perform it in Philadelphia with another director and other performers. This time we were supposed to play in a theater-in-the-round.

Milton Katselas, the new director, is a generous and cheerful man of Greek origin. He is tender and virile at the same time, and has a gargantuan appetite for all that life has to offer, up to and including the hereafter. Premonitions, former lives, and life-after-death fascinate him. As soon as I met him I wanted to work with him.

To the same degree that Harold Clurman directed us to be immobile and impassive, delivering our lines as in a Greek tragedy, Milton made us writhe and turn, like caged animals. Astonishing experience. It became another play. What it lost in nobility, it gained in humanity. Two interpretations of the same work. Both of them staggering.

Two years later, Milton asked me to be in a play by Tennessee Williams, *Camino Real*, at Lincoln Center.

In an imaginary country, a purgatory, where men and women of different nationalities and different eras are waiting to be sent to Paradise or Hell, several characters wander: Casanova (whom I played), Marguerite Gautier (beautifully acted by Jessica Tandy), Lord Byron, Don Quixote, and a young sailor of today, Kilroy—a rowdy, foul-mouthed youth who sells his heart to be able to buy a pair of boxing gloves. Everything takes place in the square of a town which might be somewhere in South America, with a dried-up fountain and an immense staircase which leads to nothing. The play, with its lightning, lyric flights and shocks, seems like a nightmare, a trip on LSD.

Tennessee was in a clinic. He couldn't come to the rehearsals.

Milton was directing us, at ease in these strange meanderings. Certain directors—a lot of them, to be truthful—try to impose their own personality. Reduced to the condition of a flock of sheep, the actors are given intonations, gestures, feelings, and reactions whose curve and intensity have been drawn up in an office by the director, before he has even had a chance to meet the actors and learn about their personalities. Milton, on the contrary, always tried to obtain the best of us, without ever imposing anything upon us. He had, like Truffaut, a respect for our individualities. He knew how to let us go, to deliver us, spur us on, all without taking away the feeling that we were free. Just like Diaghilev years ago to Cocteau, Milton's main piece of advice to us was: "And now, surprise me."

More than anyone else, I appreciated this kind of independence. Milton, who knew me well, joked about it. One day he asked me what I thought of a certain director.

"I can't stand him," I answered.

"I see," said Milton, winking. "He wanted to direct you."

Al Pacino played the sailor-boxer. Next to him I felt heavy,

conventional, theatrical, but Milton never stopped complimen-
ting me. Each day he took me aside and declared, "You're *so
fucking good.*"

I believed him.

There were five preview performances before the official
opening. On the fourth evening, during the intermission, the
stage manager announced that Tennessee Williams was in the
house, was taking notes, and would read them to us afterwards.
It seemed there were a lot of last minute changes that he wanted
us to effect. We performed the second half of the play better
than ever, in a great burst of enthusiasm, and love for this man
whom we so admired.

When the play was over, we waited on stage for Tennessee.
We waited and waited. As time passed, the more nervous we
became, wondering what changes or cuts the author was going
to require. Finally, Tennessee arrived, a stout man with a hesitant mustache.

He placed himself in the center of the stage. We formed a
respectful circle around him. Tennessee smiled. We held our
breaths. Tennessee scratched himself. We craned our necks forward to watch. Tennessee remained silent. No one dared to fill
the void. The minutes passed. You could hear a pin drop. Finally he opened his mouth and bleated out: "Good night, baaaa-
biiiies."

Then he left.

On opening night my entrance, like everybody else's, was
applauded, and since this rarely happens to actors in France, I
felt particularly happy. Oh, yes!—we are made of such pitiable
fabric. Instead of ignoring this phenomenon, we light up, we
bloom, whenever it occurs.

In our eyes, applause signifies recognition, affection. To be
applauded is a testimonial, a prize, a Legion of Honor, a blast of
oxygen, a shot of vitamins, a crown, a benediction, a kick in the
ass to send you forward.

As things seemed to have gone well, I conformed to that
masochistic practice which New York actors have of dining after
the show at Sardi's. Around one in the morning, the first edi-

tions of the papers come out. The maitre d' buys a dozen, which he distributes around. When the reviews are good, there are kisses, swoons, and toasts from one table to the other. But when they are bad, no task is more cruel than having to hide your grief while your acquaintances throughout the room are spying on you.

As soon as the unfortunate author or actor raises his eyes from the paper, he notices a great emptiness around his table. His best friends have fled. Used to this cannibalistic ritual, the maitre d' tries to console him. "Such-and-such a play ran for three years despite a bad review by Clive Barnes . . ."

Nobody listens to him. They all know that Barnes, as theater critic for the New York *Times*, is the prophet of rain or good weather . . .

Well, Clive Barnes liked the play and Jessica Tandy, who he thought was moving. I quickly skimmed the rest of the article, searching for the paragraph which concerned me. It was short:

"Mr. Aumont seemed to me slightly out of dramatic focus."

I looked for Milton. "What does that mean, 'out of focus'?"

" 'Out of focus?' I haven't the faintest idea . . ."

"Come on, Milton, try a little harder. Clive Barnes thinks I'm 'out of focus.' "

"I swear to you," said Milton, "on the heads of my children, [he had no children] that I do not know what, in this context, 'out of focus' could possibly mean."

I wandered through the streets, desperate. I had been waiting for this evening for so long! This play by Williams was such a masterpiece! . . . Milton had complimented me so! . . . One more time I tried repeating to myself, "Think of the millions of Chinese, Hindus, and Laplanders who will never read that review." But somehow, the ignorance of the Chinese and the Hindus had no effect on me. The Laplanders weren't any comfort either.

The following day, I performed in a depressed mood. I was bad and I knew it. I couldn't say one line without seeing "out of focus" dancing in front of my eyes.

Milton Katselas was in the audience. After the show, he called us all on stage. He was beside himself. He shouted at us that we should be ashamed, that we had played without any passion, freshness, or inspiration. If certain of us were idiotic enough to allow ourselves to be influenced by a bad review, then we didn't deserve the chance ever to set foot on a stage. Everyone lowered his eyes, like guilty children, but I knew that this entire lecture was meant for me.

I wasn't wrong. Milton came into my dressing room, chased out my dresser, and exploded: "You were awful! You were thinking of other things, and I know what they were, imbecile! How dare you? How dare you let yourself be hurt by the opinion of one man, whoever he is? When will you understand that any actor knows instinctively a thousand times more about his trade than the most eminent critic?"

Unnerved, humiliated, miserable, I shouted back: "It's your fault! You shouldn't have complimented me so much during rehearsals. I wouldn't have expected any praise and I wouldn't have been disappointed. Why did you say to me every day—and these were your very words—'You're so fucking good'?"

Milton stood up, looking grander, stronger, and more terrifying than ever. He was Moses about to dash the Tablets against the rocks. Gazing at me with a mixture of tenderness and hate, he bellowed, "Because you are . . . SO . . . FUCKING . . . GOOD . . ."

Then he stalked out of my dressing room as the other one had descended Mount Sinai, closed the door with a bang, and plunged into the night.

Just like *La Machine Infernale*, *Camino Real* gave birth to fanatics. The same people came back several times. Either you understood nothing of the strange, poetic beauties of the play, or you allowed yourself to be swallowed by its magic, its druglike power.

Al Pacino and I went out together often. We understood each other well, at least outside of the theater. On stage, I had to constantly hold myself back from strangling him. Al never said his lines without adding or deleting something, without transforming them into a slang which came to him naturally. Since he was playing a sailor-boxer, he could get away with it. I, however, was playing Casanova, whose role was written in an archaic and lyrical language. I couldn't permit myself the slightest deviation.

At the end of each evening I would beg Al to respect the text of the author.

"You're right, you are absolutely right."

The next day he'd be more brilliant than ever, without ever giving me a line I could respond to. I tried to reason with him:

"Listen, Al. I know your role's a lot different from mine. You're wearing jeans and I'm in eighteenth-century costume. I know you have to improvise grunts and cusses. If you want to add the word 'fuck' to every line, it's all the same to me. I have nothing against the word 'fuck.' But at least give me the last sentence . . ."

"You're right, you are absolutely right."

The next day, instead of saying to me: "Nobody thinks romance is more important than me," to which I was supposed to answer, "Except possibly me," he would belch out something like: "Shit, man, romance is fucking important."

How could I answer, "Except possibly me"?

Far away from my family on Christmas Eve, I had the blues. I dragged myself to two or three parties but my heart just wasn't in it. Then I came back home on foot through a snowy and deserted New York.

No matter how much I tried to bury it, that article by Clive Barnes kept eating at me.

During this nocturnal and solitary walk, I kept telling myself that I hadn't a shred of talent, that the critics were always right, that I'd do better to abandon the theater for good . . .

I went into a bar. It was empty. Only the barman and the dishwasher were there. As I was leaving, they recognized me and struck up a conversation.

Both of them are apprentice actors. They struggle along, working as waiters, or truck drivers, or sweeping the very theaters in which they one day hope to shine.

They watch me with envy . . . I'm an actor! I'm in a Broadway play! My name is spread out across the front of a theater! For them I am the symbol of everything they are dreaming about.

So we are always a great man for somebody! But rarely do we meet that person who could boost our self-esteem; and when we do, it's almost always too late.

I offer them a drink, but they insist that I be their guest. They continue to look at me as if I had just descended from Olympus.

"A star . . ." They revel in that term. "You don't seem to realize it, but you're a star."

Just like Schiller's Don Carlos, who complained, "I'm twenty-two years old and I haven't done anything yet for immortality," they sigh, "We're twenty years old and we're still unknown. At what age did you become a star?"

"Stop saying that ridiculous word. Nobody becomes a star. You are or you are not. What I mean is, you're born a star, just as you're born Chinese or Norwegian, or with the gift for math, or with blue eyes. It's a grace that you receive without being aware of it. I know actors with a lot of talent who don't have it. I know grocers and telephone operators who have it."

I assured them that they would succeed. They had all the trump cards. They were young, eager, passionate, devoured by their love for the theater . . . One glass followed another. The snow was no longer falling.

If I paused, they waited, mouths hanging open, for me to continue. They wanted me to tell them all about my early years, my career, my successes, my failures. I told them.

I knew periods when I was a star in the eyes of the producers but didn't feel like one myself. (I refrained from telling them that tonight, for instance . . .) At other times, I wasn't worth a penny to the producers, and I felt like a star. Why? I don't know. Because I was in love, maybe . . . because it was a nice day . . .

We talked the whole night: Shakespeare, Moliere, Sophocles, Beckett. And Stanislavsky, and Kazan, and Joe Papp.

Before parting, we drank to the New Year.

They were happy. I'd comforted them and made them believe in their guardian angel.

I strolled through the streets again. Dawn appeared. I felt twenty years younger. Mr. Barnes could write whatever he pleased. I was no longer out of focus.

20

"Day for Night"

∾∾∾∾∾∾∾∾∾∾

I had met François Truffaut on a few occasions. We had greeted each other vaguely. Though I had a strong desire to know him, he seemed to have an attitude of the most total indifference toward me.

Thus, I was as surprised as I was happy when I received a letter from him, asking me to be one of the principal characters in a film that he was writing: *La Nuit Americaine* (*Day for Night*). We met in a café on the Champs-Elysées.

Our conversation was laborious. After I had told him how much I wanted to work with him, there were long and numerous pauses. At times he would glance at me and then lower his eyes. I ordered cup after cup of coffee in an attempt to animate the conversation, but it only seemed to make me more nervous and him more silent. A half-hour dragged on endlessly. Perhaps he had changed his mind when he'd seen me and would begin looking for another actor for the part. I felt sad about not making this film, even sadder at having been incapable of establishing the slightest contact with Truffaut.

Two days later, I received an extremely friendly letter from him in which he told me what a pleasure it had been to meet me. This warm letter, following up such a glacial interview, gave me my first clue to Truffaut's character: reserve.

We filmed in Nice, at the Victorine studio, using the scenery that had been constructed for *The Madwoman of Chaillot*. Although damaged by numerous storms, it was still standing.

"I examined this setting from all possible angles," wrote Truffaut. "Each day it seemed more fascinating and beautiful, especially when viewed from the rear. Thus, my old, vague notion of making a film about the making of a film came back to me with a renewed force. After visiting the entire premises—the production offices, dressing rooms, make-up rooms, auditorium and projection rooms—I realized that the whole story could take place within the confines of the studio. This would lend it a unity of place from which I would be able to obtain the unity of time (i.e., the shooting of a film, from the first day of filming to the moment when everybody goes their separate ways; and, *a fortiori*, the unity of action . . .

"Hundreds of times I was asked the question: 'Aren't you afraid of demystifying a profession that you are so fond of?' And I answered each time that an aviator can always explain all he knows about piloting, but he will never succeed in demystifying the rapture of flight."

Every morning at about seven-thirty we find ourselves in the make-up room of La Victorine, cups of coffee in hand.

The women arrive first: Jacqueline Bisset, with those Scottish lakes she has for eyes; Alexandra Stewart, a Minerva recently descended from her pedestal, and Valentina Cortese, looking gorgeous despite a vaporous scarf pulled down to her eyelashes. She swallows her comrades in her arms: "Tesoro mio, how lovely you look . . . Io sono una vecchia puttana . . . but you . . . che meraviglia . . ."

Truffaut enters. He kisses the three women, not without having noticed their real faces, before they have time to conceal them under pancake. Whether they display impatience, lassitude, or abandon, Truffaut will incorporate these feelings into their roles.

I even suspect him of filming us without our knowledge, before or after the shooting of a scene. There is a bit of Machiavelli in this Savonarola.

Jean-Pierre Léaud arrives.

Yesterday was not one of his good days. When I asked him, "How are you?" he looked at me with a stern glance which signified, "Really, there are subjects that you just aren't supposed to bring up." But this morning, when I ask, "How are you?" he doesn't seem irritated by the question. He thinks for a long time, weighing the pros and cons, and answers, "Well."

The similarity between Truffaut and Léaud is striking. Not only the features, but the presence, the way of approaching others, of lowering the eyes out of delicacy only to raise them again abruptly, in a piercing, inquisitive, merciless glance.

In *The 400 Blows*, the character Antoine Doinel, who suffers from the indifference of his parents, and feels like a burden to his own family, ends up running away from a reform school to go see the ocean. He is a synthesis of Truffaut's and Léaud's childhoods, one as difficult, solitary, and full of revolt as the other. The details don't really matter. I don't know which of the two went to countless boarding schools, which stole Ray Charles' records, which racked up debts or ran away during his military service. If it wasn't Léaud, it was Truffaut. In any case, it is Antoine Doinel.

In mixing his own memories with certain episodes from the life of Léaud, Truffaut has created this character, with his blunders, infatuations, enthusiasms, and depressions, and his way of seducing the world into pardoning him.

We find him in *The 400 Blows*, *L'Amour à Vingt Ans* (*Love at 20*), *Baisers volés* (*Stolen Kisses*), *Domicile Conjugal*, *Les Deux Anglaises et le Continent* (*Two English Girls*), and *Day for Night*.

All three personages are a part of our mythology. I can imagine them well enough: Jean-Pierre, Antoine, and François, costumed by Watteau (with, of course, a few shadows added by Goya), crossing the Place de la Concorde with their noses to the wind, without taking the least precaution to avoid the cars, and, by some grace, without suffering the slightest scratch. Cocteau wrote: "Beauty affects even those who don't notice it." What about grace?

Who else except Antoine Doinel could answer "Yes, sir" to the woman he desires? Who else could appear at a hotel desk dressed in a nightshirt (as Léaud does in *Day for Night*) inquiring: "Can someone loan me two hundred bucks to get laid?" And still be more touching than ridiculous.

"I was a boy who sat hiding in a corner, dreaming," says Truffaut. "Sometimes, but rarely, I skipped the movies to go to school." He goes on: "I have no life outside of films. I detest dinner parties. It's too painful for me to watch eight or ten people talking at the same time and moving without my being able to direct the dialogue and the action. If one of them cuts off another, I get sick. I want to jump up and tell them who is supposed to speak and when. I can't stand the fact that in life everything is so badly directed."

Truffaut claims that he can't tolerate anything but the presence of a pretty girl after seven o'clock in the evening. Still, I think that if Orson Welles, Renoir, or Hitchcock were calling him, he'd drop the most beautiful woman to have dinner with them.

Because he was a virulent critic, he has the reputation of being ferocious, but how warmly he speaks of Lubitsch, Bergman, Bogdanovich, Godard, or Cocteau.

We shoot for two months. Truffaut-the-Inscrutable, Truffaut-the-Reserved, Truffaut-the-Secretive, sometimes lets us know with the smile of a child that he really likes us.

In any case, I don't know a film director who knows more about putting an actor at ease, about letting him improvise. The confidence which he shows in us gives us wings.

Truffaut expects—in fact, he insists—that we come to the rushes. Not after him, but with him. This attitude is much more rare than one would think. Even there, he listens to our reactions and criticisms, though he may challenge them. He makes us feel that we are all in the same boat, that he depends on us as much as we depend on him.

Will this attachment to us last once the film is over? Do we really interest him as human beings, with our problems, characteristics, faults, or is he only interested in what we can contribute to his film?

In a scene from *Day for Night* Valentina Cortese is about to leave the company. During a party in her honor, she becomes emotional: "Is there any life stranger than ours? We work together, fall in love with each other, and then . . . and then we go on to other films, to other loves . . ."

It's sadly true. Since we finished *Day for Night* I have rarely seen my co-workers, although I have a deep feeling for each of them, especially for Truffaut. Am I his friend? I don't really know. I only know that he is mine.

The success of *Day for Night* in America was a phenomenon beyond the domain of cinema.

In Washington, New York, Los Angeles, people stopped me in the street, not to ask for my autograph, but to talk to me about the film and Truffaut.

Of course, *Day for Night* won all sorts of prizes in France and in other countries. But these were tributes from the profession to a deserving work. Young Americans saw something far different in the film. Something hidden, something poetic . . .

They were most moved by the scene in the car in which I explain to David Markham, who plays Jacqueline Bisset's husband, that all artists, but especially actors, are vulnerable.

"As soon as we meet someone we ask ourselves, 'What does he think of me? Does he like me?' "

I no longer remember whether it was Tuffaut or I—maybe it was both of us—who had the idea of adding these lines: "When Mozart was a child, and someone would ask him to play the piano, he would answer, 'I'm going to play whatever you want, but first tell me that you love me . . .' "

It was in a cafe on rue de Buci that I met Joan Littlewood. She had arrived in Paris, preceded by a flattering reputation for her direction in *A Taste of Honey* and *Oh! What a Lovely War*, among other things. The director of the Théâtre National had invited Miss Littlewood to direct a show of her choice at the Palais de Chaillot.

Miss Littlewood had chosen a play by Conor Cruise O'Brien, *Murderous Angels*, a retracing of the events which led to the independence of the Congo. It depicted the secession of Katanga, the intrigues of the Belgians to maintain their interests in their old colony, the tribal hates and rivalry among Lumumba, Kasavubu, and Tschombe, and the desperate efforts of Dag Hammarskjold, Secretary General of the United Nations, to prevent this local conflict from turning into a nuclear war between the U.S. and Russia. Conor knew his subject well. He had been one of Hammarskjold's assistants, and had gone with him to the Congo. It was during this trip that Hammarskjold had died in a mysterious airplane accident.

When I saw Miss Littlewood, sipping a cognac at 11 A.M., I was reminded of Winston Churchill. She had the same sulky, bulldog looks. She was younger than he, however, much more attractive, and smoked a cigarette.

She took my hands, looked at me for a long time, and declared that she saw a striking resemblance to Hammarskjold. I told her that he was one of my heroes and that I was flattered by her offering me the chance to portray him. I also added that I had read the play by Conor O'Brien and had found it remarkable. Everything fell: the cigarette, the jowls, the eyes, and the cognac: "Don't talk to me about that play . . ."

I was a little surprised. "I thought that was the play you were planning to direct."

She threw me a dark look: "Plays . . . since when do we need plays?"

I didn't know what to answer. Later on, I learned that Miss Littlewood didn't care too much for authors. I was told she dreamed of a world where neither Molière, nor Cervantes, nor Goethe would be allowed. If it was absolutely necessary, she tolerated Shakespeare, several of whose plays she had directed with singular success. But she considered his texts more or less as raw material for her inspiration.

Authors were not the only ones who irritated her. She

didn't care for actors either. When she cast her shows she used to go into the streets and sign people whom she encountered by chance, and whose faces interested her. With them she felt secure. She could knead and mold them at her ease. London actors were acquainted with this trait of hers. Many of them, knowing that Miss Littlewood would not cast them if she discovered their profession, disguised themselves as tramps and hung around her door until she noticed them. The more miserable they seemed, the more Miss Littlewood liked them. If they swore to God that they had never set foot in a theater and had not the least desire to do so, she hired them immediately. How she ever thought of employing me or those of my colleagues who couldn't hide the fact that they were actors is a miracle.

We rehearsed three months for a limited engagement of three weeks. On the first day we asked for our scripts. An indignant look from Miss L. gave us to understand that such a request was a breach of good manners.

Surrounded by fifty people, made up of four or five bewildered professionals, some black dancers, and singers from Madagascar or Martinique, Joan Littlewood blossomed. We were a family from this day forward, she declared, we were her children, her parents, and her lovers, all at the same time, and we would have our meals together, and camp together in the gardens of the Trocadero. For those Senegalese who had nowhere to stay, the proposition was attractive, but for those of us who had private homes, it posed a few problems. It didn't seem practical to abandon our wives and children for the Trocadero gardens (not very hospitable in winter) just to snuggle up in Miss Littlewood's generous arms.

Each day she would lecture us on the Congo, then ask us to let ourselves go, leap, cry, crawl, and clown. Because I had little talent for leaping and crawling, she had me improvise. Sometimes I was a witchdoctor, sometimes a baobab or a crocodile. Improvising is a very worthwhile exercise. I would have been glad to do it, had I seen some rapport—no matter how distant— between a baobab and the character I was supposed to play. But to spend the whole day expressing the inner emotions of a tree or a toad didn't seem reasonable to me. From time to time I would remind Miss L. that I had signed a contract to play Dag Hammarskjold. She would look at me dazedly, and then, suddenly realizing whom I was referring to, answer that I was hurting her feelings by mentioning such details.

Two weeks away from opening night, and weary of impersonating my baobab, I took her aside. "We appeciate what you're doing, Miss Littlewood, but we think it's urgent that we get a script now so that we can learn our lines."

"But haven't you understood that I'm your mother . . . ?"

"We understand that, and we are grateful to you, but . . ."

". . . your sister, your daughter, your mistress . . . ?"

I was a little more fortunate than my colleagues since, knowing English, I was able to translate O'Brien's play and learn it secretly. The other actors began inventing lines, as well as they could. Miss Littlewood listened to us with a slight contempt.

"If these French actors are incapable of playing without a script, they can say what they want." She ignored us and lavished her love on the dancers. "Here are artists who don't need words to express themselves!" She had them working twenty-four hours a day. She was happy.

Outside of Hammarskjold there were two important roles. For Amyn, Miss Littlewood, after hesitating among a number of dancers, waiters, and scavengers, finally chose a fellow from Madagascar, who played the saxophone and had a slight penchant for alcohol. Miss Littlewood adored him because he was totally inarticulate.

It was nine days from opening night when Miss Littlewood declared with a triumphant air: "I've found our Kasavubu. He's an admirable man, a leader, a humanist, a saint."

"Is he an actor?" I ventured timidly.

"Of course not."

As this was a role with thousands of lines to learn, I permitted myself a second question, indiscreet as it was: "Does he speak French?"

"Not a word."

Thus, our Kasavubu arrived. Before even glancing at his role he demanded, in Swahili, to see his dressing room. He had never set foot in a theater, but he knew that actors got dressed in dressing rooms. They showed it to him. He threw a fit because it was smaller than mine. "A saint . . . he's a saint . . ." Miss Littlewood continued. In the eyes of this saint, my having been favored with a larger dressing room was an act of racism.

His sentiments toward me mattered little. What was important to me was that a week before we opened none of the performers with whom I had my scenes were capable of giving me one line.

The last two days of rehearsal Miss Littlewood made up little notes for us and left them with the doorman. "At long last," I thought, "I'm going to get some directions about my role." The first note contained only the following: "Your shoes make noise." The second and last said: "It's good to hate. Oh! you . . . spoiled panther of pleasure."

I didn't quite understand. I didn't hate anyone. As for considering me a panther of pleasure, spoiled or not, I found that a bit exaggerated.

Just then our author arrived from Ireland. Detached as she was from the real world, Miss Littlewood nevertheless confusedly sensed that Conor O'Brien would not be satisfied. Thus, she sent all her assistants to Orly Airport. Their mission was to drag Conor from bar to bar and keep him from coming to the theater.

We hardly saw Conor Cruise O'Brien. Neither did we see the assistants again, whose presence might have been useful during the final rehearsals.

Meanwhile, the Minister of Foreign Affairs was asking us to cut a scene in which King Baudouin was ridiculed. Not only did Miss Littlewood refuse, but she devoted herself to making the Belgian court appear more grotesque. She would have been happy to have the show banned, since she knew the leftist press would fly to her aid. The government smelled the trap and didn't insist.

We opened on a Wednesday evening. That afternoon we rehearsed the show one last time, or at least part of it, since Amyn had forgotten to come. Miss L. didn't seem to notice his absence. He arrived around six o'clock, wild-eyed and reeling, and overflowing with affection. I tried to make him work but he was even less capable of it than he had been on other days. We had only two hours before the play began. I went out into the night and walked toward the Eiffel Tower, trying to invent some lines to cover for the silences I anticipated from Amyn. At eight o'clock I returned to the theater. Whatever happened, I decided to maintain an Olympian calm. I couldn't afford the luxury of stage-fright.

Miracles do exist. The play progressed, somehow or other, to the final curtain. As would be expected, the dramatic scenes, containing dialogue concocted separately by each of us, appeared a bit hybrid. But the movements of the crowd, which had been lovingly developed for three months by Miss Littlewood and her dancers, turned out to be quite effective.

At midnight we waited in our dressing rooms for our director. Then we went to look for her in the wings. We wanted to know if she was satisfied, if she was planning to stay in Paris, if she felt like having supper with us. Miss Littlewood wasn't to be found anywhere. None of us ever heard from her again.

It's a bit hard losing, in a single blow, your mother, your sister, your daughter, and your mistress . . .

One Sunday matinee two gentlemen who had been sitting in the front row came to see me in my dressing room. One of them was T. E. Hambleton, the director of the Phoenix Theater in New York. The other was Gordon Davidson, a young director. Hambleton was whimsical and absent-minded: Gordon was precise, warm, and enthusiastic. I liked them both immediately. They had already produced Conor O'Brien's play in California and, although they had a hard time recognizing it at the Palais de Chaillot, they decided to bring it to Broadway with me playing Hammarskjold.

Gordon reinstated the original script by Conor, who was finally invited to take part in the rehearsals. The casting was superb. It included Barbara Colby (who was to meet a tragic end, killed on the street by a lunatic), Richard Easton, Herb Jefferson, and Lou Gossett. This time the conflict between Hammarskjold and Lumumba was aptly illuminated. Both of them esteemed each other, liked each other, and tried to kill each other. One considered himself the "Angel of Peace" while the other considered himself the "Angel of Liberty."

The performances were turbulent. The black community was offended. Every evening pickets strode back and forth in front of the theater, denouncing us as imperialists, reactionaries, and racists. Inside the theater, blacks made their thoughts known, booing Hammarskjold and clamoring their devotion to Lumumba. We organized debates at the end of the performances. In principal, I have a horror of this kind of ceremony, which demystifies the theater. I experience a profound sadness in seeing Phaedra or Lady Macbeth take off her wig and appear before the audience with her hair knotted in a scarf and a cigarette dangling from her lips. In wrangling about what Shakespeare or Racine wanted to say, the dream, the illusion, and the magic are destroyed. But for a political play like *Murderous Angels*, debates can really become exciting.

In any case they were impassioned. The blacks accused O'Brien of canonizing Hammarskjold at the expense of their hero. They couldn't accept the reference to Lumumba by his enemies as a "boozy goat." They were offended by his affair with a white woman. When we replied that this was an historical fact, they insisted that the white mistress in the play shouldn't have had a more important role than the legitimate black wife.

In any case, acting in the same play, the same year, in French and then in English, experiencing such a radical change in text, direction, and partners, and participating in those turbulent debates was a rich and bracing adventure.

27

Miracles

The years 1975 and 1976 were active and, at times, hectic. For many months, I played *Private Lives* with Danielle Darrieux in France, and then in Belgium, Switzerland, Tunisia, Morocco, and Portugal. Danielle was just as enchanting in the part of Amanda as she was in real life. It was hard to keep from laughing as soon as we walked on stage, because we could see hundreds of opera glasses pointed at us. The women in the audience wanted an accurate count of the number of creases, wrinkles, and furrows that we'd acquired through the years. That's the one disadvantage of becoming well known when you're very young. Danielle was a star at fourteen. I had my first success at seventeen. Everyone had been used to seeing us for such a long time that they assumed we were octogenarians. In every town we played, the critics would politely compliment our performances, without, however, failing to mention "how amazingly young we looked."

As a joke, I typed up an article which was supposed to have appeared in a Geneva paper, and sent it to Danielle through the mail. It read:

"Ever since they made *Tarass-Boulba*, so many, many years

ago, Miss Darrieux and Mister Aumont have never ceased to thrill generations of spectators. Seeing them last night, looking so dashing, dapper, and debonair, who could have guessed that they have reached the age when most people are patting great-grandchildren with trembling hands. During the scene in which the two lovers fight, when Danielle breaks a record over her co-star's head, everyone in the audience quivered. When Jean-Pierre fell to the floor, we gasped, fearing that he would not be able to get up again. But we were wrong. Both of them returned to play the third act. Though they looked exhausted, worn, pale, and a bit disheveled, they managed to toss out their lines with a kind of gallant bravery. During the curtain calls they were still smiling. I urge you to see them while they last."

Danielle's response to the article was one tiny, wounded cry. A week went by before I had enough courage to confess my little joke.

As a way of boosting her morale, I would sing lines I was learning from *Gigi*, which I had been asked to play in the States:

> Too old for a wedding day in June,
> But not for a weekend honeymoon,
> What better life could heaven have in store?
> Oh, I'm so glad that I'm not young anymore . . ."

I flew to New York. It was Milton Goldman's sixtieth birthday. Milton, a legendary figure in New York, is more than my agent, he's also my friend. When he gives a party, he is so anxious to make sure you have a good time that he insists on introducing everyone to everybody. Pretty soon he forgets whom he has already talked to, and ends up introducing wives to their husbands or mothers to their sons. Then he's a little hurt when they tell him that they already know each other.

His office is bedlam. Five telephones ring constantly and he carries on five conversations at once. The last time I went to see him, he was talking to Anthony Quayle. I sat listening to this amazing monologue: "Anthony, those seats you wanted for *A Little Night Music*, they'll be at the boxoffice tonight in *your* name. Write it down. Have you got a pencil? Q-U-A-Y-L-E."

The birthday party was brilliant, with Ethel Merman and Martha Graham carrying Milton to the buffet (I was going to write baptismal font) as if it were his christening. Everyone was weeping, the dry martinis were flowing like holy water.

I tore myself away from these revels to go applaud Nureyev, who was dancing in *Sleeping Beauty*. At the end of the performance he received a fantastic standing ovation. These tributes are almost nonexistent in France. I remember being at the Théâtre des Champs-Elysées with Marisa and standing up to applaud Maurice Chevalier. People stared at us reproachfully, thinking that we were in a hurry to leave.

Nureyev continued to bow. A dancer's bow is almost like a musician's encore. He puts all his skill into it, and because he is fatigued, his movements take on a hidden grace and abandon which I find almost as interesting as a brilliant performance.

"How nice it would be," I mused, "Just once, to get a standing ovation . . ."

I left for rehearsals of *Gigi* in Chicago. My Jean-Claude came there to be with me on the evening of his eighteenth birthday.

Several months before, when I had been offered this contract, he had said in a grieving, reproachful tone, "Oh, Papa, you're not going to start singing again . . ."

"Yes, I am."

"And you mean to say you get paid for it?"

For a kid who was grinding away at his studies in preparation for graduation, I could understand how this might seem strange!

On August thirteenth, he was there in the first row. During intermission he came into my dressing room. "It was terrific. You didn't sing one wrong note, not once."

After the last act, during the curtain calls, as I stood bowing, the unbelievable happened. . . . I received a standing ovation.

As I bowed again, all I could think of was that sometimes it is sufficient to dream in order for dreams to become reality. Of course it wasn't on a level with the storm of applause which had engulfed Nureyev, but a standing ovation is a standing ovation.

And my son was in the first row . . .

And it was his birthday . . .

And it was the thirteenth of August . . .

In the meantime I had received a script called *Mahogany*, and I was very excited about doing a Brecht play. I soon learned, however, that the script had nothing to do with Brecht.

Mahogany was Diana Ross, extraordinary singer and extraordinary actress. Her elegance, her royal gait, something both proud and secretive kept her apart. Even those who called her Diana did so in a respectful tone. At dawn, each day, she would leave the Hotel Excelsior in Rome and curl up in the back seat of her car. Two hours later she would appear on the set. There was a strange discrepancy between the awe inspired by her presence and the humility she displayed during rehearsals. She followed devotedly the direction of Berry Gordy, the mogul of Motown who had discovered her as a singer and made her a star with *Lady Sings the Blues*.

The film was shot in Italy, which delighted me, since my daughter, whom I hadn't seen for several months, was living there.

After three weeks in Rome I left for Spoleto, where I asked Tina to join me. She promised to be there. Each day I waited for her, but still no Tina.

One evening Diana Ross told me, "Tomorrow in our breakup scene you offer me some diamond earrings. I've seen them, they're really incredible . . ."

"Fine," I said.

"Bulgari loaned them to us. He's the best jeweler in Rome."

The next day we filmed the scene. I hadn't opened the box during rehearsals, so that they wouldn't have to wrap the package again.

First take: I open the box and seize a cluster of precious diamonds. Suddenly, I stop short, stupefied.

They were the earrings I gave Maria twenty-four years ago.

Of course, I knew that Tina, who had inherited them from her mother, rightly perceiving that they didn't suit her, had exchanged them for something else at Bulgari's. But I never imagined that I would see them again.

Being suddenly confronted by this memory and by all the happy hours it evoked was the result of a singular coincidence. But there were more surprises still to come. I heard a muffled gasp followed by rapid footsteps. Tina had just arrived. She had come directly to the chateau where we were shooting and entered the room at the precise moment when I was taking the earrings out of their case to offer them to Diana Ross.

When the scene was over, I went looking for Tina. She had disappeared.

I don't really know what she thought, because when I found her, she refused to talk about it. I didn't press her. In this bizarre stroke of fate, I felt a friendly glimmer from another world. It seemed as if Maria had just chosen to manifest herself to us. She must have been happy, because Tina and I were spending a few rare moments together.

Jouvet often said: "In life, my boy, one meets the same people over and over."

With what joy I found Madeleine Renaud and Jean-Louis Barrault again.

After the Comédie Française and the Odéon, after Marigny, the Bouffes, and the Récamier, after theaters and big-tops, they had ended up on the roof of a railroad station that was still in use, on the banks of the Seine, in the very center of Paris. There, in three months, they had imagined, designed, and constructed an unbelievably beautiful theatrical space.

It is an octagonal hall, warm and vibrant, enclosed by a framework of wood, like a Shakespearean stage or the enchanted forest of Brocéliande.

Trains continue to come in from Orléans or Pithiviers, but the station master is in love (and who isn't?) with Madeleine Renaud. He has arranged for those trains which make too much noise while Madeleine is playing a particularly delicate scene to arrive off-schedule.

I can see this worthy man on the lookout for one now, red flag in hand, shunting the cars to another track (shh! Madeleine's speaking) so that their entrance into the station will coincide with the intermission.

It was in this theater, church, hive, that I was asked by Madeleine and Jean-Louis to appear in a play by Marguerite Duras, *Das Journées Entières dans les Arbres* (*Day in the Trees*).

The Jean-Louis of *Beaux Jours* and *Drôle de Drame* has not changed. If his look has become more piercing and his speech flows easier, he has kept the same candor, the same enthusiasm. He is as committed to his career as a peasant to his plow. This healthiness, this capacity for work, this instinct for great texts . . . what pure and rare qualities.

Madeleine does not content herself with merely sharing his overriding passions. She inspires them, lives them. Their personal love is wedded with their love for the theater. It is their oxygen, their reason for being.

At the very first reading of *Days in the Trees* she gave of herself as if it were opening night. Whenever I would hesitate, figuring out a line, script in hand, she would say, "Don't worry about it. If the line doesn't come to you, I'll cover for you."

"But, Madeleine, it will come to me. We're not playing this evening. We still have two months of rehearsals ahead of us."

"Ah, yes, that's true."

At the beginning of each performance she would murmur in my ear: "Look, it's full. There are people sitting on all the steps. My God, what a responsibility! Tell me the truth, are you sure that I can be heard at the back of the house?"

Every morning she telephones me: "Don't smoke too much. Don't stay out too late. Don't forget that you're playing to-night."

But her tender admonitions have a lot more grace than is required of the rough character she plays in Duras' work.

Onstage, mother and son confront each other in a kind of duet—or duel—composed of hate and love. She has worked all her life to emasculate him. He has struggled all his life to owe nothing to her, not even his own ruin.

But sometimes waves of tenderness cleanse away the bitterness: "I don't love anybody but you, Mama. I wish you could live forever . . ."

At that moment, every evening, you can hear the faraway strains of the Blue Danube Waltz. I hold out my hands to my mother: "Come on, Mama, three little turns, I'd promised myself, come."

She stands up slowly—timid, proud, uncertain.

And with the same exact smile that Madeleine had in *Maria Chapdelaine*, in which we waltzed together so many years ago, with the same look full of love, pride, and gratitude, she comes forward awkwardly and nestles in my arms. Lifting one foot every three beats, which she believes is good form for dancing the waltz, she abandons herself little by little to her son, her lover . . .

And I don't know any longer if it is the abusive mother of Marguerite Duras, or Madeleine Renaud herself, at the summit of her glory, who now feels the trembling heartbeats of a young girl.

In the daytime we were filming *Days in the Trees* with a dialogue completely different from the one we were playing at night, for Marguerite Duras was terrified that anybody would accuse her of just photographing her play. She went so far as to suppress many lines that were beautifully written and essential to the action. Sometimes I was shocked at seeing her destroy her own creation. On the other hand, used as I was to authors who refuse to cut a single comma, I couldn't help admiring that great woman for attaching so little importance to her text.

In May 1976, the French Government sent us to play *Days in the Trees* in French in Washington, Boston, Montreal, Quebec, and New York. At times, the public was baffled. They didn't dare to laugh for fear of being disrespectful toward two such sacred institutions as Marguerite Duras and Madeleine Renaud. At other times, they would laugh at each line. "Tonight, we are playing Neil Simon," said Madeleine. "Tomorrow, it will be Eugene O'Neill."

But, tragic or comic, the play had a singular power over any audience. The public believed so completely in our characters that, one night, at the stage door of the Ambassadors Theater on Broadway, an old lady, after having asked Madeleine to sign her program, faced me with hatred and said in a trembling voice:

"And *you* . . . I am not going to ask you for your autograph. You are too mean to your mother."

I took it as a rare compliment.

In a few days it will be my birthday. Each year the fact that I am over thirty becomes more and more surprising. For me the increasing number of candles on my cake is a mystery.

Aging is the activity which I find most boring. I think of it as little as possible. Fortunately, my children are there to keep my feelings and my reflexes young. Fatigue, melancholy, or any of the regrets which encumber adult life are impossible with them around.

As long as they continue to trust me, to ask questions, as long as they allow me the sweet illusion that they still need me, I will never feel old.

My friends make fun of my euphoric disposition.

"To refuse to grow old! . . . To think the number thirteen brings luck! . . . To marvel at finding some old earrings again! . . . How superficial you are!"

Yes, I am superficial, and I'm proud of it. It took me a long time to get there. This isn't given to everybody. You need enthusiasm, a solid balance, wisdom, and cheerfulness.

"It's polite to be cheerful," said Eve Curie during the war, in the midst of the bombardments. Our sordid earth is full of sad things, but being serious won't make them any less sad. Dwelling on the ravages of time doesn't make you younger. Complaining doesn't improve your fate.

The war taught me to judge things at their true value. It was during the war that I learned to appreciate a single cup of coffee, a single letter, a single proof of friendship. Since that time I haven't stopped being astonished by all that God offers us. The wind is blowing through a tree, right here before my eyes; I don't even know what kind of tree it is, but I can watch it for a long time, fascinated by the trembling of the leaves . . .

In a few minutes the television will carry images to me. I'll be astonished again, without trying to understand.

"Come on, there's no miracle in that. It's a matter of electromagnetic waves, nothing more."

Away, infidels! I want to believe in miracles. And miracles occur daily as long as we are willing to acknowledge them.

I ask only one thing from Heaven: the power to keep, as long as possible, this faculty—or rather this need—to admire and to love.

I look for happiness.

I try, when it is given to me, to deserve it.

In any case, I say thanks.

With La Fontaine:

> J'aime le jeu, l'amour, les livres, la musique
> La ville et la campagne. Enfin, tout.
> Il n'est rien
> Qui ne me soit souverain bien,
> Jusqu'au sombre plaisir d'un coeur mélancolique.*

---

* I like books and love, music and leisure,
  The city and the country. Everything, in fact.
  To my sense,
  All is made of excellence,
  Including the somber pleasure of a melancholy heart.

Appendix

The Plays and Films of Jean-Pierre Aumont

Year	Plays	Films
1934	La Machine Infernale (F)*	Lac aux Dames (F)
	As You Like It (F)	L'Equipage (F)
1935	Design for Living (F)	Tarass Boulba (F)
1936	Le Veilleur de Nuit (F)	La Porte du Large (F)
1937	Le Coeur (F)	Le Messager (F)
		Drôle de Drame (F)
1938		Hôtel du Nord (F)
1939	L'Amant de Paille (F)	S.O.S. Sahara (F)
		Belle Etoile (F)
1942	Rose Burke	Assignment in Brittany
1943		The Cross of Lorraine
1945		Heartbeat
1946	Design for Living	Scheherazade
1947		Atlantis
1948	Design for Living	Hans le Marin (F)

* (F) = production in France

1949	L'Empereur de Chine (F) My Name Is Aquilon	La Vie Commence Demain (F) Three Men and a Girl (England)
1950	L'Homme de Joie (F) Le Voyage (F)	L'Homme de Joie (F)
1951	Le Voyageur sans Bagages (F)	La Vendetta del Corsaro (Italy)
1952		Lili Koenigsmark (F)
1953	Les Pavés du Ciel (F)	Charge of the Lancers Si Versailles m'était conté (F)
1954	L'Arlésienne (F)	Napoléon (F)
1955	Heavenly Twins	Mademoiselle de Paris (F)
1956		Hilda Crane The Seventh Veil
1957	Amphitryon 38 (F)	
1958	Sodome et Gomorrhe (F)	John Paul Jones
1959	Ange (F) Mon Père avait Raison (F)	The Enemy General
1960	A Second String	The Devil at Four O'clock
1961	Anatole	Seven Deadly Sins
1962	Flora (F)	Horse without a Head Vacances au Portugal (F)
1963–64	Tovarich	
1965	Madame Mousse	
1966	Once More with Feeling Incident at Vichy	Present Laughter (F)
1967	South Pacific	Blind Man's Buff
1968	Nightclub Act	Castle Keep
1969	Girl in my Soup Carnival The Tempest (F)	Chevaliers du Ciel (F)
1970	Camino Real	Biribi (F)

1971	Murderous Angels	L'Homme au Cerveau Greffé (F)
1972	Nous Irons à Valparaiso (F) Jacques Brel Is Alive . . .	La Nuit Américaine (Day for Night) (F)
1973	Carlos et marguerite (F)	Captain Luckner
1974	Private Lives (F) Perfect Pitch Gigi	The Happy Hooker Les deux missionnaires (F)
1975	Janus On croit rêver (F)	Mahogany Le Chat et la Souris (F) Catherine and Co (F)
1976	Des Journées Entières dans les Arbres	Des Journées Entières dans les Arbres (F)

Index of Names